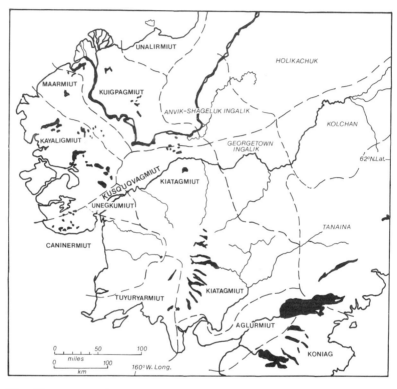

The Kusquqvagmiut area and the surrounding Eskimo and Indian populations

Bashful No Longer

An Alaskan Eskimo Ethnohistory, 1778—1988

by Wendell H. Oswalt

University of Oklahoma Press   :   Norman and London

By Wendell H. Oswalt

Mission of Change in Alaska (California, 1963)
Napaskiak: An Alaskan Eskimo Community (Arizona, 1963)
This Land Was Theirs (New York, 1966)
Alaskan Eskimos (California, 1967)
Understanding Our Culture (New York, 1970)
Other Peoples, Other Customs (New York, 1972)
Habitat and Technology (New York, 1973)
An Anthropological Analysis of Food-Getting Technology
   (New York, 1976)
Eskimos and Explorers (California, 1979)
Kolmakovskiy Redoubt (California, 1980)
Life Cycles and Lifeways (California, 1986)
Bashful No Longer: An Alaskan Eskimo Ethnohistory, 1778–1988
   (Norman, 1990)

Library of Congress Cataloging-in-Publication Data

Oswalt, Wendell H.
   Bashful no longer : an Alaskan Eskimo ethnohistory, 1778–1988
/ by Wendell H. Oswalt.
      p.   cm. — (The Civilization of the American Indian Series:
v. 199)
   Includes bibliographical references.
   ISBN 0-8061-2256-0 (alk. paper)
   1. Yupik Eskimos—Alaska—Kuskokwim River Valley—History.
2. Yupik Eskimos—Alaska—Kuskokwim River Valley—Cultural
assimilation.   3. Yupik Eskimos—Alaska—Kuskokwim River
Valley—Ethnic identity.   4. Kuskokwim River Valley (Alaska)—
Social conditions.   I. Title.
E99.E70786   1990
979.8′4—dc20   89-37036
                                                          CIP

In memory of:

Sergie Andreanoff
Anania Theodore
Crow Village Sam
Wasley Jones

Contents

Illustrations

Acknowledgments

As I assembled the sources for this study, I turned to numerous persons for aid in locating pertinent materials. I especially am grateful to the following persons for their valuable help: Taylor Brelsford, Frank Darnell, Janet A. Fredericks, Gerald A. McBeath, Timothy Miller, Phyllis Morrow, Jim Payne, Mary C. Pete, Kathryn H. Shelton, and Teddy Wintersteen.

Working drafts of the manuscript were reviewed by Lydia T. Black, Ann Fienup-Riordan, James W. VanStone, Kurt H. Vitt, and an anonymous reviewer. My debt to each of them is great, not only for calling errors and omissions to my attention but for their insightful comments about my interpretations. Finally, I wholeheartedly thank Helen Louise Taylor Oswalt for her editing of the manuscript through its numerous drafts.

WENDELL H. OSWALT

Los Angeles

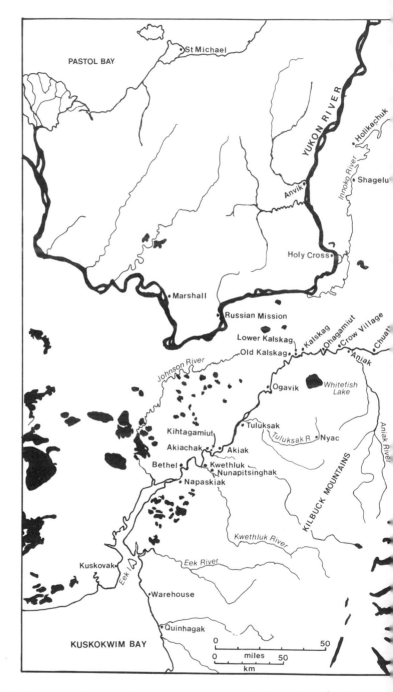

The Kuskokwim River region of southwestern Alaska with historic settlements indicated

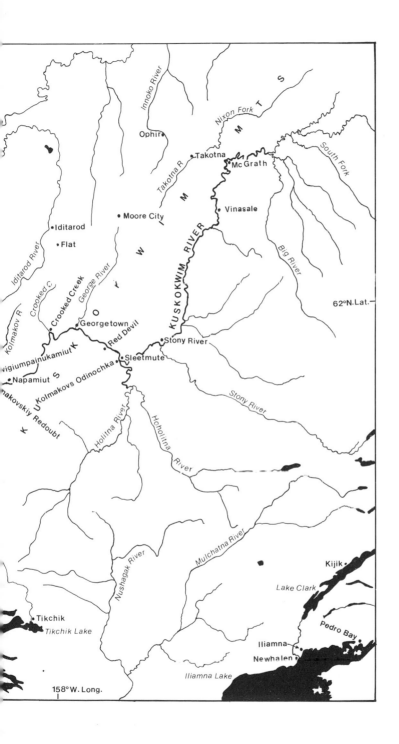

Introduction

Bashful No Longer encapsulates a new and dominant attitude held by modern Kuskokwim Eskimos toward whites that is the opposite of their traditional attitude toward outsiders. Traditionally these riverine Eskimos in southwestern Alaska placed an inordinate value on restraint. Villagers typically were modest and reserved, listened attentively as older people spoke, made requests indirectly, were nonaggressive, and strove mightily to avoid confrontations among themselves and in dealing with strangers.[1] Aggressive acts by individuals or groups were infrequent and were motivated by highly unusual circumstances. Contrawise, the Westerners with whom they have had expanding contacts characteristically have been authoritarian, self-assertive if not aggressive in their behavior, and have expected specific answers to questions rather than deferential ones. In an attempt to express their self-image these Eskimos adopted the English word *bashful,* although the word *self-effacing* might be more fitting. As intercultural conflict expanded and became increasingly critical in their lives, these Eskimos eventually reached a point at which they no longer were willing to defer to Westerners. In a far-reaching collective response, Kuskokwim Eskimos have become bashful no longer.

As an ethnohistory about Kuskokwim Eskimos, this study begins in 1778 and concludes in 1988. *Ethnohistory* itself deserves comment since it focuses this work and is a relatively new concept, having formally emerged in the 1950s from its previous position as an aspect of culture history.[2] As with any newly established subject focus, reviews of its aims and methods have been frequent.[3] In 1961 Richard M. Dorson noted that "ethnohistory employs the chronological and documentary method of conventional history, but directs its attention to the ethnic groups ordinarily relegated to the shadows in the White man's view of history."[4] In addition to its documentary basis, an ethnohistory usually includes ethnographic data and oral traditions; archaeological findings, photographic material, and other sources are employed when available.

The data core for this ethnohistory comprises largely Russian-American Company records; the journals, reports, or brief notations of explorers, travelers, and missionaries; newspaper accounts, and other varied official and unofficial documents. Supplementing these is verbal information of an ethnographic and historical nature collected in the area by the author between 1953 and 1979. However, the oral history is less comprehensive than had been anticipated. The only person located who had a significant familiarity with the Russian period was Sergie Andreanoff, a Russian-Eskimo who was eighty-three years old when interviewed in 1954. Andreanoff had a keen historical perspective, but senility had affected his verbalization as well as his memory. Matthew Berezkin, born in 1881 of Russian and Aleut ancestry, arrived in the area in 1906 as a Russian Orthodox Church songleader. He became a priest in 1908 and served the Kuskokwim villages until the 1920s. I talked with him in 1955–56 and again in 1966. With his long-term familiarity with the Kuskokwim and his interest in history, he was able to provide invaluable information about the early 1900s. Anania Theodore, an Eskimo born at Vinasale about 1887, was interviewed during six summers. Theodore was an ideal informant because he has a profound knowledge of local history and ethnography. After talking with many local residents, I singled out these three men because of their unique knowledge. Andreanoff's pride in his Russian heritage, the training and interests of Berezkin as a priest, and the exceptional intellectual abilities of Theodore, honed at the Roman Catholic mission school at Holy Cross, set each of them apart from their fellow villagers. The fact that Andreanoff and Berezkin had been blind for many years when they were interviewed also may have contributed to their ability to focus on the past. I talked with literally hundreds of other Kuskokwim residents about the past, but few of them expressed a general historical awareness, although they sometimes could and did recount notable historical episodes. This is contrary to the situation in other sectors of Alaska and may relate to the minor role the Kuskokwim region played during the early American period, when educational developments were greater in other regions. In this context it is pertinent to note that when Ann Fienup-Riordan worked among the Nelson Island Eskimos in 1976–78, they referred to a "long time ago" as being about 1940.[5]

As is commonplace, the ethnographic reports about Kuskokwim Eskimos that date from the Russian and early American periods are not as full as might be hoped. A Russian explorer, Lavrentiy Alekseyevich Zagoskin, and a Moravian missionary, John Henry Kilbuck, provide most of the reliable baseline ethnographic findings. In this context, I do not feel that ethnographic accounts about traditional life among Eskimos to the west are directly applicable to Kuskokwim Eskimos; their cultural circumstances and the historical developments among them are too different. For example, the nature of traditional Nelson Island Eskimo life has been established by Fienup-Riordan, who drew upon information collected in the 1970s; however, sustained and reasonably intense contact between Nelson Island Eskimos and Americans* dates largely from the 1930s, much later than on the Kuskokwim.[6] In addition, their isolation kept Nelson Island Eskimos relatively insulated from outside influences. Although some Nelson Island data are applicable to the Kuskokwim area, I have hesitated to draw on this material systematically.

Sometimes ethnohistorians have been faulted for not expanding their data base to include an archaeological dimension. In the Kuskokwim Eskimo area an ethnoarchaeological excavation carried out at Crow Village adds information about historic changes.[7] In addition, excavations made at the Russian and subsequent American trading center of Kolmakovskiy Redoubt permit greater insight into the impact of traders on these people.[8]

Finally, a commonplace objection to ethnohistorical accounts is their habitual emphasis on changes inspired by Westerners, as opposed to the creative responses of the indigenous peoples

---

*The word *American* is used to refer to nonaboriginal persons from the United States, whereas Eskimos and Indians are identified as such, as Native Alaskans, or as members of more specific groups.

involved. Ethnohistorians are keenly aware of this failing. In the present study a concerted effort has been made to examine changes from an Eskimo perspective. This is difficult, however, since most information comes from accounts by Westerners, whose awareness of Eskimo cultural adaptations is inherently one-sided.

With the ordering of data as a distinguishing characteristic, ethnohistory is above all else a *time-oriented approach* to information.[9] A second criterion is that the material must have an *ethnic orientation*. Beyond these defining features, ethnohistories have been organized from varied perspectives, including those of technological change, ethnicity, colonial relationships, and historical eras. In previous drafts of the present study I attempted an era approach and one based on ethnicity but found them unsatisfactory, even misleading; this view also was expressed by colleagues who read these manuscripts. In considering another revision, I decided to stress a geographical factor having a major impact on ethnohistorical developments. The importance of the accessibility of a locale to outsiders had occurred to me years before. As I worked among Eskimos in western Alaska in the late 1940s, I was struck by the degree of difference in the impact of Western culture on particular settings. The contrast between the retention of traditional ways at Black River or Scammon Bay Village and the extent of Americanization at Nome and Unalakleet was impressive. Working along the Kuskokwim River somewhat later, I found that Western influences in some villages, such as Sleetmute, were far less obvious than in others, such as Aniak or Bethel. These observations, as informal as they were, suggested that access had affected Eskimo ethnohistorical developments in a significant manner.

    Access, in this context, means the capacity of outsiders to reach and subsequently frequent a locality in which they seek to achieve particular goals. I gained greater confidence in the importance of access after reading a study about Russian America by James R. Gibson.[10] He viewed access to Alaska by company agents as critical, stressing in particular the difficulty Russians had in provisioning their stations. Gibson found that after permanent settlements were established, the inability of the Russian-

American Company to insure the residents of a food supply that was both reliable and adequate negatively affected long-term developments. He noted, "The shortfall of provisions was partly responsible for the debilitation of colonial manpower, which in turn was less able to operate effectively against foreign competition and native opponents."[11]

A study by Shepard Krech III about the Eastern Kutchin fur trade at the Peel River Post and the difficulties of the Hudson's Bay Company in supplying this post implicitly emphasized access in a fur trade operation.[12] I was struck by the parallels with Russian-American Company efforts to supply its principal Kuskokwim River station, Kolmakovskiy Redoubt. Difficulties of access by company agents working at these stations suggested that access itself was a key factor in developing the fur trade in both areas. If this was so for the early fur trade, it seemed that focusing on access might be a useful perspective for articulating all of the Kuskokwim Eskimo ethnohistorical data and also for making comparisons between these Eskimos and other Eskimos and Indians in southwestern Alaska in terms of historical developments.

Even a brief review of contact settings suggests how Western access differentially affected Native North Americans. The earliest direct and substantial contacts between Indians and Westerners apparently were in Newfoundland, a product of Norse explorations from Greenland around A.D. 1000. However, reliable access to the continent proved unattainable for the Norse, and as a result they made no lasting impact on the Indians in the northeastern reaches.[13] Many years of explorations followed, with Eskimos of north-central Canada being the most recently contacted peoples. Because they were less accessible to maritime explorers than most Alaskan or Greenlandic Eskimos, their traditional way of life persisted longer than that of most others. As a result, when changes of Western inspiration did take place in the central Canadian arctic, they were tempered by the experiences of Euro-Canadians in their dealings with Eskimos elsewhere.[14] Within a region such as the American Southwest, access also might vary widely. For instance, from Mexico access was much greater to the Eastern Pueblos than to the Western ones. As a consequence, direct Spanish influence on Eastern Pueblo social, political, and ceremonial life was far more intense than on its Western Pueblo counterpart. These examples suggest the importance of geographical access as a molder of ethnohistories. Relative accessibility is thus identified as a factor that has had a lasting impact on the changing character of Native American life. Subsumed in an orientation based on access is the related factor of *goals,* the motivation behind the entry of outsiders into an area. Access has been pursued by Westerners to achieve one or more purposes, and these in turn play a role in ethnohistorical developments. Thus, the specific goals or purposes of Westerners are a secondary factor in organizing this ethnohistory.

With access and goals as the major bases for understanding ethnohistorical developments among Kuskokwim Eskimos, questions such as those that follow are addressed. Why has access to the Kuskokwim, in its varied dimensions, been relatively easy or difficult? How have historical developments affected accessibility? What have been the broad and narrow implications of changing degrees of accessibility? How has access affected outsiders in the pursuit of their goals? Why did Westerners penetrate the Kuskokwim region? Once there, why did they stay or leave? What were, or are, their particular aims? How have they attempted to accomplish their desired ends? How have Westerners of the region reacted to Eskimo reluctance or failure to cooperate? Finally, in considering the goals of Eskimos as they have affected the ethnohistory of the region, what have their creative responses been to the presence of Westerners, and why have these responses emerged?

In sum, my approach to Kuskokwim Eskimo ethnohistory is to examine it in light of differential access to the region by Westerners and differential goals of various groups of Westerners. The concluding chapter centers on a comparison of ethnohistorical developments on the Kuskokwim with those among other Eskimos and Indians in the general region. Through these comparisons the ways in which Western access and goals affected Kuskokwim Eskimo ethnohistory become more fully apparent.

Bashful No Longer

An Alaskan Eskimo Ethnohistory, 1778–1988

1

The Setting

The far-flung discoveries made by European maritime explorers began with the African voyage of Bartholomeu Dias in 1486–88 and climaxed most emphatically with the final expedition of James Cook. Cook's goal was to write finis to the "perfect craze," as the historian Miller Christy termed the English search for a northern sea route to the Orient.[1] To be the first to navigate a Northwest Passage had become an English obsession following the discovery of northern North America by John Cabot in 1497. However, success had eluded the best of seamen, and the sailing instructions for Cook's third voyage introduced a novel navigational challenge. Rather than sailing west from England, he was to seek entry via the north Pacific Ocean or some other northern waterway.[2] Cook was then to follow the passage east or west, if possible mapping his route to enable subsequent voyagers to sail from England in the opposite direction.

Cook's ship, the *Resolution,* was accompanied by the *Discovery,* with Charles Clerke as her captain. These experienced seamen sailed from England in July 1776, discovered the Hawaiian Islands in January of 1778, and arrived at Nootka Sound along Vancouver Island two months later. Repairs occupied nearly a month before the ships coursed northwest to the Gulf of Alaska. Putting in at Prince William Sound in May for additional repairs, the English were visited by the Chugach, the southernmost Alaskan Eskimos. Cook had with him a copy of *The History of Greenland* (1767) by David Crantz, and after reading it he recognized parallels in appearance, artifacts, and language between the Chugach and the Greenlanders.[3] He reasoned that since a similar way of life was found in the western and eastern sectors of the far north, this might indicate that a waterway connected the two regions, an enticing prospect considering his goals.

As the English sailed west from Prince William Sound, they sighted a broad inlet; this they thought might be the gateway to the long-sought passage. It proved to be a false hope, however, and the waterway now is known as Cook Inlet. Returning to the sea the ships again coursed west, passing Kodiak Island and rounding Unalaska Island before entering the Bering Sea. From Bristol Bay they sailed northwest to Cape Newenham and, rounding it, entered a vast and inviting estuary, Kuskokwim Bay, on July 18, 1778.[4]

At this point the wind failed, and the ships paused in lower Kuskokwim Bay. An anchor was lost from the *Resolution,* and five days passed before it was recovered and they could extricate themselves from the shoals and return to the sea. While the crews searched for the anchor and then for a channel, twenty-seven Eskimos in kayaks paddled out to the ships. They were members of the Kusquqvagmiut, "People of the Kuskokwim," the Eskimo group that lived from the tundra edging the bay inland into the forested region of the central Kuskokwim River.

As the kayakers cautiously approached the English ships, they opened their arms to show they had no concealed weapons and called out, apparently to indicate their peaceful purpose. Yet with the coordinated arrival of so many kayaks, one would suspect they had intended to attack the ships but changed their minds. They were unwilling to board the vessels but kept the small gifts tossed to them as they bobbed about in their kayaks. Cook described these Eskimos as dirtier than the Native Americans he had encountered earlier in the voyage. Their hair was shaved or cut short, with long locks left in the back or to one side, and their heads were covered with skin hoods and wooden hats. They wore lip plugs or labrets in addition to nose ornaments. The English discovered that tobacco was unknown to them and noted that "they appeared to be wholy unacquainted with people like us." The only foreign materials in their possession were the iron blades of their knives, and they were anxious to obtain metal knives in exchange for their artifacts.[5]

Cook possibly exaggerated the isolation of Kuskokwim area Eskimos and their unfamiliarity with Westerners at that time. Actually, a relatively intense aboriginal trade prevailed from Siberia to Alaska, via Bering Strait, prior to Cook's arrival. Along this route Native Alaskans received Asian and European manufactures. When the Russians arrived in the North Pacific region in the 1640s, the Siberian trade intensified. As Lydia T. Black has noted, by the late seventeenth century Alaskan Natives had some familiarity with the people of eastern Siberia, including Russians, and the Russians in turn had considerable knowledge about the Native peoples of western Alaska. Furthermore, Russians in the Kodiak Island area were familiar with Eskimos in the southern Bering Sea area by 1761. It seems unlikely that some of these Russians had not ventured farther north before the arrival of Cook.[6]

The Alaskan Eskimo desire for iron was a long-standing one that had been satisfied in a meager way by indirect trade before direct contacts were established. At the Eskimo site of Ipiutak at Point Hope, in a context dating around A.D. 400, the smelted iron point of an engraving tool was found.[7] This attests to trading ties, however remote, with iron producers in Asia. Archaeological excavations in later Eskimo sites show that the iron trade intensified gradually into the historic era. Therefore, the existence of iron artifacts among the Eskimos met by Cook comes as no surprise. Their strong desire to obtain iron from the English does imply, however, that the material remained scarce among them.

Cook's report that Kuskokwim Bay Eskimos were unfamiliar with tobacco reveals more than does the reference to iron blades. After being domesticated in South America, probably before 5000 B.C., tobacco soon spread to North America, where it eventually became popular and was traded widely, but not as far north as Alaska. Tobacco was introduced into Europe by Christopher Columbus and was popular there by 1600. Its use soon spread eastward, but tobacco did not become a regular trade item from Siberia to Alaska until after 1800.[8] The unfamiliarity of Kuskokwim Eskimos with tobacco in 1778 implies that they had been little affected by Westerners or their products.

Alaskan Eskimos in the Bering Sea region remained unknown to Europeans for so long not only because of the distance from Europe and the short sailing season in the region, but also because of navigational hazards in the area. Although a superior navigator, Cook was ill-prepared for the conditions he encountered in Kuskokwim Bay. The bay is a vast funnel-shaped alluvial outwash plain, and its muddy waters flow over a relatively flat bottom threaded by elusive channels that may shift not only from year to year but as quickly as from one tide to the next. To compound the difficulties arising from this condition, a maze of changing visible and invisible sandbars lace the bay. A navigator might locate a deep channel, follow it for as many as twenty miles, and then find that it ended abruptly. Furthermore, the twelve-foot tides in the bay create a serious hazard; ships dare not proceed too far at high tide for fear of being grounded on the ebb.[9] Soon after the English entered the bay, Clerke wrote that this was "a damn'd unhappy part of the World," a restrained comment for a mariner in his position at the time.[10]

The waters of Kuskokwim Bay continued to be considered extremely dangerous by later navigators. The Russians, when they expanded into the region, thought it unsafe to send oceangoing vessels into the bay. They supplied the Kuskokwim along difficult inland routes even though this meant the use of small boats, which limited their imports. After the Americans purchased Alaska in 1867, the company that assumed control over Alaskan trade sent its supply ships into the upper bay, where they anchored and off-loaded into small vessels that were paddled or sailed up the river; this again made the cost of imported goods high and their availability limited.

THE RIVER

The Kuskokwim River system drains about 49,000 square miles, or ten percent of Alaska, yet it would be surprising if one percent of what has been written about the state concerns this region. The river's obscurity, despite its respectable size, results from its being overshadowed by the Yukon River drainage immediately to the north. The Yukon is vast compared with the Kuskokwim, but more important, it became the most famous waterway in northern America when it served as a major access route to the Klondike and Fairbanks area goldfields; the gold deposits discovered along the Kuskokwim have been modest by comparison. Being called the *Kuskokwim* likewise has not contributed to the popularity of the river. English speakers often find it hard to remember the name and even harder to learn the correct pronunciation (KUS-ko-kwim). To local Eskimos it is the Kusquqvak, which can be translated "a big thing [river] with a small flow." [11]

A widely accepted index to the magnitude of a river is the amount of water discharged from its mouth. In this respect the Kuskokwim ranks tenth among rivers of the United States; it discharges an average of 62,000 cubic feet of water per second. The Yukon River, which ranks fifth, discharges 240,000 cubic feet per second. The distance from the mouth of the Kuskokwim to the farthest headwater stream is about 850 miles, 582 of which comprise the named river. The Yukon, including an area in Canada, covers about 327,000 square miles and is about 1,900 miles long. [12]

Compared with many Alaskan rivers the Kuskokwim has a moderate, even gentle flow. The riverbed drops less than one foot per mile, and its waters seldom flow faster than six miles an hour. Waterfalls do not impede river travel, and rapids are confined to tributaries and headwater streams. Short sections of boiling water may rock small boats, but they are unlikely to upset anywhere along the river unless the weather is stormy. The diurnal tide measures about three and a half feet at Bethel, which is eighty-six miles upstream, and affects the water level more moderately for another forty miles. Under normal conditions a large oceangoing vessel can reach Bethel during any summer month, and a boat with a four-foot draft usually can ascend as far as the town of McGrath, 511 miles from the mouth. Thus the Kuskokwim is navigable for tugs and barges along its entire length. [13]

The watershed nearest the river mouth at Eek Island is characterized by a monotonous panorama. The flatness of the landscape is broken only by the river channel with its low, eroded banks. Where ice lenses in the banks are exposed, the summer melt produces oozing sections of muddy shoreline. Beyond the riverbanks, peat ridges provide minimal relief. The landscape is of a type called wet tundra. Here the low-growing vegetation includes cottongrass, birch or willow shrubs, and other low-lying plants. Beneath the mantle, which is about a foot in depth, is permafrost. On the north side of the river permafrost usually is continuous, whereas to the south it more often occurs in scattered pockets.

The land is poorly drained, and countless ponds and lakes make it difficult to walk very far in a straight line during the summer. Dense thickets of Sitka alder grow in protected spots along the riverbanks and on islands, while small draws shelter substantial stands of willows.[14]

From the river mouth to Bethel the channel narrows gradually, and the landscape is transformed. The north bank becomes higher and more stable, and it supports stands of quaking aspen and American green alder. Beyond these stands, tundra vegetation resumes its dominance. On the many islands near Bethel aspen and alder again are found. Another species, white spruce, has spread in a narrow corridor from the interior to beyond Bethel as the treeline edges seaward. Some sixty miles above Bethel scattered stands of spruce become increasingly common along both banks of the river and on islands; however, beyond the riverbanks tundra vegetation again dominates. Upriver another fifty miles at Kalskag, the channel narrows abruptly, and large spruce stands become more common. Here, for the first time, the north bank is backed by rounded hills reaching as much as 1,500 feet in elevation; immediately beyond the south bank the terrain remains low, although it is more undulating than farther down the river.[15]

The river surface, be it water, ice, or snow-covered ice, has been and remains the primary thoroughfare for local travelers. The river begins to freeze in early November, and it remains ice-covered until about mid-May. During periods before freezeup and breakup, travel can be dangerous. It may take new ice a few weeks to thicken enough to support a dog sled or snowmobile, and the spring meltwater can prove troublesome as well. Breakup brings hazards and problems not only for travelers but also to residents in low-lying settlements. The greatest fear is that an ice jam at a river bend will cause an immense amount of water to back up, flooding a broad area and sometimes inundating villages.

Away from the main river, lakes, sloughs, and streams enhance the mobility of travelers, and Kuskokwim tributaries provide a more extensive access deep into the adjacent countryside. Most major tributaries flow northward from mountainous areas and are one hundred miles or considerably more in length. Rivers such as the Kwethluk, Aniak, and Holitna were, and to a lesser extent are, important routes to hunting, fishing, and trapping areas.

THE REGION

Climatic summaries for the far north tend to be misleading because they imply that it is cold throughout the year, as reflected in the mean annual Kuskokwim valley temperature average of about 28° F. (-2.2° C.).[16] Yet for the central river town of Aniak the temperature averages are well above freezing from May through September. At Aniak the mean temperature for the warmest month, July, is about 55° F. (12.8° C.); a record high in June is 92° F. (33.3° C.). It can be and often is quite cold from November through March. The coldest month is January with a -0.6° F. (-18.1° C.) average, and a record low is -62° F. (-52.2° C.). In relative terms, it makes little difference to the people whether the temperature is 0° F. (-17.8° C.) or -30° F. (-34.4° C.), provided it is windless. They carry out their normal winter activities except when the temperature and winds make the air extremely cold. People then avoid outdoor activity, especially of a strenuous nature. This is reasonable since fish and game typically are inactive when the temperatures are low, making food-getting activities unrewarding at these times. Total snowfall at Aniak is about 60 inches a year, yet total precipitation is low, about 18 inches a year, most of it falling as rain.[17]

Contemporary plant and animal species along the river are much the same as they have been over the past 150 years, yet certain changes have occurred. The most dramatic is the disappearance of virgin stands of spruce as a result of fires in historic times. The first extensive burn for which we have a record occurred in 1842, soon after Kolmakovskiy Redoubt was established. Within days the woods around the redoubt had been reduced to ash.[18] The worst burns date from the opening decades of this century and are associated with the presence of gold seekers.[19] Today virgin stands of spruce exist only on a few islands; the forests elsewhere are dominated by second growth spruce.

The distribution in historic times of economically important animals has been less stable for large species than for small ones. Animals living along the river in general, in early times as well as now, include arctic ground squirrels, ermine, land (river) otter, mink, muskrat, pine marten, red fox, wolf, and wolverine. Beaver and land otter have lived along the central and upper river from early Russian times to the present. Black bears are confined largely to the forested area, and other species, including arctic fox and tundra hare, are limited largely to the wet tundra near the coast. In spruce stands and uplands hoary marmots, porcupines, and snowshoe hares are found. Coyotes, the only wild land mammals new to the region in historic times, began to arrive along the upper river drainage in the 1920s, and by 1931 they had reached the Stony River.[20]

The most dramatic historic decline in the distribution of wildlife has been in two large species, beluga and caribou. Beluga commonly ascended the river in the last century.[21] Along the lower river they were hunted as late as 1911.[22] In 1844 a countless number of Barren Ground caribou roamed the Kuskokwim Mountains south of the river some distance behind Kolmakovskiy Redoubt and north of the river around modern Sleetmute.[23] Caribou were hunted within sight of Bethel in 1887, and in 1910 one observer reportedly saw a thousand caribou in a single day below Little Russian Mission (Chuathbaluk).[24] After the introduction of reindeer in 1901, caribou disappeared gradually, in part because they attracted reindeer and were considered a nuisance by herders, who killed them indiscriminately.[25] By the late 1920s their number had declined dramatically as a result of such killings, the relatively recent and widespread availability of effective firearms, and the miners' reliance on caribou meat as food. Caribou seldom were seen in the area by the 1950s, but today small numbers again are found along the central river.

The most striking increase in the big game population during this century has been that of the Alaska moose. Although unknown numbers lived along the central river in the 1840s, they did not appear at the headwaters until somewhat later.[26] By the 1920s they had become numerous along the central and upper river, presumably because of the good pasturage in the aftermath of forest fires. Moving downriver, the first ones began filtering into the Bethel area by about 1940.[27] Since then they have become relatively abundant and have continued to spread westward.

Moose hunting is now an important means of obtaining meat for many residents of the region.

Waterfowl and game birds have been important seasonally to the people living along the river. Many species of waterfowl pass through the region in the spring and fall; most nest elsewhere, but some breed along the river system. Game birds that remain in the region all year include the Alaska willow ptarmigan on the tundra, Yukon ruffed grouse in alder and willow thickets, and Hudsonian spruce grouse in forested areas.

At the time of contact, the economic mainstay of riverine Eskimos was salmon, and this has remained true to a lessening degree into the present. The species currently most important is the chinook (king) salmon, followed by chum (dog) and coho (silver). Smaller runs of sockeye (red) and pink (humpback) salmon also occur.[28] Other fishes plentiful on a seasonal or local basis include the inconnu (sheefish), several species of whitefish, Alaska blackfish, northern pike, and burbot (lush).

The Kuskokwim region may have been "a damn'd unhappy part of the World" for English explorers, but the Eskimos living inland found the river to be a great and highly dependable provider. They relied on fish, especially salmon, as their primary staple. In addition, they depended heavily on the upland tundra as hunting and trapping grounds. For whites, apart from gold seekers and a few trappers who have lived along the river, the Eskimos themselves have been the primary resource attracting them to the area. Whites settled among the Eskimos to transform them into consumers of Western products as well as Christians, to educate them in schools, and to administer varied social, economic, and political programs intended to change the quality of their lives.

2

The Eskimos

Eskimos typically are associated with northern coastlines fronted by icy seas and backed by a tundra zone, yet most of them did not occupy settings of this nature. They were the most far-flung aboriginal population in the world, and the dramatic regional differences in their habitats led to the emergence of lifeways that differed appreciably while remaining clearly Eskimoan. This diversity seldom is noted in general writings about them, and therefore, Eskimos most often are thought of in terms of the stereotype established when explorers first discovered and described the coastal-dwelling peoples of northern Canada and northwestern Greenland. In this high arctic setting Eskimos lived in small family groups, hunted sea mammals and polar bears, occupied snowhouses, wore fur garments, and traveled widely by dog sled. Numbering about 4,400 in early historic times, they represented only a small proportion of the estimated 51,000 Eskimos then in existence.[1] Not only were the stereotypic Eskimos comparatively few, but their lives were impoverished, especially when compared with Alaskan Eskimos. The culture of "snowhouse Eskimos" was so exotic, however, and their manner so congenial that they readily captured the imagination of those who read about them. Because of this, most people think of Eskimos in terms of the stereotype even though far more has been written by now about those who live in a much different environment. Included in this larger group are riverine populations such as the one to be considered.

This presentation focuses on the Upriver People or Kiatagmiut living along the Kuskokwim, who represent an Eskimo subculture that belies the stereotype. Typically, the Upriver People

12

never saw icy seas or a living polar bear, and they rarely hunted seals. Salmon was their primary staple. The Upriver People were intimately familiar with tundra country, exploiting it intently for fish and fur, but they were equally at home among spruce-forested riverbanks. Among all Eskimos, the Upriver People had the distinction of ranging farthest inland in a continuous line of stable settlements, and their riverine adaptations possibly were the most refined.

Although unlike the stereotypic Eskimos in many ways, the Upriver People were similar in most respects to other Alaskan Eskimos, especially those living in the southwestern region. They distinguished between the house life of females and children and the *qasgiq* living of males; the nuclear family did not prevail as the year-round residence unit. Their emphasis on fishing and their dependence on salmon as the major food source throughout much of the year made their subsistence orientation similar to that of the Yukon and Nushagak Eskimos. They also shared with these Eskimos a highly developed religious life that focused largely on annual ceremonies. Many of their manufactures, such as their stone artifacts, tool kits, and objects of personal adornment, were types made widely by other Alaskan Eskimos. In these and other cultural dimensions the Kuskokwim Eskimos blended harmoniously into adjacent Eskimo groups and contrasted greatly with their counterparts at the northern fringes of the continent.

Along the Kuskokwim drainage at the time of historic contact, there were two distinct aboriginal populations, Eskimo and Indian. The Indians, represented by the Georgetown Ingalik, Kolchan (McGrath Ingalik), and Tanaina lived along the upper reaches of the river and in the adjacent inland area. The Eskimos were subdivided into two cultural groups, the Downriver People and the Upriver People. Eskimos living from the Kuskokwim Bay area to Bethel called themselves the Unegkumiut, meaning Downriver People. Those called the Kiatagmiut, meaning Upriver People, lived from Bethel to the vicinity of the future Russian post of Kolmakovskiy Redoubt, a distance of about 170 miles.[2] (This is not the upriver area geographically but was considered to be by its inhabitants.) The farthest Upriver Eskimo village was Crow

the Aleutian Islands; the separation between Aleut and Eskimo, meaning Inuit and Yupik, is about three times as great as the difference between English and German.[7] Inuit-speaking Eskimos, who may have numbered about 31,000 early in their history, lived and continue to live from northwestern Alaska across northern Canada to Labrador and Greenland. No major subdivisions occur within Inuit. Yupik, which is subdivided into Central, Pacific Gulf, and Siberian languages, may have been spoken by about 20,000 people in early historic times. It prevailed from eastern Siberia to the shores of Norton Bay, south along the coast and up some rivers to Controller Bay, which fronts the north Pacific Ocean. Central Yupik is divided into seven dialects, including the one identified with the Kuskokwim Kiatagmiut.[8]

The Eskimo-Indian boundary is marked by the remains of Kolmakovskiy Redoubt, a major trading station built by the Russians. From that point inland into western Canada lived Northern Athapaskan Indians. One Athapaskan group, the Georgetown Ingalik, had settled along the Kuskokwim from the vicinity of Kolmakovskiy upriver to the Stony River. This group had branched off from the major Ingalik population, which was centered to the north along the Yukon drainage. Beyond Georgetown Ingalik territory, upstream from the Stony River mouth to the Kuskokwim headwaters, lived the Upper Kuskokwim Athapaskans, also termed the Kolchan or McGrath Ingalik.[9] The Stony River drainage was the home of other Athapaskans, the Tanaina, whose greatest population concentration was in Cook Inlet drainages.[10]

Upriver People, at the time they were first contacted by Westerners, were unusual but not unique among Eskimos in the influence Athapaskan Indians had on their lives. These Eskimos shared a common inland boundary with the Georgetown Ingalik and were in the process of peacefully assimilating them. A similar situation was found on the Yukon, where the Anvik-Shageluk Ingalik came into contact with Yukon Eskimos as they moved upriver.[11] Whereas most Anvik-Shageluk Ingalik have retained their ethnic identity into the present, the Georgetown Ingalik have been absorbed into the Kuskokwim Eskimo population. Joan B. Townsend has demonstrated other Eskimo-Indian blendings, to the south along the Pacific Rim, that again were basically harmonious, with trading ties and intermarriages far more common than hostile encounters. Townsend acknowledges that the distinction between Eskimo and Indian languages remained meaningful in this area, but she stresses that a cultural mosaic had developed because of the intensity of friendly contacts.[12]

Eskimo-Indian interactions along the central Kuskokwim in early historic times quite possibly were similar to those described by Townsend. However, Kuskokwim Indians were relatively few compared with local Eskimos, and the 1838–39 smallpox epidemic depleted the Indian population proportionally more than that of the Eskimos. It is thus not surprising that the Georgetown Ingalik eventually disappeared as an ethnic group. Another factor enabling Upriver Eskimos to assume control over this interior forested region was their ready adoption of Indian technological forms.

It seems reasonable to assume that the extensive use of bark by Upriver Eskimos was stimulated by contacts with Athapaskan Indians. Both netting and bindings were made of the inner bark of willows. Slabs of bark from spruce or birch trees covered the frames of structures. Birch bark also was used to cover large and small canoes and was fashioned into baskets. At the historic Upriver Eskimo site of Crow Village birch bark was the raw material most commonly recovered.[13]

All aboriginal Eskimos used wood in their manufactures when it was available, but the Upriver Eskimos had an especially well-developed spruce splint technology, presumably as a result of Indian contacts and ready access to forests. The most complex spruce splint manufactures of these Eskimos were funnel-shaped fish traps set with weirs fashioned largely from the same material. At each of the numerous openings in a weir they set a fish trap that was eight or more feet in length, thereby creating a highly efficient means for taking salmon in the main river. Setting smaller traps of similar design in conjunction with weirs in streams was a reliable means of harvesting many blackfish and whitefish during their runs. This intense use of flexible materials is especially notable when the technology of the Upriver Eskimos is compared with that of most other Eskimos.

Early in their history Upriver Eskimos were well established in small communities scattered along the banks of the Kuskokwim River. Residents of a village possibly averaged 120, and all had a

strong attachment to their settlement. For a family to move away
or for an individual to die elsewhere was considered unfortunate.
At times entire villages were relocated because of changing conditions, but under such circumstances kinship ties were not broken.
Upriver People occupied their villages in the winter, moving elsewhere to live the balance of the year. Nonetheless, the village was
the setting of greatest importance since it was the only place
where all the people gathered for any period of time.

Settlements were built on well-drained high ground close to
productive salmon-fishing sites. A nearby clearwater stream to
supply drinking water added to the desirability of a site, as did a
good beach and a commanding view of the river. A village might
include five or six sod-covered houses and always had one much
larger mound, beneath which was the men's house or qasgiq. The
men's house, which was the heart of any village, served as the
residence of most males and as the ceremonial center. Only
shamans lived permanently in the houses occupied by their wives.
Compared to a qasgiq, the dwellings of women were humble
structures.

Near each house stood a cache, which was set on four corner
posts, framed with poles or hewn spruce logs, and covered with a
bark roof. A notched log provided access. Long sills extended
beyond the front and back walls to hold sleds and other bulky
items; the closed-in storage area was filled with supplies at the
approach of winter. Salmon that had been dried and smoked were
stored in woven grass bags, fishskin bags, or sealskins. Pokes of
seal oil and beluga stomachs stuffed with blubber and oil were
piled in one section. Elsewhere were wooden or birchbark vessels
filled with berries and bundles of dry grass for mats and other
purposes. Near the houses pits might be dug and lined with bark
for the storage of fish caught too late in the season for drying. If a
house was near the riverbank, trash was likely to be dumped on
the bank, where it would wash away with the floodwaters of
spring; alternatively household debris might be thrown onto a
pile near the structure, where it formed a kitchen midden. Elsewhere in a village were fish drying racks made from poles; other
racks made from poles were used to store boats during the winter.

Men identified closely with their qasgiq and worked together to
build or repair it. It was framed with stout spruce logs recovered

as driftwood. The walls, as much as thirty feet in length, were set into an excavated foundation, and the framed structure was covered with grass or slabs of bark before being sodded. The semi-subterranean design helped keep out the cold as did the anteroom or tunnel entrance. The main room, dominated by a large central fire pit, had a spruce plank floor; additional planks covered the pit when the fire was out. In the ceiling directly above the fire pit was a skylight with a removable cover made of sewn gut stretched over a wooden frame. When the skylight was covered, there might be so little oxygen in a hot and crowded qasgiq that a burning ember could remain lit only near floor level. Persons unaccustomed to such living would find their eyes watering soon after they entered the ammonia-filled room. The fumes came from large open tubs of urine collected for personal bathing and for processing skins.

The life stages of a male were symbolized by the location of the bench on which he slept, worked, or rested in the qasgiq. Young boys were given space beneath the benches until they became old enough to occupy the bench or benches opposite the entrance. Middle-aged men were assigned benches on the side-walls, and old men had benches adjoining the entryway, the oldest being nearest the entry. Apart from the benches and urine tubs the only other furnishings were a large tub of drinking water and two bowl-shaped clay lamps mounted on wooden stands toward the back of the building. Filled with oil, the lamps provided nighttime light, and in a prosperous community they never burned low.

The early morning routine in a qasgiq was ritualistic, unlike activities during the balance of the day. While everyone remained in his sleeping place, an old man delivered a monologue; alternatively, two old men participated in a dialogue. In either case, the discourse concerned the behavior of youths and adults while at home or away, how to act in emergencies, and what to do differently as times changed. Residents also might be reminded how to behave in the men's house. For instance, conversations were to be subdued, horseplay was prohibited, and quarreling forbidden. Young boys learned that they were to drink from the water tub only after asking a man's permission and were expected to consume little water, which was thought to increase their endurance.

In effect, boys were reared collectively by the men of a qasgiq, and because of this, they learned to respond promptly to any man's request for assistance. The morning teachings ended when the shaman arrived to perform a daily ritual, the nature of which is unknown. After the shaman was finished, the day's activities began. These included departures for hunting and fishing, settling in to make or repair equipment, eating meals at customary times, and bathing.

Aboriginal Eskimos seldom have a reputation for personal cleanliness, but in this sector of Alaska the men were avid group bathers, sometimes taking repeated hot baths in their qasgiq during a single day. To prepare for a bath some of the men removed the boards above the fire pit and stacked lengths of dry spruce in the hole. After setting the skylight cover aside, they started a fire, a signal for all bathers to undress. As the room filled with smoke and heat, each man bit on a bundle of wood shavings that filtered the hot air before it reached his lungs. Ears were the part of the body most likely to burn, and to protect them some men wore skin headbands. When the smoke had cleared, the skylight cover was set in place, causing the heat to intensify. If a bather's skin began to burn, he would daub it with urine from a small container nearby. If the heat proved unbearable for a bather sitting on a bench, he eased himself onto the floor and stretched out, to be cooled by the air rising between the floor planks. Bathers became lightheaded and exhilarated from the heat and felt refreshed afterward. In the winter a man might end his bath by walking to a nearby hole in the river ice and having someone ladle ice water over his naked body until he was chilled. Most bathers, however, remained in the building, where they washed in urine, pouring the unused portion from their containers on the coals of the dying fire. One of the most pleasurable aspects of life for these men was bathing and sitting around talking in the warm room afterwards.

The dwellings that formed the principal part of a village were built of spruce logs set partially beneath the ground in a square or rectangular outline. Covered with bark topped by a layer of sod, such houses were entered through narrow, pole-lined tunnels dug into the ground to serve as cold traps. Family dogs often stayed in these tunnels to escape mosquitoes in the summer and cold weather in the winter. A ground-level entrance, either temporary or permanent, might be used in the summer; if it was permanent, an anteroom for storage often was attached. Above the stone-lined fireplace in the center of a house was a skylight. Wood burning in the fireplace heated the room and cooked the food; an oil-burning lamp provided light during the evening. Logs separated the grass-covered walking area in the room from the fireplace and from the low earthen platforms along the side and rear walls. Residents worked, lounged, and slept on these platforms, which were covered with grass and grass mats.

A typical household included an old woman, her daughter or daughters, and their daughters, plus boys under about nine years of age. The work routine was supervised by the old woman, who lived at the back of the house on her own platform. Such older women had the reputation of being outspoken critics of villagers in general, yet to their granddaughters they were loving and faithful allies. Young boys respected their grandmothers but remained aloof from them; their loyalties were reserved for male relatives in the men's house. This living arrangement did not foster close conjugal bonds; a man always was something of an outsider in the house where his wife lived, although he might stay there overnight or when he was ill. Women and girls visited a qasgiq to attend ceremonies but never remained there overnight.

The daily routine began in a household when a child, usually a boy, lit the oil-soaked moss wick of the household lamp. He searched the fireplace for a glowing coal, and if none had lasted the night, he obtained a live coal from a neighboring house. After the lamp was lit, women began preparing the morning meal. Conscientious wives watched for the shaman to return from the men's house to his dwelling; this meant that the males of the village awaited their morning meal. The woman who appeared first with food, usually a young woman, gained the reputation of being a good provider. After the women distributed food to their family members, they sat on a bench with their heads bowed. When the men had finished their meal, wives, sisters, or daughters left with the empty bowls.

On those mornings when a man planned to use his dog team, his wife helped harness the loose dogs to the sled. Afterwards she might go off with small children to collect wood for her household and for the qasgiq. While older boys and girls checked snares set in thickets for ptarmigan and along the trails of hares, elderly adults performed other chores. Late in the day but well before dark, men who returned from hunting or fishing went directly to the qasgiq while their wives unharnassed the dogs, secured the sleds, and either stored or began to process the take. A woman had full control over the harvests delivered by her husband. A man usually ate the morning meal at the house of his wife and then returned to the men's house, perhaps to go back to her dwelling later.

MATERIAL CULTURE

The Upriver Eskimos could obtain locally all the raw materials required for their artifacts, but they sometimes preferred materials and manufactures from elsewhere. Since resources differed from one sector of the river to the next, a well-developed aboriginal trade had emerged. For instance, the Upriver People obtained from interior Indians birch-bark canoes and a particular type of slate that made good whetstones. They traded with coastal and bayside Eskimos for the sealskins they valued for containers, boot soles, and boat covers, and for walrus hides from which to make ropes. In return, most riverine Eskimos could offer wolverine pelts for garment trim and beaver or otter skins obtained either locally or in trade from interior Indians.

As has been noted, Kuskokwim Eskimos were receiving trade goods from Siberia before the arrival of Russians. The Chukchi of Siberia and Eskimos in the Bering Strait region were the middlemen responsible for introducing iron and copper manufactures, as well as personal adornments and reindeer skins, to western Alaska. It appears that the indirect trade was through trading partners, individuals in other villages with whom a special socioeconomic relationship prevailed. In addition, some local Eskimos had become part-time traders, and their annual visits to different villages, combined with the yearly markets held near Bethel and Sleetmute, provided numerous trade opportunities in pre-Russian times. After the Russians opened their trading station at Nushagak, Kuskokwim Eskimos could travel south to do their trading directly, but apparently few chose to do so because of the distance involved.

The material adaptations made by Eskimos as they moved in-

A Kuskokwim Eskimo family photographed at Mumtrekhlagamute Station (Bethel) in 1884. *Courtesy of the Moravian Archives, Bethlehem, Pa.*

land are well illustrated by their garments. Upriver People did not wear fitted parkas, and they depended rather heavily on fish skin as a raw material. Here, unlike on the coast, both sexes wore the same style of loose-fitting, ankle-length frock. It most often was made of ground squirrel skins sewn together, with the tails and paws left dangling as ornamentation. In cold weather people added hoods made from caribou or squirrel skins. Both parkas and the separate hoods could be trimmed with different kinds of fur. A fishskin parka cover might provide additional protection against the cold and prevent snow from blowing into the fur. Sea mammal intestines were preferred for rainproof parkas, but fish skins were more readily available and served as an alternative material.

Mittens presumably were worn, and possibly leggings. A person's feet were protected by socks made of woven grass or sewn skin and by boots commonly fashioned from fish skins. Caribou skin boots with sealskin soles were also worn. The advantage of fishskin boots was their lightness and warmth, but they tore easily. Despite the drawbacks of fish skin, its use in clothing represents in innovative utilization of a locally abundant material.

As among Eskimos elsewhere, the most sophisticated handwork of women went into garments, which required more production steps than any other artifacts. The making of clothing was the last and most difficult technological skill acquired by a young woman. She learned how to process the skins through numerous stages as well as how to shape and sew them. The delicate stitches required for a fishskin rain parka and the blind stitches for waterproof boots were the greatest tests of her abilities. In addition to clothing, women made birch-bark baskets, stitched the coverings of canoes, and wove mats and baskets of grass. They also formed clay into cooking vessels and lamps, which they might decorate with line and dot designs before firing.

With skin garments covering most of their bodies beautification was concentrated on the head. A woman wore her long hair parted in the middle and braided. Tattoos of vertical blue lines might decorate her chin, and milky blue beads were strung on a cord that hung from a hole in her nasal septum. A small hole on each side of her mouth, just below the lower lip, held an ivory labret with beads and other adornments attached. Women also pierced their ears and wore ivory earrings decorated with dangling strings of beads. The hair of men was either tonsured or worn long over the shoulders. Men did not tattoo their faces, but they often wore labrets and earrings similar to those of women.

Eskimo men are justly famous for their craft skills, and those along the river were no exception. Elsewhere antler, bone, and ivory were the materials used most often, but along the Kuskokwim, manufactures of wood dominated. For most purposes, men preferred the dry spruce driftwood abundant along many riverbanks. For artifacts that would be used in connection with water, such as net floats and dippers, or those requiring particular care in crafting, spruce root was the favored material. It resists waterlogging and tends not to crack when carved into forms such as dance masks and ladles. For other purposes, spruce logs were split into sections by using a wooden maul to drive wooden wedges inserted along the grain. A stone-bladed adz served to shape the wood further, and refined carving was accomplished with a beaver-tooth knife. The most precise finishing was made with a crooked knife, so named because it had a curved iron blade fitted into one side of an antler handle. Artifacts crafted from wood ranged from large ones, such as structures, sleds, canoe frames, and fish traps, to smaller ones such as gauges for nets and cups.

Men flaked chert to make scrapers and arrowpoints or basalt to fashion net sinkers. They chipped slate and then smoothed it on grinding stones to produce adz blades, scrapers, and some whetstones. Stone also was flaked and polished to produce blades for end-bladed knives or to make the semilunar knives that are so typically Eskimo. Other hard materials sometimes were worked, including antler and bone; each was processed with burins and crooked knives. Antler was made into arrowheads, knife handles, and wedges, whereas bone was worked into awls, net sinkers, and sledshoes.

Eskimos are well known for their capacity to produce artifacts from a wide variety of materials and with highly appropriate designs. The Upriver People aptly are included in this characterization. They, and their Eskimo neighbors, are further acknowledged to excel in the production of particular forms considered by Westerners as especially pleasing. Their ceremonial masks, which are imaginative in design, painted with varied colors, and elaborated with moving appendages, have attracted widespread attention. The same is true, but less dramatically so, of their small containers, which have varied decorative motifs added to highlight the design. The elegance of their manufactures clearly represents one of the many cultural achievements of these riverine Eskimos.

OBTAINING FOOD AND FUR

To exploit local resources efficiently, most families probably lived at three different places each year. These were their village, tundra camp, and fish camp. While at their winter village, they did comparatively little hunting or fishing, depending on cached fish and game taken before freezeup or soon thereafter. By the end of winter these supplies and the local sources of edibles often had been depleted, and families anxiously awaited the longer days of spring, when they could set off for their tundra camps. Here they concentrated on harvesting waterfowl, fish, some game, and furbearers. A tundra camp might be less than a day's trip from a winter village, although some families traveled to tundra camps along distant tributaries. To make the spring journey a family used a freight sled, which they loaded with all of their equipment, including a large boat. The sled was pulled by four or fewer dogs harnessed at the sides and by a man pulling on a towline attached at the front; in addition, the man's wife pushed from behind. Very small children might ride on the sled, but older children and other family members followed on snowshoes. Related families and friendly ones often camped at traditional sites, living as nuclear families in sod dwellings or tents covered with skins or grass mats.

After settling in at a spring camp, women and girls carrying birch-bark baskets searched for last year's berries that still hung from bushes. As soon as nearby streams shed their winter ice, women fished for northern pike and whitefish with hooks and lines. At the same time men tended gill nets and fish traps for both species and hunted on an opportunistic basis. The males also ranged widely in small canoes to hunt and snare migratory waterfowl. Equally important they hunted, trapped, or snared furbearers, especially beaver, land otter, and muskrats. These species were obtained not only for their pelts but for the meat they provided. After about two months, families grew weary of camping and were ready to return to their villages. As soon as the waterways were free from ice and any flood waters had subsided, they boated home with their equipment.

The Kuskokwim was a reliable provider during the summer. The first evidence of this each year was a run of smelt, a small fish that frequented shallow coastal waters until early summer, when it swam upstream to its spawning grounds between Tuluksak and Kalskag. Smelt arrived in the lower river in vast and churning masses that disappeared upstream within a few days. The local Eskimos, who had prepared their long-handled dip nets after returning from camp, were ready to take advantage of the run as soon as someone spotted the first churning of the water. Sometimes the fish could be netted from shore, but more often men paddled their boats to the cutbanks that tended to be the best netting spots. As long as the weather was good and the run heavy, people were reluctant to stop fishing for any reason. They never knew when winds might make it dangerous to use their boats or when the smelt might disappear. Individual smelt were strung through one gill on willow branches stripped of their leaves, and by the end of a run dozens of loaded willow branches hung from caches or fish-drying racks. Some fresh smelt were boiled and eaten whole, but most were dried and cached, to be dipped in seal oil and relished the following winter.

With the summer fishing season ready to begin, families often moved from the village to nearby camps along the riverbanks. Early June brought warm and lengthening days, when the weather generally was calm and there was little rain, and people began to work harder than at any time since the previous fall. Even the laziest men spent days making and repairing equipment in preparation for the fishing soon to begin. Gill nets were set in river eddies to intercept inconnu, which might weigh twenty or more pounds. Everyone looked forward to catching these fish because they were a fatty species that made good eating and also because their arrival was a sure sign that salmon soon would appear.

The stability, quality, and success of Upriver Eskimo life depended most heavily on salmon, their primary staple. These and other fish were prepared in many different ways; as one observer noted, they might be "boiled, pickled, fried, iced or shredded, and dried." [14] The annual salmon runs were predictable and usually were bountiful. Apparently the runs never failed entirely, although weather and river conditions caused the size and quality of the catch to vary from year to year. Restrictions centering about the salmon harvest were relatively few but not unimportant. They applied particularly to chinook, which were the first as well as the largest salmon species to run. The first one caught in a village was treated in a special manner, which included using every part of it. Fresh chinook were not to be prepared as food for twenty-four hours after they had been taken, and in general, fresh salmon were never to be touched by dogs. Finally, when salmon were running, making noise near the river was prohibited.

If time, equipment and circumstances permitted, men fished

intently for chinooks, which might be from 30 to 60 inches in length. Early historic accounts do not mention the number caught using aboriginal gear, but in the recent past a man who fished with a commercial net from a powerboat might take eighty chinook in a single drift. In all likelihood, in aboriginal times a heavy run meant that a man could harvest enough chinook in a week to satisfy the winter needs of himself, his family, and guests. When the chinook catch was abundant, fishermen were far less diligent in taking other species, if only because their ample supply diminished the importance of the smaller fish.

Two salmon fishing strategies prevailed, with the use of drift nets less popular than weirs and traps set in combination. Drift nets were relied on when water and riverbank conditions were such that weirs and traps could not be used effectively. To harvest salmon with a drift net a man in a kayak or canoe drifted a gill net down a relatively straight and snag-free stretch of river. He paddled quietly along as he paid out the net, keeping it extended at right angles to the current. If a large chinook struck the net, the impact was great. When this happened, the fisherman untied the net line from his boat and moved as silently as possible to the spot. With a wooden club in hand, he lifted the section of net slowly, and as the fish broke the surface, he struck it a sharp blow on the head. The goal was to kill the fish immediately so that it would not cause the net to tear. A single drift spanned a mile or two of river, and when it ended, any smaller salmon caught in the mesh were removed. The fisherman then paddled back upstream and began the process anew. He fished throughout much of the day and continued to do so day after day until the run ceased or he was satisfied with his total catch.

Although drift netting was an efficient means for taking salmon, most were caught in funnel-shaped traps set at weirs. The building of a weir and traps was difficult, but once this was done, the combination operated untended and continuously, which meant that with little additional effort, great numbers of fish could be taken during a heavy run. A weir was built from a riverbank at right angles to the current at a place where the channel was approximately four feet deep for a distance of about fifty yards. The builder drove one stout spruce pole after another into the riverbottom as he moved away from the bank. When he had covered the desired distance, he tied sections of woven spruce splints on the upstream side of the poles and backed them with brush held in place by the current. At periodic openings in the weir, he set cone-shaped traps so that their mouths faced downstream. As salmon or any other fish swam upstream, their course was barred by the weir, and many entered the traps, from which they seldom escaped. Hundreds of salmon might be taken in a single night. A major disadvantage was that driftwood logs could destroy a set in a few minutes, as could a surge of floodwater. Another potential problem was that a drop in the water level could render a weir-trap set ineffective.

Whenever a fisherman paddled back to his village or nearby fish camp with his catch, he unloaded the fish into a rectangular wooden bin and covered them with grass mats as protection from the sun's heat and egg-laying flies. At this point the women's work began. Throughout the day they removed one fish after another from the bin, put them on boards, and partially filleted them with a semilunar knife. The prepared fish, held together by the uncut tail, were dried on pole racks that had smudges set beneath them to ward off flies. In rainy weather women covered the fish with grass mats to prevent them from turning sour from excessive moisture. After being dried thoroughly, the fish were bundled and cached for winter.

A small family may have required about five hundred salmon a year to feed themselves, their dogs, and visitors, especially those who came for ceremonial events. This is not a great number of fish considering the aptness of their retrieval technology, but it was not always possible to meet this goal. If a season's first run began earlier than usual because of weather conditions in the bay, fishermen might be so unprepared that they could harvest com-paratively few chinooks. Large numbers of salmon usually could be caught if the runs came when the river water was relatively high and muddy, but if summer rains were light and the water remained relatively clear, salmon fishing could be poor. When the water level was low, salmon tended to swim in the middle of the river and consequently became more difficult to catch. An-other factor affecting the supply of winter food was the weather following a run. If the summer was rainy, fish might rot before they dried, no matter how carefully they were protected. Thus even though annual salmon runs were assured, many variables separated a fisherman from a cache filled adequately with dried salmon at the end of the season.

The Upriver People also exploited other aquatic species on a regular basis. Harbor seals and beluga (white whale) found migrating salmon easy prey, and they pursued them upriver for many miles, only to be taken themselves by the Eskimos. Smaller mammals in the rivers and streams likewise made a significant contribution to the economy. Land otter, mink, and muskrats were caught in funnel-shaped traps set in conjunction with weirs built across narrow streams. When locally available, beaver were shot with arrows or snared. These furbearers were taken at any time of the year and were valued as a source of food and fur.

In the fall other fishes, especially burbot, blackfish, and whitefish, were hooked, trapped, or netted as winter food. Generally alternative or supplemental edibles, these fish were critical to the food supply when the salmon harvest was light. Another fall activity was caribou hunting. While great herds roamed the area, they could be difficult to take because their movements were not entirely predictable. Hunts, which might be planned far in advance, had to be launched quickly when herds appeared nearby. Some caribou were snared or stalked by individuals during these hunts, but more often the animals were shot with arrows after being corralled cooperatively. Hunts of this nature were exciting and strenuous but seldom dangerous. Caribou most often were taken late in the fall when their meat was prime and the skins best for garments and bedding. The thick layer of fat was rendered into oil, which was used as lamp fuel and as a dip for food. The meat, like that of beluga and seals, might be dried if the weather was too warm to freeze it for later consumption.

In the late fall many families boated to the camps they had occupied in the spring. Here they obtained additional food for winter. Women filled many containers with blueberries and salmonberries to mix later with congealed fat into *akutaq,* or Eskimo ice cream, a favorite dessert for special occasions. Men set traps at their weirs in small streams to intercept blackfish and whitefish as well as an occasional mink, muskrat, or land otter. If families arrived at camp soon enough, they could capture molting waterfowl by surrounding them and closing the circle. Hundreds of birds were taken in this manner, but there were few nesting grounds near the river. At this time and somewhat later, furbearers were sought for their pelts and as food. Depending on the locality, ground squirrels, marmots, beaver, land otter, and marten were hunted, snared, or trapped. As the days shortened, families sledded back to their home villages and settled in for the winter.

If food caches were bulging by late fall, villagers could relax and look forward to the winter festivities. Those men who had not yet obtained enough food for winter kept working to expand their provisions. Throughout the fall they could chip holes in stream or river ice and net whitefish, hook burbot, and trap blackfish without great effort. They could also snare ptarmigan and hares or spear a black bear to death in its den. As winter progressed, however, food-getting declined. Weir-trap sets were used for catching fish, but it became increasingly difficult to chip through the thickening ice to tend these traps or the nets that were set. Furthermore, the cold caused species to become relatively dormant. Only extenuating circumstances led men who had been ill to hunt or fish in the coldest months. Few families were likely to experience food stress during the winter, though it might occur in the early spring if supplies became depleted before the weather was suitable for hunting and fishing. This period could be especially lean if the people had been overly generous hosts during winter ceremonies.

SOCIAL LIFE

Although Upriver Eskimos did not live in nuclear family units, adults preferred to be married, primarily for economic reasons. It was nearly impossible for an adult male or female to function independently in this culture. A man depended on his wife to prepare his meals, preserve the fish and game he caught, process the pelts, and make as well as repair his garments. A woman relied on a man to provide food and skins for herself and her children and to supply most of the artifacts she required in daily living. Yet marriages were unstable. Divorce was expected if a young wife did not conceive because children, especially boys, represented the greatest hope of a couple for support in old age. A woman might reject a lazy husband, and a man might leave a wife who hoarded food for herself. If a man desired another man's wife, he might challenge the husband to a wrestling match and thereby win the woman. If a man was dissatisfied with his wife and sought to end the marriage, he typically left the village for an extended period and made no provision for her welfare. A woman seems to have initiated a divorce by not preparing meals for her husband. On occasion men exchanged wives, more as a gesture of friendship and an acknowledgment of social and economic ties than for sexual gratification. In addition, a man who was an exceptional provider might have more than one wife.

Apart from marriage and divorce, pregnancy, especially the first one, was a milestone of adult life. Customarily a young woman made no obvious preparations for the birth, fearing that to do so might cause the baby to die. The birth of a couple's first child introduced them to parental responsibilities while also conferring a higher status, especially if the offspring was a boy. Symbolically, they were no longer referred to by personal names but became known as the parents of their firstborn, a convention known as *teknonymy*. As a couple succeeded in their parenting, they gained standing among fellow villagers. A mother did her best to satisfy every need of her offspring, and a father became far more conscious of his role as a provider.

As children grew, they were integrated into the community through everyday activities and also through special ceremonies. After a small boy killed a member of any animal species, even an insect, for the first time, his parents hosted a special meal to mark the event. Each celebration apparently was proportional to the value placed on the species taken, with the greatest feasts held for caribou and seal kills. Young males were further acknowledged at an annual villagewide ceremony honoring their skill as hunters. Mothers stuffed and kept the skins of birds, mice, and other animals their young sons had killed during the year. At religious festivities held in the late fall or early winter, these skins were hung from a wooden carving of a bird with movable wings, which was suspended from the ceiling of the men's house. When the villagers had assembled for the festivities, the fathers of the honored boys performed to the accompaniment of tambourine-like drums. As they took turns dancing and presenting gifts to the audience, their wives served vast amounts of food. Not only was this a means to note the boys' achievements, but it appeased the spirits of the skinned animals, thus helping to insure an abundant harvest in the forthcoming year.

After a small girl first picked a berry, a feast was held to acknowledge her initial contribution to family welfare. Similar meals honored her as she contributed other edibles for the first time. Within the next few years a girl was expected to be increasingly helpful to her mother, and by the age of nine she was well integrated into the household routine. A girl's childhood ended when she reached puberty, a point marked by her observance of new taboos and by a ceremony called Putting Away the Doll. In preparation for this event the girl and her mother made fishskin boots, woven grass mats, socks of woven grass, and other articles to be presented to guests. The family prepared large quantities of food, and villagers were invited to the festivities, as were friends from nearby communities. This puberty ceremony, like the celebration after a boy killed a major animal, served to acknowledge the attainment of adult status.

Not long after a girl participated in the Putting Away the Doll Ceremony, her parents and other near relatives arranged her marriage. The marriages of youthful persons were especially unstable; they often served as "trial" marriages through which each participant sought to find a compatible mate. Marriage was marked by a special feast and the presentation of a new set of garments to the bride and groom, but no formal ceremony was performed. The bride continued to live in her mother's house, and the groom stayed in the qasgiq; thus, the marriage residence pattern was matrilocal. Although the husband's abilities as a provider were watched with care by the girl's parents and villagers in general, there was little change in the status of the partners at this time, especially if the man came from another village. A new son-in-law was neither asked nor told to do anything, but if he did not maintain his wife and her parents in a satisfactory manner, he was dismissed by his in-laws. All the fish, fur, and game that a new husband obtained apparently went to his in-laws until they felt he had proven himself able to provide adequately for his wife.

Some men became such highly successful providers that their families did not require all the food they had available. These men gained honor at home and abroad by hosting both social and religious events during which they shared their food with others.

In each village one man was singled out as the most outstanding provider as well as a dependable and generous person. Called "a man indeed," his authority was great in matters of community-wide concern. For instance, he decided the timing of major festivities, if only because he was the one most obligated to provide sufficient food for the event. He was an informal or consensus leader until his abilities failed as a result of accident, bad luck, old age, or a combination of these factors. He then would be displaced informally by a new, more capable leader.

Cooperative male labor was uncommon despite the shared living arrangements for men. In the food quest a man usually worked alone or with one or two others, most often a brother, friend, or son. Youths learned how to do a man's work largely by observation as they were growing up. As adults, men most often seem to have worked as equals, regardless of their age. Yearly drives of waterfowl, hares, or caribou and building or repairing a qasgiq were the only occasions on which unrelated males coordinated their efforts, and these activities occupied relatively brief spans of time. For women the cooperative unit was the household in which they shared food processing obligations. More formal cooperation prevailed when they crafted artifacts as gifts for ceremonial occasions and prepared foods for these events.

Just as villagers usually did not work together to make a living, neither was there a formal body to make political decisions. Political action within a village depended primarily on extended families functioning independently. The extended family, usually meaning an elderly couple, their sons and daughters, and their grandchildren, was the most important kin group among the Upriver People. Two or three relatively large extended families plus a number of smaller ones seem to have been typical in their villages. An extended family buffered members when they came into conflict with outsiders and provided aid in times of need. All villagers identified primarily with these units. A friendly rivalry prevailed between extended families, but they also were bound together not only by common identification with a settlement but by economic exchanges that occurred in social and religious contexts. Economically successful older persons within and among these families functioned as leaders, primarily of their own relatives. They did their best to assert their authority in a nonforceful manner, depending most heavily on reason and persuasion. Conflict might occur within a village if leaders of the large extended families disagreed so much on some matter that they became aggressive. Because the leaders were generally good providers who were able to offer aid to relatives and others, the respect for them that originated within their families gradually extended villagewide.

When serious problems arose in a village, its population responded in unison only when numerous kin groups were affected. If a drastic disruption in normal life, such as murder, occurred within an extended kin group, it was not a community-wide concern. However, the murder of a nonrelative seriously disrupted relations between families and might involve an entire village and nearby settlements. At the center of this type of homicide was the victim's family, who reacted by attempting to kill the murderer or a close male relative. While they sought revenge, the perpetrator's kin tried to convince nonrelatives to support their cause; if enough people became pitted against one another, a feud emerged. Influential neutral parties usually tried to intervene before this point was reached, lest large segments of the population become engulfed in retaliations that would devastate the community.

RELIGION

The natural world, represented by plants, animals, people, the landscape, and heavens, was intimately joined with the supernatural sphere represented by spirit beings and forces. Integration of the natural and supernatural was the key to Upriver Eskimo religious life. An individual was well aware of this linkage through his or her personal name. When a person died, his or her name was bestowed on one or more infants, depending on the social standing of the deceased. This was achieved readily since names had no gender. This naming pattern resulted in continuity between the souls of the dead and those of the living. Furthermore, rituals were performed to achieve the continuity of animal species and perpetuate their spirit essence. Through propitiation hunters were able to harvest the physical bodies of the species involved without destroying their souls. Thus the death and rebirth of people and animals were integrated through the belief system of these Eskimos.

Magico-religious activities were vested most clearly in the village shaman, who was the primary interpreter of spirit beings and forces. A Kuskokwim Eskimo shaman could be male or female, but since little is known about female practitioners, only male shamans are considered here. These individuals hunted and fished as other men did, but they did not live in the men's house. Instead, a shaman and his family occupied a separate residence. People respected and might fear a shaman because of his reported rapport with supernaturals. Shamanism was an achieved status, and the goal of an apprentice was to gain power over spirits. Once this was accomplished, he could seek advice from them in dreams or visions. Spirit helpers could be found in animate forms, such as birds, or in inanimate ones, such as mountains or ponds. With their help shamans reportedly could change the weather, cure some forms of illness, attract edible species, and prevent disease or disaster.

Among Eskimos those of southwestern Alaska are especially well known for the richness of their ceremonial life. Clever staging effects, drama, humor, and elaborate symbolism characterized their ceremonies. Kuskokwim Eskimos held ceremonies of this nature, which often were highlighted by men performing as masked dancers. The wooden masks often were painted several colors, and they might be small, face-sized images or much larger ones with appendages attached that shook as their wearers danced. The masks most intimately associated with shamans depicted their spirit aids and were carved by the shaman himself or an expert carver. Another cluster of masks was worn by men when telling stories or making humorous presentations. A third type of mask depicted animals or plants whose characteristics were mimicked by dancers in rituals designed to insure the continuing abundance of the species involved.[15]

The ceremonial season, extending from late fall through early winter, was a favored time for these riverine people. They gladly settled in for the winter, not dreading the darkness and cold but anticipating the good times to come. Numerous festivities were held before spring arrived. The Berry Festival that marked the end of summer was the first ceremony held each fall. It and the Bladder Festival that followed were major religious ceremonies in which honored species were propitiated so that the people might thrive for another year. New harvests were required each year in this region. Frozen meat typically decayed if uneaten by summer,

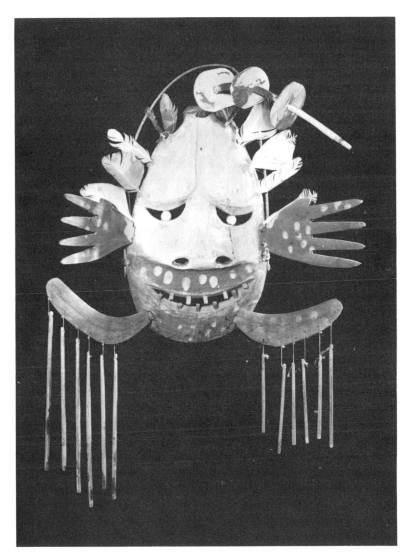

This Upriver Eskimo wooden mask, made between 1875 and 1900, represents a spirit being named Walaunuk, meaning "bubbles as they rise through the water." *Photograph courtesy of the Museum of the American Indian, Heye Foundation, Neg. No. 29614.*

and dried fish became too dehydrated after a year to provide satisfactory nourishment. Since food surpluses could not be carried
over from one year to the next, people literally began each subsistence year anew; for this reason they held fall and winter ceremonies to insure that their needs would be met when it was again
time to hunt and fish intently.

One ceremony held during the winter was so elaborate that it
was not performed in each village each year. This was the Great
Feast for the Dead, which honored those villagers who had died
since the ceremony last was held. There was comparatively little
ritual involvement at the time a person died. The body was flexed
and placed on its side in a small plank coffin that was then carried
to a nearby cemetery and set on four posts. Figures might be
painted on a headboard to represent an outstanding achievement
of the deceased, and the person's personal belongings were placed
near the grave, either on the ground or attached to the posts. For
individuals buried away from their village or for those who died
by accident and whose bodies were never found, carved wooden
figures were erected as memorials in the cemetery. The dead were
honored later at minor annual rituals, but the final tribute, and the
most elaborate one by far, was the Great Feast for the Dead.

Intense preparations preceded a Great Feast for the Dead. For
each of the deceased adults honored, the closest relative became
the principal host. He or she was aided by kinpersons in making
hundreds of gifts; in addition, the hosts worked especially hard
the summer before the feast to obtain the best foods in vast quantities. The ceremony was held during the early winter, and hundreds of guests arrived from surrounding villages. They as well
as their dogs were fed during the several days of their stay. At
ceremonies performed during this time all visitors received gifts
of food and crafted articles in honor of the dead, and the name-
sake of each honored dead was given the finest clothing. After the
celebration was completed, the honored souls were content and
required no further concerted attention.

SUMMARY

With the advantage of hindsight we may briefly review cultural
conditions among Upriver Eskimos on the eve of Russian entry
and emphasize those aspects that would foster successful penetra-

tion of the area by Westerners. The presence of home villages meant that the Russians would be dealing with relatively concentrated and stable clusters of people. However, the amorphous nature of village political organization and the absence of formal intervillage alliances favored Russian penetration and reduced the likelihood of widespread resistance. Likewise, being small and scattered, the villages had no developed means for defense. These Eskimos already harvested all the furbearers that the Russians desired, and short and long-range trade networks already prevailed. Local Eskimos were pleased with the trade goods they had been receiving indirectly from Russian sources, which suggests that the Russians, if they were prudent, would be welcomed.

RUSSIAN PROBES

All was not tranquil in the Kuskokwim region on the eve of Russian penetration. An unfortunate accident and its consequences led to an exceptional and prolonged display of violence known later as the War of the Eye. The confrontation spread north and south from the lower Yukon area, giving rise to countless bloody encounters and producing a major Eskimo population shift before it finally ended. Historically the war played a pivotal role in Russian colonization of the region, and for that reason it is examined.

The war began in a men's house as the result of a dart game being played by boys. One of the players threw a bone-pointed dart so wildly that it missed the target and struck another boy, blinding him in one eye. Their fathers were present, and when the father of the injured boy realized what had happened, he seized the dart and the offending boy. In what would be considered just retribution, he put out one of this boy's eyes, but in his fury he unjustly blinded the other eye. Afterwards the fathers began to fight; one was armed with a beaver-tooth knife and the other with a bone bodkin. The duel led to the death of both fathers, and the villagers immediately formed two revenge-seeking factions. Each was identified with one of the fathers, who apparently represented competing groups of kin. This suggests that the villagers had different backgrounds and that the blindings had in fact triggered long-standing feelings of mutual hostility. Most of the males representing one faction were killed, and the survivors fled.[1]

The blindings and homicides soon involved Eskimos of surrounding communities because closely related males living elsewhere were duty bound to avenge the deaths of their kin. The only way for the men of either faction to insure their future safety, and that of their sons, was to kill all males of the opposite group. Before long the war enveloped thousands of Eskimos as it spread across the Yukon River delta, south to Bristol Bay, and inland along the Kuskokwim River. The extent of the conflict suggests the range of overlapping regional kinship groups and the inability of these Eskimos to settle problems of this magnitude by peaceful means.

When the war reached the lower Kuskokwim region, the Aglurmiut Eskimos living there planned attacks on central river villages. Ordinarily these Eskimos traveled upstream during the summer by way of the main river, but for a surprise attack they chose an alternative route. In this case they planned to reach Old Kalskag by kayaking up the Johnson River, which parallels the north bank of the Kuskokwim, to Mud Creek, which enters the main river near Old Kalskag. Forewarned of the plan, men from Old Kalskag and nearby Ohagamiut hid along the banks of Mud Creek near its junction with the Kuskokwim River. As the kayakers approached, paddling slowly and quietly along the shallow waterway, one of the men lying in wait gave a raven's call as the signal to begin shooting. The waterway was so shallow and narrow that the kayakers were unable to maneuver their boats quickly enough to escape the arrows. All of the invaders were killed except one old man with poor eyesight who had lagged behind the others. When he finally reached the junction, the victors were gathered to meet him. The old man got out of his kayak to look around, and seeing the strangers, he asked which way the river flowed to the coast. As they helped him back into his kayak, one man cut off his right ear, threw it into the river, and told him to follow his ear home. According to one account, when he reached his home village, the old man shouted, "Valor and victory," but on questioning him, the people learned of the defeat and in their rage tore him apart limb from limb.

The victors stuck their paddles into the creek water, and blood coated the lower half of the blades. Henceforth these men and their descendants painted a red line around the middle of their paddle blades to commemorate their victory. It is said that the waters of Mud Creek, also called Bloody Creek, turned red from the blood shed that day and have remained that color ever since. Some men at Upper Kalskag, descendents of the victors, continued to paint a red ring around their paddle blades into the 1960s. By the mid-1970s, however, the custom had been dropped, and few people recalled the Bloody Creek Massacre.[2]

Following this episode the Upriver People apparently gained the initiative, and they decided to attack the village of Quinhagak along Kuskokwim Bay. The invaders raided the village men's house at night as the men and boys slept. After blocking the entrance, the raiders removed the skylight cover and threw burning embers into the building, suffocating the residents. Soon after, the Quinhagak survivors joined families from allied villages and fled south.[3] Migrating to the Nushagak River drainage and settling there, the escapees, who were known as Aglurmiut, came into conflict with the local Kiatagmiut Eskimos, who had close relatives along the central Kuskokwim. The invaders apparently killed many Nushagak-area Kiatagmiut but at considerable cost to their own number. In a major confrontation in 1816, as many as two hundred Kiatagmiut were slain.[4]

As the Kuskokwim-area Eskimos most affected by the War of the Eye, the Aglurmiut lost not only their homeland but much of their population. Attacks on them were so successful that by the time of the 1816 massacre, only sixty Aglurmiut men reportedly remained alive.[5] When the Russians explored the Nushagak area, they learned of the situation, and after they had built Aleksandrovskiy Redoubt (modern Nushagak) in 1819 they tried to protect the newcomers from their enemies. Some Aglurmiut settled near the Nushagak station and became allied with the Russians, while others journeyed farther south and west to the Alaska Peninsula.[6] Russian expansion into the Kuskokwim drainage clearly was facilitated by having Eskimo allies who were familiar with the region. Although these Eskimos initially proved unreliable guides for explorers, they soon became faithful employees in the fur trade.

The presence of Russians in Alaska was based on their frenzied quest for furs. They first became familiar with the Aleutian Islands and, finding the region rich in the most desired pelts, those of sea otters, hastily organized trading companies that competed for the greatest profits. In the process they ruthlessly exploited the local Aleuts and Eskimos. The Russians founded their first permanent station on Kodiak Island along Three Saints Bay in 1784, and in 1799 the surviving companies were consolidated as the monopolistic Russian-American Company. As its general manager, Alexsandr Andreevich Baranov, an energetic and skillful administrator, devoted his many talents to furthering the fur trade and advancing Russian interests in the Pacific. After founding an administrative capital at Sitka in 1804, the Russians ranged to California and to the Hawaiian Islands in an effort to expand their dominance of the Pacific region. However, obstacles to expansion southward proved overwhelming, and an alarming decline in fur resources along the north Pacific soon affected the northern trade. At this point Baranov began shifting his attention northward, hoping to expand the fur harvest by exploiting the Bering Sea drainages of Alaska.

An exploratory probe into southwestern Alaska had been launched in the early 1790s, soon after the Russians had established themselves on Kodiak Island. Vasily Ivanov set off one winter from Iliamna Lake with a group of Lebedev-Lastochkin Company employees and Native Alaskans. Skiing northwest they crossed the Nushagak River drainage and continued on to the "Tutna," or Kuskokwim River. They traveled downstream to the community of Ohagamiut and then probed north again, crossing over to the "Balsanda," or Yukon River. After following the Yukon to the sea, the explorers traveled a short distance up the coast before turning back toward their home base. During this trip of nearly four months, Ivanov noted an abundance of fish and fur animals but recorded little else. He did remark, however, that the people encountered had some copper and iron tools and a few beads, evidence that they were receiving artifacts from Siberia along aboriginal trade networks.[7] Some fifty years after this remarkable probe into unknown lands, people along the Kuskokwim still recalled the "military behavior" of these men who were identified as *Kosyaks* [Cossacks].[8]

Following Ivanov's trip, the next concerted northward probe was launched by Petr Korsakovskiy in 1818 with Fedor Lavrentevich Kolmakov as the co-leader. Their purpose was to explore the mainland north of the Alaska Peninsula to learn as much as possible about the local peoples and the resources of the region.

Departing from Kodiak Island the party crossed the Alaska Peninsula to explore the coast as far as Cape Newenham and to probe adjacent sectors of the interior. A detachment of the party led by Eremy Rodionov set out for Lake Clark in a skin boat, possibly crossed the Mulchatna River drainage to the Hoholitna River, and from there went on to descend the Holitna River to the Kuskokwim. They apparently boated downstream to Ohagamiut, where it is reported that they met an old man, Kylymbak, who talked as if he had encountered Russians during his travels to the north. Kylymbak and other Kuskokwim Eskimos accompanied Rodionov south to talk with Korsakovskiy, who listened to the old man's story but did not find it credible.[9]

The following year, 1819, the Russians built Aleksandrovskiy Redoubt at the head of Nushagak Bay, a site favored because of its high bank and accessibility from the sea.[10] In the late fall Korsakovskiy again set out to explore the coast, this time traveling as far as Goodnews Bay. He had hoped to ascend the Kuskokwim River but changed his plans after meeting Eskimos who advised against the trip, pointing out the lateness of the season and the probable difficulty in obtaining food.[11] With the founding of Aleksandrovskiy the Russians not only had established their presence along the Bering Sea but were in a better position to obtain pelts from the area and to expand their explorations farther north.

THE NUSHAGAK POST

Fedor Kolmakov was the company employee most involved with the Nushagak post during its early years. After helping to select the site and construct the buildings, he became the manager. Unlike many company employees, Kolmakov was a Russian, not a *creole,* a French loanword applied by Russians to people who were of aboriginal and Russian ancestry.[12] During his exploratory work in 1818 and 1819 Kolmakov had become aware of the animosity between different groups of Eskimos in the area. He soon learned that the Aglurmiut, some of whom lived near the Nushagak post, were refugees who had come from the Kuskokwim region and were being harassed by the local Kiatagmiut. Both being outsiders, the Russians were sympathetic with the Aglurmiut and attempted to bring an end to the disputes. Once the conflict was muted, other Eskimos felt reasonably safe in traveling to the Nushagak post to trade. This expanded the fur trade and led to close feelings of identity between the Russians and Aglurmiut. As a result these Eskimos ranged widely to obtain pelts and contributed significantly to the furs received at Nushagak in its early years.[13]

By 1828 trade at the Nushagak station was thriving; reports listed 4,000 beaver and land otter pelts obtained early in the year.[14] Many of the skins came from the Kuskokwim region, which company administrators regarded as a rich and largely untapped source of furbearers. However, by this time the Kiatagmiut, especially those along the Kuskokwim, were serving as local traders in Russian goods, and they opposed the entry of company agents into their area.[15]

As company administrators became dissatisfied with the location of the Nushagak fort, they contemplated a move to a better area. A major disadvantage of the Nushagak site was the shallow coast, which made supplying the fort from deep-draft vessels difficult. In addition, the beach and lower portions of the station flooded intermittently. Although a short-lived station was built on Hagemeister Island, it was decided not to make a more permanent move until the region to the north, in particular the Kuskokwim River, had been explored.[16]

KUSKOKWIM EXPLORATIONS

Ten years after founding the Nushagak station, the Russians launched their first major exploration to the northern interior as a prelude to expanding the fur trade. Their 1829 expedition was organized on Kodiak Island and led by Ivan Ya. Vasilev, an ensign in the Corps of Navigators. His party crossed by ship to the Alaska Peninsula and then boated and portaged to the Nushagak station, where a larger, fifteen-member party was organized. This group included Aglurmiut and Kiatagmiut guides, whose number varied as some deserted and others were recruited along the way. The party boated up a Nushagak River tributary to Tikchik Lake and Tikchik Village; this was the closest they came to the Kuskokwim. Most of their guides deserted at this point, having learned that the Eskimos at Tikchik planned to kill all of the party. When

Vasilev heard of the intended attack, he left the Tikchik area, and because he no longer had guides, he was forced to return to the Nushagak post without accomplishing his primary purpose.[17]

In organizing a second expedition intended to reach the Kuskokwim, Vasilev asked for more men, but his request was rejected by Petr Egorovich Chistyakov, then general manager of the company. Chistyakov felt that a large contingent was more likely to encounter difficulties than a small party and that the people along the way might think a large group was bent on conquest. Since such a misunderstanding could create problems for the party at the time and also might inhibit future relations, it was decided to take ten or fewer men from the Kodiak area, plus guides. Because the previous expedition failed when the guides deserted, Chistyakov instructed Kolmakov, still the manager of the Nushagak station, to enlist Eskimos from the Kuskokwim itself as guides and to hold their relatives and friends hostage at the post. Advising Kolmakov not to be concerned about the expense of caring for the hostages, Chistyakov stressed that when "the wolves are satiated . . . the sheep are safe." [18]

With these instructions in mind, Kolmakov sent word to the Kuskokwim Eskimos that they were invited to spend the winter of 1829–30 near the Nushagak redoubt, and more than two hundred men responded. When it came time to organize the expedition, he selected guides for Vasilev from this group and held others hostage. On June 19, 1830, the Vasilev party left the Nushagak station on a second inland expedition.[19] The group included two creoles, Petr Fedorovich Kolmakov, the eldest son of the manager, and Semen Ivanovich Lukin, a creole who was to interpret, as well as eleven Eskimo guides. They boated up the Nushagak River until they reached a pass leading to the Kuskokwim. Before this point all but four guides had deserted, and the ones who remained did so under duress. After a difficult five-day portage the party came to the Holitna River and descended it to the Kuskokwim. Efforts to induce the local people to guide them upriver failed, and they hesitated to proceed in that direction without a knowledgeable person to lead them. The party began paddling downstream and at various points along the way was threatened by the local people. Apparently it was only because the men were

well armed and alert at all times that they avoided a confrontation. Vasilev finally won over some prominent men, and under
their protection he was able to reach the mouth of the river. After
arriving at Kuskokwim Bay they traveled south along the coast
until they could portage between Kuskokwim and Togiak bays.
They returned to the Nushagak redoubt on July 29. The Kuskokwim Eskimo guides who had not deserted had worked out reasonably well, and Chistyakov praised Fedor Kolmakov for his
part in the successful exploration of the central and lower river.[20]

Neither Vasilev's original 1830 travel journal nor copies of
it are known to exist, but fortunately both were consulted and
commented on at the time by other Russians.[21] From their accounts we learn that Vasilev outlined central and lower Kuskokwim area geography and reported an abundance of furbearers,
only a small number of which were being harvested. There were
reports of his difficulties with the people, especially with a man
named Iliugnali, described as a "famous robber"; Vasilev eventually had made peace with him however. These contacts between
Vasilev and the people indicated to the company administration
that although the people were initially unfriendly, they could
be won over. This information and the encouraging reports about
the number of furbearers led the new general manager, Ferdinand
Petrovich von Wrangell, to formulate further plans for a northward expansion.

LAUNCHING THE LOCAL FUR TRADE

In 1832 Wrangell issued precise orders about the development of
Kuskokwim trading and made Fedor Kolmakov directly responsible for the enterprise. Kolmakov was to assemble a trading outfit and recruit as many men as he wished to accompany him. He
was to obtain the skins of beaver, land otter, lynx, and fox, especially dark brown and black ones; red fox and other furbearers
of little value were to be ignored. Kolmakov was to leave the
Nushagak station before winter and follow the most direct route
to the Kuskokwim, not stopping to trade along the way. Once
there he was to tell the people that Vasilev had praised them and
that he, Kolmakov, had come to trade and establish peace between hostile groups. Kolmakov was to ascend the river, barter-

ing for pelts and stressing that the Russians would return the following year with additional trade goods. The party also was to build winter quarters from which to range in obtaining furs. Finally, Kolmakov was to select a site for a permanent station, to which he or someone else would return the following summer.[22] Wrangell obviously had confidence in Kolmakov since his party was to be the first to winter in the area and to carry out active trading in Eskimo and Indian settlements.

On August 30, 1832, Kolmakov, Semen Lukin, and six others, including Aglurmiut guides, left the Nushagak station for the Kuskokwim. They traveled in kayaks (baydarkas) that held from one to three persons. Ascending the Nushagak River to a headwater stream, they portaged to the Holitna River and descended it to its junction with the Kuskokwim. Here they built the first Russian station along the river, a "winter hut." This station became an *odinochka,* the smallest administrative post used in the Russian fur trade, and was called Kolmakovs Odinochka.[23] On December 1, Kolmakov and most of the party left the odinochka and reportedly traveled up the Kuskokwim to the most inland Indian village, where they traded for furs during the winter. Lukin and a few men ventured up the Stony River in January. This splitting of the already small party indicates the trust Kolmakov and Lukin had in the local people. In the spring Kolmakov and those men with him retraced their route to the Nushagak post, and Lukin's group followed the same route on their return in July.[24]

Kolmakov reached the Kuskokwim with an inventory of goods valued at 2,776 rubles, and returned with 1,150 beaver skins, having used goods valued at 1,574 rubles to give as gifts or trade for skins. The previous year the Nushagak station had taken in 2,232 beaver and land otter pelts; total trading the year of Kolmakov's initial trip brought the take up slightly, to 2,900 skins. This indicates that the initial inland trading venture was not an overwhelming success as far as the year's fur take was concerned. Wrangell reported to St. Petersburg that the returns were less than expected because the people had not realized the Russians would return to trade and they had few pelts on hand. He stressed, however, his certainty that more skins would be obtained the following year.[25]

Kolmakov and Lukin traveled to the Kuskokwim again in August of 1833, but they did not venture as far from the odinochka to trade as they had the previous year. Additional men arrived by dog team in early January as had been arranged, and all appear to have returned to the Nushagak station in February except for Lukin, who traded at the odinochka until later in the year. The Russians obtained nearly 1,500 beaver skins with an outlay of about 4,000 rubles; this meant that the cost per skin was far greater than in the previous year.[26] Despite their efforts, the overall fur trade at Nushagak dropped from the high of 2,900 in 1833 to about 2,750 the next year. The general manager wrote to his superiors in St. Petersburg that the take for a particular year varied because of local conditions and that the inland trading ventures had improved the overall harvest. However, when writing to Kolmakov, he expressed displeasure at the small number of pelts received.[27]

As the fur harvest along the Nushagak drainage declined, the inland trade became more important and was expanded. During Kolmakov's two trips to the Kuskokwim, the party members had not only traded for pelts but had hunted animals themselves. Their success led to the practice of sending company hunting parties into the interior, partially because the local people did not seek out furbearers with the diligence the Russians expected. The pattern was to place creoles in charge of Eskimos from the Nushagak area, presumably most often Aglurmiut, who received traps, guns, and ammunition as an inducement to participate. The first such group appears to have operated along the Innoko River in 1836–37, and more were added in the spring of 1839. Each functioned independently; their only stricture was that they were not to alienate the local people.[28]

After his trading trips Kolmakov recommended a new means for supplying the Kuskokwim odinochka. The Nushagak-Holitna route the Russians had been using could be undertaken only with small boats in the summer or lightly loaded dog sleds in winter. Kolmakov proposed sending a large oceangoing vessel to the Kuskokwim River mouth in the late spring to rendezvous with small boats arriving from upriver loaded with skins. Kolmakov's suggestion was rejected because of the expense involved and because it was thought that Kuskokwim Bay was shallow and dangerous to navigate.[29] Instead, supplying the Kuskokwim from the Nushagak station was facilitated with the founding of another odinochka, this one along the Nushagak near the King Salmon River junction. In addition, more dwellings and warehouses were built at Kolmakovs Odinochka.[30] This provided more adequate shelter and storage on each side of the pass separating the Nushagak and Kuskokwim drainages, but it did not solve the problem of limited transport.

Kolmakovs Odinochka was a convenient resting place but was not well situated for trading furs. Although beaver were plentiful here and along the upper river, the local population was small and scattered. The number of Eskimos and Indians was far greater downstream, where, in addition, good trails led to the Yukon, with its substantial Indian population and many beaver. Therefore, Kolmakov founded a second Kuskokwim station downriver at the junction of the Kuskokwim and Kolmakov (Kwik) rivers, a far more favorable location. Here at the village of Kwigiumpainukamiut, Kolmakov built a three-room structure in the fall of 1833. It came to be identified as Lukins Odinochka because Semen Lukin most often stayed there.[31] As unimpressive as this post must have been, it was the most important inland trading center until the founding of Kolmakovskiy Redoubt.

The northward thrust for furs led to continuing explorations. After his Kuskokwim travels in 1830, Vasilev had recommended founding a station to the north of the Yukon River mouth, and his suggestion was followed in 1833.[32] Built on St. Michael Island, Mikhailovskiy Redoubt (St. Michael) became the farthest north redoubt in Alaska and led to the growth of the fur trade in the region between the island and the Yukon River.[33] In the same year the creole Andrei Glazunov pioneered a route from St. Michael to the Kuskokwim. Traveling by dog team, Glazunov guided his party to the Yukon River, crossed from there to the central sector of the Kuskokwim, and traveled upstream to the Stony River. He ascended the Stony, planning to cross over to Cook Inlet, but food scarcity and personal illness forced the party to turn back.[34] In early 1835, Glazunov again set off, this time on foot, from St. Michael to the lower Yukon River. His purpose was to select a site along the Yukon for an odinochka, and he chose the Eskimo settlement of Ikogmiut (Russian Mission), where a post was built later in the year. It did not flourish as a trading center, however, because the local people were accustomed to taking their furs to Lukins Odinochka, which served the same general area.[35]

1839

In varied ways the year 1839 was a critical one for the Russians and for the Upriver Eskimos. Fedor Kolmakov received permission to found a new trading center along the Kuskokwim, but he died on August 20, before any action had been taken.[36] His death ended a career of about twenty years devoted to guiding the Russian company's fortunes in southwestern Alaska with a resourcefulness seldom matched by his successors. When Wrangell, as general manager, had visited the Nushagak redoubt in 1832, he met Kolmakov, who was then station manager, and commented on "the intellect, the experience, the boldness, the zeal, and the shrewdness of this old company campaigner."[37] Although this praise of Kolmakov is expansive, he is little more than a shadow in the company's recorded history.

The loss of Kolmakov's leadership occurred at the time of another serious setback, a devastating smallpox epidemic. The disease had reached the Kuskokwim area in 1838. Although the creole Afanasiy Klimovskiy was sent north from Nushagak to vaccinate people, his efforts seem to have been largely unsuccessful.[38] How many Eskimos died along the river is not known, but of the Aglurmiut and Kuskokwim people familiar to the Russians, at least 60 percent had perished by mid-June 1838.[39] Estimates of the nearby Yukon Ingalik Indian population before and after the epidemic suggest that two-thirds of these Indians may have died from smallpox.[40] Since the epidemic continued at least until the fall of 1839, we might suspect that a third or less of the Upriver Eskimos lived through it.[41]

The Eskimos of this region had two theories to explain the origin of any disease. One involved "soul-loss," and the other was the intrusion of a foreign substance.[42] Presumably they applied the intrusion theory to the smallpox epidemic, but the shamans were unsuccessful in their attempts to expel the harmful substance. Since the Russians had been vaccinated, none of them died, and the Eskimos, seeing that the newcomers survived, assumed that the disease was introduced purposefully to kill them.

This engendered a great deal of bitterness, which led to attempts at revenge. One group of Eskimos attacked the company employees at Russian Mission; a further motivation for this attack apparently was the arrogance of the traders. The Eskimos traveled from the lower Kuskokwim to the station, killed the employees, and seized all the furs.[43]

The success of the attack on Russian Mission led the same Eskimos to plan a second attack on Lukins Odinochka. According to one account, Lukin was forewarned, and when the Eskimos entered his house, he threw one of them out the window, causing the others to flee.[44] A different and detailed version was recounted about fifty years later by the elderly Russian Nikolai Dementiev.[45] He stated that the attackers paddled up the river to the station in kayaks, not knowing that several men from the Nushagak redoubt were with Lukin. Dementiev described the planned assault as follows:

> "The fleet of kayacks arrived, in the night, and all except three went up the creek [Kolmakov River] back of the station. The three kayacks went on the Kuskoquim, to the station, and the men, leaving their kayacks on the beach, went up to the house, and entered it. The trader [Lukin] and the visitors were drinking tea, but without waiting, the trader, seeing that something was wrong, asked them their business. They replied that they had come to trade a kayack, and wanted a wolverine skin. The trader without rising again said—'That is not your errand. Your faces show that you have come for some other purpose. May be you come to do some killing.'
>
> 'No, No.' —they answered, —'we want to trade. We are not thinking of anything else.'
>
> 'Well if you want to trade, buy this; and the trader took an ax from under the table, and showed it to them.
>
> 'No, no, we don't want that.'
>
> 'Well I will put it back, because I may have to use it myself. Well let me finish drinking my tea, so that when you stick me with a knife, water will run out instead of blood.' With that the trader kept on with his tea drinking. Some of the people of the station mounted the house, and kept watch, lest other natives would come upon the station unawares. After the trader was thro', he bo't the kyack, with a wolverine skin, and then he stepped out to the middle of the floor, and said: —'Now, here I am, if you want to take hold of me, here I stand ready. Quick and do your errand.'

'No, no—we have no such intentions.'
'Well, then go, we are thro'."

The three men left, only to return shortly because the one who had traded his kayak had no way to go home. Lukin returned the kayak to the man and also gave him a kick. After the men left for the second time, Lukin told one of his men to follow them, using the heavy mist as a cover, and find out anything he could about their plans. When the scout returned, he reported that they intended to go south to the Nushagak station and attack the employees there. Lukin quickly sent messengers to alert the Nushagak post. They arrived at the same time as the company supply vessel, and after the company agent heard the warning, he forbade the consumption of alcohol that was customary when the yearly allotment of alcoholic beverages arrived on the supply ship. In addition, the men readied their weapons. That same evening the Kuskokwim Eskimos arrived, but when the local Eskimos told them of the Russian preparations, the would-be killers abandoned their plan and returned home.

In the aftermath of Fedor Kolmakov's death, the smallpox epidemic, the massacre at Russian Mission, and the abortive attack on Lukin, the Russians became more circumspect in dealing with their clients. The general manager conveyed this new approach in his instructions to Petr Kolmakov, who succeeded his father as the Nushagak station agent. Petr was to be firm yet cautious in his dealings with the inland peoples. He was to set a positive example but at the same time was to be armed, especially when traveling. It was hoped that these policies would lead to a renewed Eskimo respect for the Russians. However, the general manager intended to punish those who had sacked the Yukon odinochka. They were to be apprehended, by their own people if possible, and sent to Sitka, not only because they were guilty of murder and theft, but because they might be disruptive in the future. If the guilty men resisted, they were to be shot, wounded rather than killed if possible, since "God and the sovereign permit the use of arms in the defense of our lives." [46] There is no indication that the guilty were apprehended, but no more attacks were attempted by Kuskokwim Eskimos.

When the Russian-American Company began trading in the interior, it was operating under the charter granted by the Russian government in 1821. This was replaced by the Charter of 1844, which specified that before an outpost could be founded, company representatives must obtain permission from the local inhabitants. In addition, they were to respect the independence of the local people. They were prohibited from extracting tribute or taxes from them and could take hostages only if physical force was not involved.[47] The rigor with which these and other constraints were observed is not known, but contemporary records suggest that company agents were even-handed when dealing with the Kuskokwim peoples. Apart from official policy, employees were well aware of their tenuous position. They were few in number and could not rely on effective aid if attacked. Equally or perhaps more important was the attitude of company employees toward the indigenous people. The workers were primarily non-local Eskimo and creole men who were likely to identify with the local population, in some cases marrying local women.

To expand the fur trade and insure stability in long-term trading relations, company managers pursued a number of well-formulated policies. First, they settled intervillage feuds and resolved the animosity between the Aglurmiut and other Eskimos. Second, they sent company parties comprised of creoles and Aglurmiut northward from Nushagak to trade for pelts and to hunt furbearers. Third, they appointed influential local men as *toyons,* a word used by the Yakut of Siberia to designate tribal leaders. Both Fedor Kolmakov and Semen Lukin appointed known leaders as local company representatives. Each toyon received a silver medal, a certificate of appointment, and no doubt extraordinary gifts as well. The primary obligations of toyons apparently were to keep the local peace and to encourage villagers to obtain pelts for the company. The Russian goal was to develop a stable group of trading chiefs among the Upriver Eskimos. This plan was thwarted when all ten of the appointed toyons died in the smallpox epidemic.[48] A fourth but poorly documented policy seems to have been to encourage the local people to become dependent on the company. Providing trade goods to them directly was expected to undercut the aboriginal Siberian trade. It is possible that company agents encouraged their Kuskokwim clients to obtain credit against future fur harvests and thus become indebted, a common company policy, especially when faced with competition.[49]

The Russians did not seek to disturb the tempo of local life, yet it became apparent that teaching some Eskimos to read and write was desirable if the trade was to expand. This did not affect Kuskokwim Eskimos directly but was a notable innovation nonetheless. A school was founded at Nushagak in 1839 to provide a formal education for a few promising males. The rest were expected to live much as they had in aboriginal times except that they now would obtain furs for the company and receive trade goods in return.[50]

Most Upriver Eskimos seem to have accepted the intermittent presence of Russian-American Company employees in their area because they did not pose a physical threat and made at least a small amount of new trade goods available locally. After being encouraged to go south to trade, Kuskokwim men journeyed to the Nushagak post, but they objected to the distance involved. Now that local contact had been established and hunters were found to be cooperative, it is not surprising that the Russians decided it was safe and economically feasible to make a further move, that of establishing a year-round inland trading station.

4

Russian Presence

The trading post the Russians built along the Kuskokwim in 1841 brought the first permanent settlement of company traders in the area. It therefore introduced a novel life-style to the people living nearby. For the first time, Upriver Eskimos saw how people very different from themselves lived. The redoubt that was built became a principal contact community. Here Eskimos received much of their Western trade goods, and they also saw how new artifact forms, ranging from log cabins and bathhouses to tools and utensils, were used. They observed the daily social life of the foreigners, and soon they were urged to participate in the religious activities carried out at the site.

The new Russian post was named after Fedor Kolmakov in recognition of his efforts to develop the regional trade.[1] The man in charge of its construction and the first manager was Kolmakov's long-time associate, Semen Lukin.[2] The choice of Lukin, who has been mentioned earlier, was highly appropriate. The Russian-American Company had been a major influence on his life from childhood. His father, Ivan Lukin, an associate of Baranov's, was stationed at the company's Yakutat post. He, his Kodiak Eskimo wife, and others were killed when the Tlingit destroyed the station in 1805. Semen, then about five years old, survived the massacre and was rescued the next year by an American trader, who took him to Kodiak. He grew up at Sitka in Baranov's household.[3] In 1816 Lukin was sent to Kodiak Island to work, and in 1819 he became a member of the exploring party led by Korsakovskiy. When the Nushagak post was founded, Lukin became the interpreter. He used the same skills when he accompanied Vasilev during his explorations in 1829 and 1830 and later when he joined Fedor Kolmakov on his trading ventures to the Kuskokwim. Subsequently stationed intermittently at the odinochka bearing his name, Lukin was to become the company representative most intimately associated with the Kuskokwim trade.

KOLMAKOVSKIY REDOUBT

Because the location of Lukins Odinochka had proved favorable for trading, the new station was built on a spruce-covered plot across the river and slightly downstream. During the planning stage the company manager, Adolf Karlovich Etolin, emphasized the need to build a stockade, probably because of the massacre at the Russian Mission station and the abortive attack on the post of Lukin.[4] However, company headquarters in Sitka were far off, and by the fall of 1842 the stockade had not been built. Expressing his concern to the Kodiak office, Etolin wrote, "At the first opportunity it is necessary to bear in mind the building and encircling of it [the redoubt] with a secure fence for sheltering people of importance from the savages."[5] Lukin no doubt felt it was more valuable to build other structures and begin trading than to erect a stockade. He also may have reasoned that a stockade would provide little protection unless a constant watch was posted, which was beyond the capacity of the few employees at the fort. He possibly felt, as did Zagoskin, that a stockade could be set on fire by attackers and that winter snow drifting against the outer face would provide easy access to the interior.[6] Furthermore, and possibly more importantly, Lukin was unafraid of the local people. Yet he recognized Etolin's authority, and a stockade was built, possibly in 1843.[7]

In the 1960s adult Eskimos, who had been told by their elders how the fort was constructed, readily recalled that the Russians first built an eight-sided blockhouse. These Eskimos also reported that Russian workmen were uncertain how thick to hew the wall logs and resolved the matter by firing a musket into a log at point-blank range. They measured the musket ball's penetration and made the thickness of the wall logs double this distance. In addition to the protection afforded by a blockhouse, with its seven-inch-thick walls and slots through which guns could be fired, the redoubt was armed with two light bronze cannons and

The configuration of buildings at Kolmakovskiy Redoubt in 1884. From left to right are the store, blockhouse, kashim, Separe's house (with the church behind), Old Andrew's house, the creole barracks, and Eskimo barracks. *From Henry W. Elliott 1886.*

two muskets. The administration felt that it was unnecessary to import heavy cannons.[8] At no time during the redoubt's history were the small cannons or muskets fired at Eskimos.

In the long run the store was the most important building; over its threshold passed the furs and trade goods responsible for the station's very existence. The store, or more properly store-warehouse, was completed by the fall of 1843. Lukin, a religious man, converted the building into a chapel each Saturday evening so that the employees and their families might attend Russian Orthodox services. Lukin himself read the prayers and psalms.[9] Thus, from its beginning this Russian establishment brought new religious as well as commercial practices to the Kuskokwim.

Soon after the store was built, two hewn log barracks were completed for the employees. The first included one section for creole workers and another for the manager. The second barracks was for Aglurmiut workers and their families. A third building was constructed as a hostelry for visitors. Clients who came to trade often traveled considerable distances, and bartering for goods usually spanned a number of days. The accommodation for customers was called a *kazhim,* the Kodiak Eskimo word for men's house and the term adopted by the Russians for a building that provided temporary shelter. Unlike the men's house in a local Eskimo village, the one at the redoubt housed families. There also was a Russian-style bathhouse, which we may presume was one of the first structures built at the site.[10]

The importance of the Russian Orthodox religion to the redoubt's personnel is clear from the number of structures built over the years to serve religious needs. A prayer house constructed during the early years was replaced by the Transfiguration of Our Lord Jesus Christ Chapel in 1849.[11] By the early 1860s this chapel had become a virtual ruin, and in 1863 a plot was consecrated for a church that probably was completed during the next two years.[12] Buildings constructed for religious purposes possibly fell into disrepair more rapidly than others because of their intermittent use. The only other major structure built during the Russian era and recorded in any detail is the house for a priest. The foundation was built in 1861, and construction apparently was completed the next year.[13]

Despite its stockade, blockhouse, cannons, and designation as a redoubt, Kolmakovskiy was not a bastion of Russian power; quite to the contrary, it began as a small peripheral outpost and never expanded appreciably during the Russian period. The settlement had no resident population unconnected with trading. During the late construction phase, the occupants included seven male employees who were creoles, eight others who were Aglurmiut married to Kuskokwim women, and twenty-seven women and children.[14] After about 1844 ten or fewer creoles and Eskimos worked at the redoubt; occasionally one or more Russians were stationed there as well.

Life at Kolmakovskiy during the early Russian period is recorded best in company records and in accounts written by L. A. Zagoskin during 1843 and 1844. As a lieutenant in the Russian Navy he had served on the Caspian and Baltic seas before requesting assignment with the Russian-American Company in Alaska. Zagoskin traveled widely on behalf of the company in western Alaska during the early 1840s. One goal was to identify the Native American trade routes leading into Siberia so that the company could determine how best to replace this means of exchange. He hoped also to explore the Yukon and Kuskokwim rivers.[15] Although he did not realize his goals fully, Zagoskin traveled widely and was one of the first to write knowingly about Upriver Eskimos.

Zagoskin and his party set out from Russian Mission, sledded from the Yukon to the Kuskokwim, and reached Kolmakovskiy in December 1843. His initial impression of the post is revealing: "Here everything differs from our other settlements in the colonies—food, clothes, customs, the people themselves. In all trading posts the Russians, Creoles, and Aleuts who are on the payroll cannot get on without their ration of flour, or so they say. Here they do not refuse flour, but so little is freighted in that they forget all about bread for three months at a time."[16] In addition, the post had practically no trade goods, and Lukin was delighted when Zagoskin offered to lend him tobacco and fat for the trade.[17] Zagoskin wrote little else about his first visit, which ended in February.

The capacity of the company to provision its workers at Kolmakovskiy is revealed by Zagoskin's comments about his second visit, made in the spring of 1844. He wrote that by mid-April the winter supply of dried fish was almost exhausted, and because of the incomplete breakup of the river at the time, some fish traps could not be tended while others caught few fish or had been swept away by the unstable ice. Furthermore, the melting snow made it difficult for dog team parties to search for game. Although caribou were nearby, the guns at the redoubt were not in working order, and, according to Zagoskin, the men at the fort were not adept at hunting with firearms.[18]

Zagoskin notes that when food stores were depleted, adults cooked and ate sealskins and bladders in which fat had been stored. After these were consumed, they had only old boot soles to eat. In early May he wrote, "The dogs as well as the men are pitiful to look at; it is a long time since there has been anything nourishing to eat." Only when this point had been reached was Lukin willing to pay the price necessary to obtain fish from people in a nearby settlement.[19]

Despite the hardships, Lukin and his workers seemed generally content with their lot. Of all the persons involved with the fort, the Russian employees living there during the early construction phase caused the most problems. In 1842 a Russian carpenter built a fire to smoke beaver meat but neglected to extinguish it when he was finished. The flames from this fire spread quickly and within days had reduced the nearby spruce forest to ash. Two of the Russian workers would not help fight the fire, and two others were accused of "insubordinate absence from the redoubt, and in general for violence and their disobedience to the local manager."[20] These four men also were punished for "licentiousness."[21] As building the redoubt progressed, the general manager realized that the Russians were the greatest source of disorder, and he instructed the Kodiak office to replace them. The Russian workers quite possibly resented being in a subordinate position to the creole manager.[22] From this time forward, it appears that Aglurmiut most often worked at the redoubt, and they performed their tasks in an acceptable manner.[23]

In the history of Kolmakovskiy one person, Semen Lukin, stands out above all others. Zagoskin, typically faint in his praise of individuals, described him as "a sort of big brother, and first among the workmen."[24] While at the fort Zagoskin wrote, "Here one man—and I am thinking of S. Lukin—was able to spread the Christian faith among many savages, and to establish such good order among them that any changes could hardly be an improvement."[25] Zagoskin obviously had a great deal of respect for Lukin, and he was so well regarded by the local people that they called him by the Russian word meaning "daddy," a term of affection.[26] Lukin died in 1855, and although other men served as capable managers of the redoubt, he clearly was the person most responsible for the harmonious riverine Eskimo and Russian relationship.[27]

THE FUR TRADE

After establishing Kolmakovskiy for the purpose of obtaining beaver pelts, the Russians found that the demand for them on the world market was declining.[28] Furthermore, other factors, each directly involving beaver, began to have a negative impact on company profits. From the Russians the people had learned a new means to take these animals. They located a lodge, blocked the exits, and broke into the top. They then could remove all the animals trapped inside by snagging them with iron hooks attached to long poles.[29] Although this method produced large catches with little effort, it destroyed beaver colonies and rapidly depleted the population. Company officials began discouraging the practice and urged the hunters to shoot single animals.[30] Yet hunting beaver with guns was not effective; of those shot only about one in three could be retrieved.[31] In 1838 and 1839 metal traps of a type developed by the English were sent to the Nushagak station; these probably were steel-spring traps like those used by the Hudson's Bay Company. Instead of using these traps, Eskimos cut them up to obtain the metal for making knives and other objects.[32] This suggests that the people felt little need for a greater beaver harvest. Finally, many of the skins received at the station were not prime or well prepared and therefore were downgraded when sold on the world market. This made it difficult for the Russian-American Company to compete effectively with the Hudson's Bay Company, whose trappers obtained pelts of better quality.[33] With all these factors against them, it is not surprising that the Kuskokwim trade proved less rewarding than had been anticipated.

With Kolmakovskiy established as a year-round trade center, the company soon established secondary stations along the river, hoping that by covering a larger region the trade would be more profitable. A temporary post was founded by 1844 at the downstream village of Ogavik; it probably was maintained by an Eskimo trader working for Semen Lukin.[34] At Kihtagamiut, located a short distance upstream from the future town of Bethel, an odinochka was built, possibly in 1853.[35] Upstream from Kolmakovskiy Semen Lukin traded with the McGrath Ingalik at their summer village of Vinasale, where a substation was established at a later date.[36] In 1849 Lukin hoped to ascend the Kuskokwim to its source and contact a new population, but he did not make the trip.[37] His plan suggests that the headwater sector had not been penetrated by that time. However, in 1861–62 Illarion, Hieromonk [Peremezhko], an Orthodox missionary who wintered at Kolmakovskiy, noted that Indians from the upper Kuskokwim, McGrath Ingalik, Ingalik from the Yukon, and Eskimos from the lower Kuskokwim all traded at Kolmakovskiy. Illarion also noted that trading trips were made by redoubt employees to distant villages. For example, in early March 1861, a group led by Ivan Lukin, who succeeded his father as the trader at Kolmakovskiy, sledded down the river about two hundred miles, possibly to the Kihtagamiut Odinochka, and returned fifteen days later. In January 1862 a company employee returned from a trip to the lower Kuskokwim, where he had gone to obtain furs and fish to help provision the station. In March of 1862 Ivan Lukin went to the Yukon drainage to trade with Indians and returned twenty days later. The same spring, he boated up the Kuskokwim to trade with Indians at the Holitna River mouth. Since this number of trips occurred during Illarion's stay at the fort, it seems likely that there were similar ones during the other years of the Russian period.[38]

Before Kolmakovskiy was founded in 1841, a yearly average of one thousand beaver and land otter pelts had been obtained by parties sent from the Nushagak station to the Kuskokwim to trade and hunt. After the Kuskokwim redoubt began functioning, from one to three thousand pelts were taken each year, and most of these were beaver skins. However, the total yearly take of beaver at the Nushagak station averaged about 1,600 pelts from 1845 to 1860, indicating that the Russians had not increased their overall beaver harvest a great deal by moving into the interior.[39] They tried raising the price they paid for beaver skins in the mid-1840s, but when they did so, the Kuskokwim take declined, much to the company's surprise. According to Semen Lukin, the people traded fewer skins because they received more for them and thus had their needs satisfied more readily than before. Apparently the goods available did not provide sufficient incentive to induce the Eskimos and Indians to increase their hunting. Lukin was instructed to explain to the hunters that the pricing was designed to benefit both the company and the people and that they should co-operate by taking more pelts.[40] Prices became a problem for the company again in 1856, but for a different reason. Eskimos trading at Nushagak complained that those in the Katmai area were receiving a better rate of exchange. The low prices also led Eskimos in the northern area to trade their pelts through aboriginal Alaskan middlemen to Chukchi traders in Siberia and to trade through intermediaries at a Hudson's Bay Company post, presumably the one along the upper Yukon.[41] These problems led the Russian-American Company to increase its payments the following year for all pelts except beaver, since the demand for beaver continued to decline. Skins now sought to meet market needs were those of bear, fox, land otter, lynx, mink, muskrat, sable (pine marten), and wolf.[42]

A major reason the company did not expand its Kuskokwim operation was that supplying Kolmakovskiy with a large inventory of trade goods and sufficient provisions for the employees was difficult. The Nushagak station served as the major supply base until 1845. From there food and goods were transported up the Nushagak River to a Kuskokwim tributary by kayaks or dog sleds. Either method required hiring many men for the sole purpose of transporting trade goods and supplies.[43] Because of this expense the company considered it impractical to increase the inland trade until better access was available.

In 1845 the company tried a new means of provisioning the Kuskokwim stations. Supplies were sent by ship to St. Michael and from there by umiak, a large, open skin boat, to Kolmakovskiy.[44] This apparently required one umiak in 1847, at least two in 1848, and three in 1866, two of which were described as large.[45] The umiaks traveled along the Bering Sea coast to the mouth of the Yukon River, ascended the river a short distance, and followed a series of waterways and lakes, connected by portages, to reach the Kuskokwim at Old Kalskag, a village downstream from the redoubt. The trip required about one month and was less costly than importing goods from Aleksandrovskiy by kayak because of the large carrying capacity of each umiak. The success of this method led to its permanence, and by 1862 boats were transporting goods to the Kuskokwim in mid-June and again in late September.[46] If an urgent need for additional supplies arose during the winter, the Kolmakovskiy manager sent a dog team to St. Michael to obtain them, but such a journey was expensive because of the amount of dog food required, especially if unfavorable trail conditions prolonged the trip. The travel time for a round trip of this nature was about forty days.[47]

A problem for the company apart from that of supplying its Kuskokwim stations was the expansion of English trading in Alaska. Direct competition between the Russian-American and Hudson's Bay companies began in the 1830s in southeastern Alaska and slowly spread north.[48] In 1847 the Hudson's Bay Company knowingly built Fort Yukon on territory Russia had claimed along the upper Yukon, and soon thereafter goods of English origin and rumors about the post began to reach the Russians.[49] In the late 1850s Russian traders who boated up the Yukon from their Nulato post to trade with interior Indians at the Tanana River junction met some who also traded with the English at Fort Yukon. As the company general manager increasingly became concerned about this competition, he decided to send Ivan Lukin, who was then managing Kolmakovskiy, to investigate the operation. In 1860 he was ordered to determine the exact location of the English post and identify the nature of the trade. He likewise was to determine the feasibility of founding an odinochka deep in the interior.[50] Lukin made the trip to Fort Yukon and in the process became the first Russian to identify the Yukon as the river the Eskimos called the *Kwikpuk,* or Big River. We know little else about his trip, since the Russian-American Company did not release his findings.[51] The company apparently decided not to pursue the matter further, possibly because Russia was considering the sale of Alaska to the United States.

THE IMPACT OF RUSSIAN TRADING

As the historic Russian trade along the Kuskokwim is examined, one general observation is noteworthy. The direct trade that began from Siberia along Native routes in protohistoric times remained strong and effective throughout the span of Russian occupation. This emphatically diminished the trade of the Russian-American Company, especially at its northern posts. Zagoskin's fieldwork in 1842–44 was carried out primarily to divert this trade to the company, but it remained prominent throughout the Russian era and later.[52] In 1878–81 the American ethnologist Edward W. Nelson noted the continuing intensity of the trade of Siberian goods, which by then were supplemented with wares from trading ships and whalers operating in the Bering Strait region. Nelson especially noted the importance of this trade between Kotzebue Sound and the Kuskokwim and commented on the demand for beaver and land otter skins in Siberia.[53]

Because supplying Kolmakovskiy and subsidiary Kuskokwim stations proved troublesome for the Russians, relatively few trade goods were available locally throughout the span of Russian occupation. Not only was the quantity of goods shipped to the northern stations moderate, but no particular effort was made to see that clients in the interior received the goods they most wanted. Zagoskin noted that items which could not be sold at major stations were shipped to remote outposts as "trade goods for the savages." [54] He likewise stated that "Along the Kusko-kwim . . . they receive third-hand merchandise, for the most part shopworn." [55] In much the same context, the traders "have paid no attention whatever to improving the living conditions of the natives themselves by providing them with different articles which would be useful to them." [56] While at St. Michael, which was provisioned by ship and therefore presumably could have received more adequate supplies than posts along the Kuskokwim, Zagoskin wrote, "The trade between the natives and the fort is limited to their demands for tobacco, European iron and copper products, and a small number of manufactured trifles." [57] When at Kolmakovskiy in 1843, he observed that there were "practically no trade goods"; the next spring he commented, "The quantity of European goods traded is negligible." [58] Of the few goods shipped to the redoubt in its early years half were used to pay for the transport and to provision local employees. [59]

By the end of the Russian period, the imported goods traded at Kolmakovskiy differed little in variety from those brought in when the fort was founded. An 1861 inventory of imports included bracelets, calico, dentalium shells for decorations, glass beads, knives, needles, tobacco, and "etc.," suggesting that the post was not a thriving trade center with a varied stock. [60] This seems to have been true of all Russian posts in northern Alaska, though to a lesser extent elsewhere. An 1860 list of trade goods shipped to the colony from European Russia included items of apparel, axes, candles, kettles, soap, tobacco and flints, lead, powder, and shot for guns. [61] Few of the useful manufactures appear to have made their way north.

One trade item of lasting importance from the time it was introduced through the direct Siberian trade, around 1800, was tobacco. [62] As the first drug to become available to Alaskan Eskimos, it became so popular that by 1862 Illarion commented, "It is impossible to achieve anything with the savages if there is no tobacco. Tobacco to a savage is the same as bread to a Russian." [63] In the late 1800s, detailed accounts about tobacco usages noted that men, women, and children used chewing tobacco and snuff, and men smoked tobacco in pipes. Snuff was prepared by shredding leaf tobacco, drying it, pounding the fragments in a small mortar, and sifting out the fine particles, which were kept in a small box. Snuff was inhaled into one nostril and then the other through a bird bone tube. Chewing tobacco was made by shredding leaf tobacco and mixing it with ash from birch fungus. A chew usually was held in one cheek and the juice swallowed. Smoking tobacco, which was shredded leaf tobacco, was stored in a small bag for use in a pipe. The pipes used by these Eskimos usually had wooden stems and stone or metal bowls. A tuft of fur was placed in the bowl, tobacco was packed on top, and tinder placed above the tobacco was lit with flint and steel. When the tobacco began to burn, the entire pipeload was inhaled with one deep breath, which was held as long as possible.[64]

Intoxicants were not used as trade items at the northern stations of the Russian-American Company. Rum was imported once a year for employees to have a single spree until 1845, when it was banned in an effort to end alcohol abuse by the Tlingit among whom it was traded and company workers, especially creoles.[65] At that time it was noted that the sale of rum had profited the company at more southerly posts. By 1866 the yearly shipment of intoxicants had been resumed in an attempt to satisfy employees, including those at northern stations, and homebrew also was consumed, at least at St. Michael.[66]

Trade good inventories indicate a minimal concern with introducing items that the Eskimos would find of clear economic utility. "Luxury items," such as brooches, bells, earrings, rings, and especially beads, played a large part in the trade throughout the span of Russian occupation. It would appear that the reason was straightforward: "trifles" were much more readily imported in quantity than were heavier and more bulky goods. Western manufactures with direct economic utility, including axes, cloth, copper and iron utensils, and hatchets, were limited in their availability. It has been suggested that some Eskimos accepted beads as a form of durable wealth, with established values based on their color and form. Robert F. Spencer demonstrates that among northern Alaskan Eskimos beads "came to be a kind of monetary unit," which probably was the case along the Kuskokwim.[67] Another approach to understanding the importance of "baubles, bangles, and beads" in the early trade has been proposed by Christopher L. Miller and George R. Hamell.[68] They argue that these forms were accepted readily during initial phases of contact because they fit into the existing ideological systems. Close parallels were drawn with the use of native copper, exotic siliceous stones, and shells as objects of ritual importance in northeastern North America. Since ritual usages such as these do not seem to have prevailed along the Kuskokwim, it is unlikely that beads were ideologically significant to the Upriver People. They do, however, appear to have been dominant trade items throughout the Russian period, especially for bodily and clothing adornments.

Another factor affecting the attitude of Eskimos toward Kolmakovskiy traders was the 1838–39 smallpox epidemic. It produced an immediate outburst of hostility against the Russians, which diminished after the epidemic ended but never disappeared entirely. Because the Siberian trade gave them an alternative means of obtaining trade goods, they could, and possible did, limit their dealings with the Russians. As the Russian period drew to a close, some Eskimos, especially those with little direct Russian contact, still felt that the foreigners were not to be trusted.[69]

Although the Russian company did not import utilitarian goods in quantity, their agents along the Kuskokwim helped meet Eskimo needs for company profit in another manner. They traded in products obtainable in one locality but not another. In the account about the abortive attack on Lukin at his odinochka in 1839, the excuse of the attackers for visiting the station was to trade a kayak for a wolverine skin, and Lukin made the exchange.[70] While Zagoskin was at Kolmakovskiy in 1844, he wrote, "The biggest turnover is in native products, such as deerskins, thongs, tanned sealskins, and fats."[71] Thus, in a very real sense company agents became middlemen in the local trade to the detriment of itinerant Eskimo traders.

The difficulties the Russians had in supplying Kolmakovskiy affected the Upriver Eskimos directly in two ways not yet mentioned. Company employees were ill equipped to live along the river throughout the year and depended on local Eskimos for much of their food. At least some of the local Eskimos worked as temporary employees to import supplies to the post from

Nushagak and St. Michael. In each instance Eskimos earned trade goods in exchange for their labor, which of course increased company expenses and did not contribute to profits in the local trade. More important, perhaps, these examples illustrate how dependent the Russians were on Eskimos for the success of their Kuskokwim trading venture.

Changes in Eskimo social life during the Russian period are not recorded, but it is apparent that any number occurred. Not only did many male leaders die in the smallpox epidemic, but village population shifts occurred. These brought dislocations in village living. Other factors, more directly related to the station itself, introduced additional change. For example, we know that traders and their employees lived with and married Upriver Eskimo women. The offspring of these unions presumably were socialized in both cultures, with the Russian aspect of greater or lesser importance. Likewise, when clients came to trade, they were exposed to alternative social norms, which must have left impressions, positive or negative. It is impossible to assess the social implications of the Russian presence since written records are virtually nonexistent on the subject, but judging from subsequent developments, the Eskimos made at least some adjustments.

Ethnoarchaeological evidence provides a means for gaining another perspective on the direct Russian impact on Upriver Eskimo life. Excavations were made at Crow Village, some thirty miles downstream from Kolmakovskiy, which was occupied throughout the Russian period and was not abandoned until about 1910. Had the local Russian trade strongly influenced the material culture of these villagers, we would expect it to be reflected in the excavated material. Some artifacts recovered do suggest the impact of the Russian presence. These include traditional Eskimo forms made from imported materials. A piece of metal was cut to fashion a salmon dart head; metal blades were made for ulus, end scrapers, and an awl. Some beads may have been of Russian origin as also was true for pieces of glass made into scrapers and imported earthenware used as containers.[72] Yet the vast majority of the finds represented traditional nineteenth-century Eskimo forms, and not a single artifact could be identified with absolute assurance as of Russian origin.

As far as the Russian-American Company was concerned, the

Kuskokwim trading operation remained useful as long as expenses were modest and the return was acceptable. Over the years, the administrators did not hesitate to reduce the status of less profitable stations and eliminate those not worth maintaining. For instance, the Nushagak redoubt was reduced to an odinochka in 1844, and the Russian Mission Odinochka, founded in 1836, was abandoned in 1845.[73] In the closing years of the Russian era the reason for maintaining the redoubt may have been to validate Russian sovereignty over a vast sector of inland Alaska. As far as the Eskimos are concerned, it appears that they could accept the Russian fur trade or do without it. Its influence on their lives at this point appears to have been minimal.

ORTHODOX MISSIONARIES

Of the Russian institutions established among Upriver Eskimos, the one with the most lasting impact has been the Russian Orthodox Church. The relationship between the Russian-American Company, the Russian Orthodox Church, and the Russian state was quite different from that of company, church, and state as seen in the United States. The Russian-American Company was an extension of the state, and the Orthodox church administration was linked closely with the state as well. When the Russians penetrated Siberia, they combined missionary work among the indigenous peoples with colonization, and they extended the same policy to Alaska. The first Russian Orthodox missionary to reach Alaska arrived on Kodiak Island in 1794, and by the time the Kuskokwim was explored, the Russian church had become reasonably well established in southern Alaska.[74]

Eskimos of the Bering Sea region of Alaska met the first official orthodox missionary when the priest Ioann Veniaminov visited the Nushagak station in 1829. In that year, he baptized thirteen men, presumably Eskimos who came to trade, and presented each with a bronze cross. Before leaving, Veniaminov authorized the manager, Fedor Kolmakov, to baptize people but cautioned him against giving presents to converts.[75] When Veniaminov returned to Nushagak in 1832, he baptized forty-six male and female Aglurmiut and seven other persons of both sexes from the Kuskokwim.[76] Kolmakov, his son Petr, and Semen Lukin had baptized people also but did not keep a record of their number.[77]

During these introductory years, relatively few persons were baptized, and their understanding of Christianity probably was rudimentary. However, a chapel was constructed at Nushagak on instruction from Veniaminov in 1832, and a church was built in 1845.[78]

In 1840 the general manager of the company urged that missionaries be stationed permanently north of the Alaska Peninsula, a recommendation favorably received by the church hierarchy.[79] In 1842 the priest Ilia Petelin arrived at Nushagak, and the following year he visited the Kuskokwim, where he baptized people and performed weddings.[80] A second priest, Iakov Netsvetov, founded the first inland station of the Orthodox Church in 1845 at Russian Mission along the Yukon.[81]

Father Netsvetov worked at Russian Mission from 1845 to 1863, and his existing journals provide an invaluable record about the first long-term Christian missionary in inland Alaska.[82] According to these writings, which cover his stay except from late 1853 to mid-1857, he made ten trips to Kolmakovskiy for visits averaging twenty days. While there he ministered to Christians and counseled as well as attempted to convert Eskimos and Indians. During his Kuskokwim trips he spent considerable time at Kwigiumpainukamiut, the village across the river from the fort, and he also visited the Eskimo settlements of Old Kalskag, Ohagamiut, and Crow Village.

In 1861 Illarion, a Russian hieromonk (which means a monk who is also a priest), from the Ukraine, was appointed to assist Netsvetov and to be responsible for the Kuskokwim area. He wintered at Kolmakovskiy in 1861–62, but in the fall of 1862 he left the Kuskokwim to replace Netsvetov, whose health was failing, as the missionary in charge of the Russian Mission station.[83] Illarion's 1861–62 journal is invaluable because it provides a day-to-day account about life at Kolmakovskiy during the closing years of Russian control.

When Illarion arrived at the redoubt on September 19, 1861, he praised God for the trip's success and then gazed with disbelief at the sight before him.

"While my things were being taken out of the baydarka, I went to see the redoubt's site on which all was peaceful, but alas, is this a redoubt? Having asked myself this question, I could not give the report. This is not a redoubt but a pitiful ruin, which is impossible to look at without pity. . . . All of its buildings are so decrepit that it seems that they are only waiting for a sizable storm in order that it is demolished with the help of the elements, not troubling the people who are few as it is. The roofs of the buildings are almost all overgrown with moss and grass. It is easy to imagine what happens during a heavy rain! . . . My God is it possible that the Company is so poor that its employees (though they are creoles) have been fated for such beggary and poverty, or are the inhabitants themselves so careless as to neglect their own comfort? God knows. . . ."[84]

Illarion noted that no glass graced the windows of the chapel; instead, sewn panels of intestines had been stretched across the frames. Inside he found the trappings in disarray. The other buildings had been similarly neglected, as was the stockade.

Illarion's 1861–62 and later journals are filled with accounts of his attempts to gain converts. Through an interpreter he lectured willing persons about the world's creation, human origins, the meaning of baptism, the sign of the cross, and the basic rules of the church. Adult listeners who indicated that they believed the lessons and would obey church rules were baptized. When Illarion met these persons again, he blessed them and if feasible taught them more about their obligations as Christians. He considered the Kuskokwim Indians much more zealous in performing Christian duties than the Eskimos. Illarion was vexed that converts continued to consult shamans in times of illness, but as the people explained, they had no other means of treatment.

Illarion's journals suggest that he made moderate progress in winning converts, but he probably was overly optimistic about his success in changing their lives. We suspect this especially after reading the reports of Feolil, Hieromonk [Uspenskii], who worked among the Nushagak area Eskimos at about the same time. Feofil wrote that because the people lived in widely scattered settlements he could visit them only a few days at a time, which was not enough to convey his purpose effectively. He was pleased that many Aglurmiut accepted Christian ideas, but he also noted that those who failed to do so continued to rely on shamans, cohabited without marriage, committed adultery, disregarded family obligations, and, worst of all, refused to listen to his teachings.[85] Feofil probably had a much more realistic view of his ineffectiveness than did Illarion, who worked among Eskimos less familiar with Russian ways and less able to understand his message.

In August of 1866 word reached Illarion, while he was at Russian Mission, that Kolmakovskiy was to be abandoned. In early December he went there for the last time to inventory the church property and to arrange for the removal of certain items. On the 9th of December, Illarion sprinkled holy water on the buildings at Kolmakovskiy, and two days later he left.[86]

Although the buildings at Kolmakovskiy were sold, the store and church would remain a focal point in the life of Upriver Eskimos for many years to come. The strength of their faith was such that Eskimos continued to hold services and maintain the church buildings until priests would again return to their midst. The Russian Orthodox religion continues to be practiced actively in numerous churches along the Kuskokwim, a strong reminder of Russian contacts that were based primarily on a fur trade that ended many years ago.

Early American Presence

The freedom of Upriver Eskimos to pursue their traditional life-way began to diminish most clearly on that June day in 1830 when Vasilev set out to explore the Kuskokwim River. The initial impact of direct penetration by the Russians was limited, but within a few years they had launched far-reaching changes. As they were replaced by Americans, the Eskimo sense of cultural differences between themselves and Westerners gradually intensified. However, the purchase of Alaska by the United States in 1867 produced neither abrupt nor dramatic changes. During the early American period, as in Russian times, traders and missionaries were the exclusive agents of change. Although Alaska was purchased for political reasons, settlement of the new territory was not a priority. For a few years the Kuskokwim trade was in a state of flux, but it soon came under the monopolistic control of a single company, again repeating the Russian pattern.

With the sale of Alaska, the assets of the Russian-American Company were purchased by the San Francisco firm of Hutchinson, Kohl & Company, later to become the Alaska Commercial and Northern Commercial companies.[1] Soon after acquiring the Russian company, Hutchinson, Kohl & Company stationed an agent along the Kuskokwim. Its first representative soon was succeeded by a Finn called "Vasenius," also known as "Brown," who had a Portuguese partner called "Joe." Vasenius left in 1870 and was replaced by Reinhold Separe, who was hired in 1869 but apparently did not go to the Kuskokwim until 1871 or shortly thereafter.[3]

Before Hutchinson, Kohl & Company consolidated its position along the Kuskokwim, merchants representing other companies also were involved in the riverine trade. For example, Taylor and

Bendel Fur Trading Company of San Francisco sent an agent, Bernhard Bendel, to the Kuskokwim in 1870 on a schooner, the *Lizzie Sha*. After arriving at upper Kuskokwim Bay the Bendel party obtained an umiak and traded along the river as far inland as Kolmakovskiy, directly competing with Hutchinson, Kohl & Company. From Bendel's journal it appears that traders operating from schooners competed vigorously with one another at that time.[4]

KOLMAKOVSKIY

For nearly twenty years following the purchase of Alaska, the person living in the Kuskokwim region who best represented American culture to the local people was the trader at Kolmakovskiy. The fort, which had been the principal Russian trading station for twenty-five years, served nearly twice as long as a major trade center in the American period. However, its impact on the local population began to diminish soon after 1900 as independent traders and small-scale trading companies became established elsewhere along the river.

In contrast with the Russians, Hutchinson, Kohl & Company soon began to supply the Kuskokwim from the bay. The company sent an oceangoing supply vessel into Kuskokwim Bay on a yearly basis, which greatly facilitated the shipment of goods to and from San Francisco. As during the late Russian period, local Eskimos were hired to transport supplies to Kolmakovskiy and other posts by umiak. This annual employment of a few men was important to the families involved. Furthermore, the amount of trade goods for the Eskimos probably increased, another favorable result of the takeover.

The first long-term agent for Hutchinson, Kohl & Company was Reinhold Separe. He and his trading outfit were transported on a company vessel that anchored in the upper bay about eight miles out from the southern shore because of shoals and tidal flats. Separe decided he could navigate the shallower waters if he built a raft from lumber he had brought along. After launching the raft and loading it, Separe headed for the shore on an incoming tide. Unable to reach land, he was carried back into the bay as the tide ebbed. A second attempt likewise failed, but before the next tide he made a small sail and with its help reached the shore.

Here he dismantled the raft, reusing the lumber to build a boat in which he could travel up the river.[5]

When Separe settled in at Kolmakovskiy, he made use of the existing structures. The stockade had disappeared years before, the logs no doubt serving as firewood, but the blockhouse remained intact. Separe probably stored dried fish in this structure. After gold seekers had become numerous and American political control of the area began to be asserted, a U.S. commissioner was stationed at the post, and the blockhouse became a jail.[6] The old Russian store remained the trading post, but Separe added a porch and decorative railing to the building. One barrack was a partial ruin, but the other served as a residence for employees and as a warehouse. The kazhim, which had been used as a hostelry for clients until it was abandoned in the late Russian period, was renovated and used for that purpose as well as temporary quarters for employees. Separe later added a new building to the complex. About 1880 he built a five-room log dwelling at the center of the station as his home. The only other dwelling was Old Andrew's house, built about 1900 and named after an Eskimo who was a long-term employee at the post.

The old church was a virtual ruin by 1878, but a few years later Separe had it reroofed. He replaced it with a chapel before 1890, an indication that he identified with the Russian Orthodox religion. As a result of Separe's efforts Eskimos not only traded at Kolmakovskiy but worshipped there as in the past. After the chapel fell into disrepair, the foundation of another church was laid, but according to local Eskimos, an Orthodox official who visited at this time felt that the site would flood and ordered that the building be constructed on higher ground elsewhere. The foundation was dismantled and taken downriver to Little Russian Mission (Chuathbaluk), where it was rebuilt as the foundation for St. Sergius Church.

Russian-style bathhouses were constructed repeatedly at the site, each one apparently replacing one that had burned or deteriorated. In addition to the main bathing room, most bathhouses had dressing rooms attached. The most important furnishings of the main room were a stove for heating stones and benches for the bathers. The benches, which were low, lined one or more walls. The earliest stoves, made of clay imbedded with stones, eventually were replaced by metal ones. Stones were heated on metal stoves by being placed on the top and at the sides. A metal bucket set in front of the stove held water that became hot and then was ladled onto the stones to produce steam. For Eskimo men visiting Kolmakovskiy, the steam baths were an alternative to the hot air baths they traditionally took in their men's houses.

Reinhold Separe was a Finn by birth and must have impressed the local people with his size. He was about six foot three inches in height, and in his later years he weighed nearly 290 pounds. Separe lived with an Eskimo woman who bore many children, but most of them died before reaching adulthood and were buried in the cemetery at the station.[7] After 1875 Separe became an independent trader, contracting to buy his merchandise from and sell his furs to the Alaska Commercial Company.[8] His health failed in the 1880s, and after making repeated trips to San Francisco for treatment, Separe reportedly died in California during the early 1890s.[9]

Before his death Separe sold controlling interest in the Kuskokwim trade to Edward Lind, an associate of long standing. Lind was trading with Separe at Kolmakovskiy by the 1880s, and he managed the station while Separe was in San Francisco. Lind was a moderately successful trader, but his life was haunted by personal tragedy. Each of his two Native wives died, his three sons drowned in a single accident, his four daughters died, and his final marriage, this time to a white woman, ended in a separation.[10] Lind's fortunes took a turn for the better when he sold the buildings at Kolmakovskiy to the Northern Commercial Company in 1912. At that time it appeared that large quantities of gold were going to be mined along the central river sector. The physical plant was sold again in 1917, when it became evident that the gold rush in this area had failed to materialize.[11] Following this sale the site was abandoned as an ongoing trading station.

Not all the Russian workers left the river after the purchase of Alaska. Some employees remained at Kolmakovskiy and worked for Separe, Lind, or both men. Ivan Lukin apparently became an independent trader for a short time but then worked for Separe.[12] Nikolai Dementiev worked for Separe at Vinasale by 1884 and for Lind in later years.[13] Sergie Andreanoff, who married Semen Lukin's daughter, Paraskeva, traded for Separe and Lind at Vinasale and Kolmakovskiy.[14] George Separe (Sipari, Sipery) retained

part interest in his father's trading enterprise when it was sold to
Lind, but later, in 1898, he sold out to Lind and moved to the
Yukon.[15] The descendents of these men had relatively little im-
pact on affairs along the river during the American period. The
family line of Lukin died out locally, while the Dementiev and
Separe families relocated along the Yukon. The descendants of
Sergie Andreanoff continue to live in the Sleetmute area and
carry on the family name but not the trading activities.[16]

In addition to trading, Reinhold Separe searched for gold, but
in this venture he never was successful.[17] He also mined a cinnabar deposit across the river and downstream from Kolmakovskiy,
but again the venture proved unprofitable.[18] In 1881 the miner
George C. King examined this and other cinnabar deposits in the
area but did not consider the prospects promising.[19] Apparently
the vein worked by Separe was mined again in the mid-1890s by
Lind, who sent the ore to the United States for processing but lost
money on the venture.[20] Subsequent mining of this cinnabar deposit and others in the vicinity of Sleetmute did not yield a great
deal of mercury.[21]

MORAVIAN PROBE

With the transfer of Alaska to American control, the Russian Orthodox Church representatives faced an uncertain future. A small
number remained in Alaska, but they had diminished support.
Most of their converts lived along the north Pacific, and isolated
sectors such as the Kuskokwim were ignored during the adjustment period. Orthodox officials became more concerned about
the Kuskokwim area when the Moravians expressed an interest in
founding a mission along the river in 1884. Upon learning of
their plan, Vasili Shishkin, the Orthodox missionary at Nushagak,
wrote to his superiors that it was absolutely necessary to station a
priest along the Kuskokwim, especially one who spoke the language and knew the local customs.[22]

The Moravian decision to launch a mission in Alaska was encouraged by the Presbyterian Sheldon Jackson, a mission advocate who had worked in southeastern Alaska since 1877. After
developing missions in the western United States, Jackson had
applied his restless energies to the northern scene, soon emerging
as the preeminent spokesman in a crusade to save Native Ameri-

cans through Protestant Christianity and directed culture change. In innumerable public addresses made during the early 1880s he emphasized what he considered the shameful neglect that had led to the dismal conditions under which Native Alaskans lived.[23] Moravian Church officials invited Jackson to speak to their members at Bethlehem, Pennsylvania, and those who heard him in February 1884 were touched by his account of Native Alaskan life. They made immediate preparations to respond to his appeal for missionaries. When members of the graduating class of the Moravian College and Theological Seminary were asked whether they would volunteer for mission work in Alaska, nearly all of them responded in the affirmative. Church officials decided to select two persons to survey conditions in Alaska that summer. J. A. H. Hartmann, an experienced church worker among Canadian Indians, was named head of the Missionary Exploratory Expedition, and one of the seminary students, William H. Weinland, was chosen to accompany him.[24]

Traveling to San Francisco in the spring of 1884, the two Moravians obtained passage to the north on the Revenue Marine Steamer *Corwin* as far as Unalaska and then transferred to an Alaska Commercial Company steamer, the *Dora*. The captain of the latter vessel told Hartmann and Weinland he thought a good place to found a mission would be along the Kuskokwim. He suggested that one advantage of this locale was that the company ship could supply the mission on its annual voyage to outfit the local trading stations. When the ship arrived at Nushagak, the Moravians talked to the resident Orthodox missionary, Vasili Shishkin, who claimed the Nushagak area as his parish and suggested they found a mission along the Kuskokwim; we know, however, that in a report to his superiors Shishkin opposed the establishment of a Moravian mission along the Kuskokwim. After hearing his recommendation in addition to the captain's, the Moravians decided to investigate the Kuskokwim, and they continued north on the *Dora*. When the ship stopped at Togiak, they recruited four Eskimo men with two three-holed kayaks to accompany them so that they would have transportation back to the Nushagak station.[25]

The *Dora* sailed into upper Kuskokwim Bay and anchored some eight miles offshore from Warehouse. Soon four large umiaks arrived, with Separe, Lind, and other traders aboard. Separe was leaving on the *Dora* for San Francisco, but Lind agreed to help the Moravians in their journey upriver. Nine thousand skins were loaded aboard the ship, and supplies for the posts were transferred by umiak to Warehouse, where they were stored in a frame building for later shipment upriver. After a delay caused by contrary winds the traders, Moravians, and Togiak Eskimos began the three-day trip to Mumtrekhlagamute Station. This small settlement, built on a high north bank with stands of spruce nearby, was separated from the main river by a slough and a large protective peninsula. The location impressed Hartmann and Weinland alike. When they arrived on June 20, the Bible reading for the day was, "God said unto Jacob, Arise, and go up to Bethel, and dwell there, and make there an altar unto God that appeared unto thee" (Gen. 35:1). They took the reading as divine guidance and eventually decided to settle there, subsequently changing the name to Bethel.

At Mumtrekhlagamute Station the Alaska Commercial Company had a log house for its trader and a second employee, a log store, and a Russian-style bathhouse. The trader was an Eskimo, Nikolai A. Kamilakozhin, who had been reared by Semen Lukin. After working for the Orthodox church from 1861 to 1866, Kamilakozhin became a trader for Separe, possibly in the 1870s.[26] The Moravians were impressed with Kamilakozhin and the standard of living he maintained.

After the trade goods were sorted by station, the umiaks were loaded again, and the Moravians accompanied Lind upriver to Kolmakovskiy. After the nine-day trip, they remained at the old fort for a week, taking only a short upriver trip to Napamiut. Lind tried to convince the Moravians to found their mission at Kolmakovskiy, but Mumtrekhlagamute Station was more attractive to them. It was near sizable Eskimo villages, could be supplied by oceangoing ships, and was close to spruce that could be cut as fuel. They could build on high ground that seemed unlikely to flood or be damaged by erosion if the river channel changed. Finally, they thought Kamilakozhin would help them become familiar with the local people. Hartmann and Weinland traveled from Kolmakovskiy to Nushagak by kayak and eventually returned to Bethlehem, Pennsylvania, to present their findings.

Church officials approved of the plan to found a mission on the Kuskokwim even though it did not satisfy one of their original requisites. They had hoped to select a mission site among heathen Eskimos. At that time Eskimos elsewhere in Alaska approached this ideal far better than did those of the Kuskokwim area, many of whom already considered themselves members of the Russian Orthodox Church. However, as Hartmann and Weinland pointed out, the Orthodox missionary who centered his work in the Bristol Bay region had recommended that the Moravians establish themselves on the river. Furthermore, when they traveled up the Kuskokwim on their survey, Hartmann and Weinland had found that although Orthodox workers had preceded them, their impact seemed negligible. While they could hardly ignore the Orthodox chapel at Kolmakovskiy, they deemed it inactive since a priest rarely visited there. Nonetheless, in founding a Kuskokwim mission, the Moravians compromised their plan to work with heathens since they knew that some of their future converts already were nominal Christians. Although scrupulous at this time about not working in the Nushagak area because of its identification with the Orthodox, they later launched a mission there as well; this station opened in 1887 and existed until 1906. In 1950 the Moravians once again established a mission in the Nushagak area.[27]

THE BETHEL MISSION

When the summer of 1885 arrived, a chartered schooner, the *Lizzie Merrill,* transported five Moravians and their supplies from San Francisco to upper Kuskokwim Bay. Lashed to the deck of the schooner was the Moravian's thirty-five-foot sailboat, the *Bethel Star,* capable of carrying nine tons of freight. In charge of the group was Weinland, a Pennsylvania Dutchman, who brought with him his bride, Caroline Yost Weinland, formerly of New York City. Accompanying them were another seminary graduate, John Henry Kilbuck, who was a Delaware Indian born on a Kansas reservation, and his bride, Edith Romig Kilbuck, the daughter of Moravian missionaries. Hans Torgersen, who was older than the other party members, was a Norwegian fisherman, lay missionary, and skilled carpenter.[28]

After launching their boat into the bay, the Moravians sailed to

The Moravians who established the Bethel mission in 1885: from left to right, John Henry Kilbuck, Hans Torgersen, Edith Romig Kilbuck, Caroline Yost Weinland, and William Henry Weinland. *Courtesy of the Moravian Archives, Bethlehem, Pa.*

Warehouse and then transported themselves and part of their outfit upriver to the mission site. Repeated trips were necessary since the boat held only a small amount of freight. When Kilbuck and Torgersen sailed with the last load, they were forced to anchor below Bethel when the wind slacked and they could not make headway against the current. They hoisted the mainsail when the wind came up, and with Kilbuck at the helm, Torgersen went forward to hoist the other sail. He stepped on a bundle of wet shingles, slipped and fell into the river, and was drowned. His loss was a severe blow to the survivors, especially because he was to supervise construction of the mission building. Torgersen's body was found on an island and was taken to Bethel, where his was the first burial in the Moravian cemetery.

Weinland and Kilbuck built a house, smaller than originally planned but adequate for the four of them. Adjusting to each other in cramped quarters required patience, and because such practical problems as obtaining fuel and water loomed large the first year, converting the Eskimos necessarily was delayed. Kamilakozhin, the person they had expected to be of greatest help, had died in December 1884, which was a second setback in their plans.[29] Lind, who replaced him as the local trader, was instructed by Separe to aid the Moravians provided they did not trade.[30] Trading was far from the minds of these newcomers as they sought to make a home for themselves and begin their work at this spot they shared with Lind and his workers.

The missionaries and their wives soon realized the enormity of the task they faced. The Eskimo life-style in general and many personal habits in particular could not be comprehended, let alone accepted, by the missionaries. One of the conditions they, particularly the women, found most upsetting was the lack of cleanliness of their many Eskimo visitors. These people did little to care for their hair, and their heads sometimes were white with lice eggs. For one person to delouse another and eat the lice was a common pastime that the missionaries found disconcerting to watch.[31] Eskimo skin parkas never were cleaned and might not be discarded until they were filled with holes and the hair worn away. Edith Kilbuck noted with dismay that the grimy parka of one old man was made from bird skins and that his hat was a raven skin opened on the underside, cleaned, and stretched over his head. She also saw a woman wearing a patchwork parka made from pieces of an old blanket combined with the skins of fish, hare, fox, and muskrat.[32] Eskimo houses were small and cramped beyond belief, as well as "dirty, filthy, and filled with an indescribable stench." [33] When Edith Kilbuck objected to people spitting tobacco juice on the floor of her house, one man spit on his boot and another spit in his hand and rubbed the juice in his hair.[34] Some Eskimos were neat and reasonably clean by missionary standards, but the others attracted the most attention, possibly because they represented the greatest challenge.

Aside from uncleanliness, many Eskimo customs affecting social behavior were not acceptable to the Moravians. Some women reportedly had as many as a dozen husbands over a period of time, and "immorality," as the missionaries saw it, was rampant. Parents were said to have made "perfect prostitutes" of their daughters by the time they were ten years old. The newcomers found that unwanted infants might be killed, an old woman accused of being a witch was murdered, and a shaman had two wives at one time.[35] To the Moravians this mode of living was "uncivilized" at best and "sinful" at worst. As Edith Kilbuck wrote, one of the greatest missionary tasks was "to get the people to *sufficiently understand the vileness of sin*" and "to leave off from doing it" (emphasis in the original).[36] Traditional Eskimo culture represented a clear challenge to these newcomers, who had come to the area with the sole purpose of teaching the Eskimos to follow an American way of life.

One of the daily occurrences most upsetting to the missionaries was that Eskimos, who came from near and far to visit them, walked in, as was the local custom, and stayed for a considerable period. As Caroline Weinland wrote when this occurred at Warehouse, "You cannot imagine how queer it seems to have a group of these people crowd about the door and into the room, scrutinizing our every movement, in genuine heathen wonderment."[37] After they settled in Bethel, the missionaries debated whether to allow people who were so riddled with lice to visit them. They decided after due consideration that Christian charity and their missionary purpose made it essential to entertain everyone, despite the lice they might bring with them.

The missionaries' first two years at Bethel were trying ones not only because they had so much to learn but because of personal health problems. Both women bore children, and the illnesses of these infants were of great concern since no professional medical care was available. Sickness among the adults was serious as well, especially in terms of time lost from their work. The health of Edith Kilbuck frequently was poor, her husband periodically suffered from a loss of vision, and William Weinland had chronic, severe chest pains. His poor health and that of his older daughter forced the Weinlands to leave Alaska in 1887, but he did not abandon the mission field. Weinland worked among the Cahuilla Indians in southern California from 1889 until his retirement in 1929.[38] The Kilbucks remained at Bethel, and the Weinlands were replaced by a series of other missionaries.

As the man most responsible for the Bethel establishment, John Kilbuck devoted his first years to expanding the physical plant. A principal project, as Eskimos moved to Bethel, was the construction of a school, which opened in 1886.[39] Supplying the mission was another of Kilbuck's responsibilities. In the summers he bought logs for winter firewood, fished for salmon, and bartered for additional fish to provision the mission workers, students, and dogs. Without quite realizing it he and the other Moravians became merchants as they traded with Eskimos to obtain food and other supplies.[40]

The Kilbucks became increasingly confident speakers of Yupik, and by 1888 John Kilbuck was able to deliver the Easter services in Eskimo.[41] In the fall of that year he had the mission well supplied for the winter and was ready to expand his activities beyond the narrow confines of the Bethel station. He began traveling to widely scattered villages by dog sled, going alone or with an Eskimo guide and delivering his Christian message in the village men's houses, where he usually slept. Over the years most Bethel missionaries traveled widely and often, but Kilbuck was on the move far more than any others. He apparently was most content on the trail or among villagers and would leave at a moment's notice to treat the ill, minister to the dying, or bury the dead.

The missionaries insisted that their converts accept the Moravian tenets and live good Christian lives, or at least try hard to do so, before being accepted as church members. A major problem in introducing Moravian Christianity was to blend it satisfactorily with patterns already accepted by the Eskimos. Kilbuck used Orthodox songs previously translated into Eskimo as a part of Moravian services, and for Eskimo brides his wife made gingham caps like those worn by married Orthodox women.[42] In 1888 they admitted the first eight individuals, each previously baptized by

Orthodox priests, to the Moravian Church, and the first couples were married.[43] In another type of transition, one related to Eskimo customs rather than Orthodox ones and therefore more important to the missionaries' goals, Christmas services became a partial substitute for Eskimo winter ceremonials, which the missionaries tolerated at first but later sought to displace.

During the first years of the mission's existence, Kilbuck and Weinland had debated their position regarding aboriginal ceremonies, often termed *plays, masquerades,* or *potlatches.* After witnessing these events and finding no obvious idol worship or wanton heathen excesses, they had judged them harmless. However, after Kilbuck learned to speak Yupik, he realized that some performances were heathen religious rituals, and at this point he took a firm stand, singling out the annual fall and winter ceremonies for particular condemnation. At these ceremonies, held to propitiate spirit beings, masked dancers performed to ensure a good food supply for the coming year. In their battle against heathenism the Moravians decided their most significant victory would be to displace this part of the traditional ceremonial round. Their first notable success was in 1889 when the people of Kwethluk burned their dance masks.[44] In 1890–91 the villagers across the river from Bethel held their masquerade, but performers wore no masks.[45] By 1894, Kilbuck reported with a great sense of accomplishment, *"There was no masquerade this year from Bethel to Ougavig, that is, the six prominent villages* (emphasis in the original).[46] As time would reveal, Kilbuck's reported achievement was ephemeral. He would come to realize that the ceremonialism he thought dead in actuality persisted with considerable vitality into the 1920s.

As the Moravians abolished the Eskimo winter ceremonial round, they attempted to replace the festivities with American holidays and Christian holy days. Christmas became the annual ceremonial highlight, with Thanksgiving second in importance. The Moravian emphasis on gift-giving at Thanksgiving had parallels in the gift presentations during some Eskimo festivities and so was accepted readily. Easter services did not fit nearly as well with aboriginal activities. A major disadvantage was that the time they usually were held conflicted with the subsistence round; in the spring people usually went to their tundra camps. Attendance at Easter services was high only during those years when they were held early in the spring. Low attendance distressed the Moravians, but only rarely and in later years were they willing to adjust the timing of these services.[47] Overall, however, the substitution of Christian celebrations for aboriginal religious ones went well as far as the missionaries were concerned. Furthermore, the Moravians tolerated, even encouraged, traditional ceremonial exchanges that were largely social, not religious. The Eskimos thus combined the old and new and seem to have kept any objections to themselves, indicating their strength but also their willingness to be accommodating.

The most formidable opponents of the Moravians were the Eskimo shamans, whom the missionaries denounced as charlatans and advocates of the devil. Not only did shamans play a prominent part in the aboriginal religious ceremonies the Moravians sought to displace, but they were the healers Eskimos had relied on up to this point. From the time their mission was founded, the Moravians became competitors of shamans not only by offering their own ceremonies but also by attempting to cure the ill. Using a book on homeopathic medicine for consultation, the Moravians treated patients by drawing on their ample supply of medicines. Quite often the missionaries' treatments were successful, and they quickly gained a widespread reputation as curers. Eskimos throughout the region were therefore drawn to Bethel when they required medical aid. Not only did Moravian medical success undermine the position of shamans, but it helped convince the Eskimos that these missionaries were sincere in their desire to improve the quality of people's lives. This was an important factor in the Eskimo acceptance of Moravian teachings. Because the missionaries helped the people fulfill their goal of being well, they were of value to the Eskimos.

Yet the missionaries themselves realized fully their inadequacies as healers and urged the mission board to send a medical missionary to the Kuskokwim. In 1893 the nurse Philippine King finally arrived. She served in the area until 1896, when she was transferred to the Bristol Bay area mission. Her place was taken by a medical doctor, Joseph H. Romig, and his wife, Ella Ervin Romig, who was a nurse. A brother of Edith Kilbuck, Romig joined the Bethel missionaries for seven years.[48] When the Romigs were at Bethel, sick people, especially the desperately ill, often traveled great distances to seek their help. His medical aid was appreciated particularly when home remedies or those of shamans proved unsuccessful. When the Romigs left, the Moravians were unable to replace them, and the people depended on shamans and the less trained missionaries as curers until a hospital was built and staffed at Akiak in 1918.

Despite efforts by the Moravians and other outsiders to heal the ill, shamans remained active as curers. Some Eskimos distrusted whites as healers; furthermore, Western medical practices were ineffective in the treatment of some widespread diseases, such as tuberculosis, and Eskimos knew this to be the case. Shamans also persisted because in practical terms there were far more shamans than whites to help the Eskimos when they were sick. A perceptive shaman, who knew his or her patients, also was in a good position to deal with problems we would label as psychological. In addition, shamans sometimes retained positions of power because they were feared as sorcerers. In sum, shamans remained prevalent and important longer than most Moravian missionaries realized.

The Bethel mission always had few workers available to spread Christianity among a dispersed Eskimo population. To expand the sphere of Moravian influence, Kilbuck initiated a program in which male Eskimo converts represented the church and preached the gospel in select villages. He appointed the first *helpers* in 1889 and stationed them at the lower river villages of Akiak, Kihtagamiut, and Kwethluk.[49] However, this endeavor suffered a severe blow the following spring.

A man named Hooker was appointed the resident helper at Kwethluk. In his initial efforts he succeeded in convincing the people to burn their dance masks. Next, many of these villagers, who had been baptized earlier by Orthodox missionaries, decided to set aside all heathen ways, and in February 1890 Kilbuck received confessions of faith from twenty-two of them. While carrying out his missionary work, Hooker also hunted and trapped to support himself and his family. When trapping in the early spring of 1890, Hooker "was seized with something like vertigo," and this problem was compounded by the death of his only son, which was a severe blow. A messenger was sent to tell Kilbuck that Hooker was extremely ill, and Kilbuck went to Hooker's spring camp to treat him. He did what he could for Hooker, and while there he realized that for some reason the people in general, and in particular a half brother of Hooker's, Mountain Boy, had become extremely hostile.

Hooker recovered slowly, and on the day before Easter he joined the other men to take a bath. As the bath ended, Mountain Boy and another individual announced that Hooker now was ready to leave them and would go to heaven a saved person. The two men led Hooker naked from the bath and ordered the others to follow. A short distance from the camp they told the others to stand still, shut their eyes, and bow their heads in mock prayer. Suddenly there was a howl and shriek, and when one man opened his eyes, he saw dogs tearing Hooker to pieces.[50] On later investigation it appeared that the local shaman, who resented Hooker's success, expected his murder to eliminate Christian influence from the village. This did not follow, but Hooker did become the only Christian martyr among these riverine Eskimos.

Undeterred by Hooker's fate, Kilbuck expanded the helper program. He instructed these men on an informal basis, and in 1895 he initiated an annual summer Moravian Conference for the purpose of shaping local policy, discussing common problems, and furthering the education of helpers. At the first conference the helpers plus one to three delegates from each of the helpers' villages attended. The riverine villages represented included Akiachak, Akiak, Bethel, Kihtagamiut, Kwethluk, Ogavik, and Tuluksak. Under Kilbuck's guidance the members of the first conference considered the future of potlatches, especially the Great Feast for the Dead. Following a presentation by one delegate about the origins and development of potlatches, they were discussed. When it came time to decide future policy, the representatives unanimously voted to abolish them. Kilbuck and the other Moravians considered this a great achievement even though the voters were not representative of all the villagers in their communities.[51] Potlatches were not abandoned entirely along the lower river for another twenty-two years, but this was indeed a major step in that direction.

The Bethel mission thrived under the leadership of John Kilbuck, who more than any other missionary represented the white man's world to Eskimos along the lower Kuskokwim and in the adjoining areas. He was the outsider most active in the Eskimo world, visiting all the villages in the area to win converts, hold church services, help the ill, comfort the dying, and bury the dead. Kilbuck strived most effectively to Christianize and Americanize these people, yet in 1898 he was forced to resign as a Moravian missionary. Kilbuck's resignation resulted from an admission of adultery with an Eskimo woman and with an unmarried female missionary at Bethel.[52]

That the Moravians were able to alter overt Upriver Eskimo religious life significantly in about seven years was an accomplishment in which the earlier Orthodox workers played an indirect role. These men had spoken out against non-Christian aspects of local living and had been the first to encourage major historic changes in religious life. They were handicapped, however, by their lack of regular contact with the people and by the poor support system of the Orthodox in Alaska, especially after the purchase of Alaska in 1867. Moravian interaction with Eskimos was far more sustained and operated from a stable physical base. The Eskimos knew that their own belief system did not always achieve its goals, and they also realized that the Orthodox workers who had offered them an alternative approach seldom visited them. Therefore the Moravians met less resistance than they might have expected.

Becoming Moravians brought not only religious conversion to these Eskimos but changes in social customs. In the aboriginal social system, daily living was integrated with religion only loosely: traditional beliefs had a far less pervasive effect than those to which they now were exposed. When Eskimos decided to accept the Moravian religion, they faced dramatic changes in their manner of living. Their casual attitudes toward premarital and extramarital sexual activities, plural marriages, and divorce are ready examples. Furthermore, the Moravians found Eskimo manners, their sense of propriety, and concepts of cleanliness less than satisfactory. They insisted that their converts change these attitudes and behaviors to conform with Moravian ideals.

Another area, that of economic activities, had to be altered as well if Eskimos were to become good Moravians. It was not easy for the Eskimos to accept and follow the Moravian prohibition against work on Sunday since it had a negative impact on their most important subsistence pursuit, salmon fishing. It became useless for men to fish on Saturday because women could not process the catch on Sunday, nor could men fish on Sunday. This meant that the better part of two days was lost each week, irrespective of how great or small the runs might have been on those days. Likewise, the Moravian effort to replace the winter ceremonials affected Eskimo economic life, but in a less direct way. When these ceremonies were an intimate part of the yearly routine, a great deal of effort was channeled into accumulating food for serving at that time. The reputation of families depended to a great extent on their generosity. As the traditional ceremonial round was abandoned, the incentive to accumulate a food surplus declined. The result was that people apparently lowered their productivity and also began selling the surplus fish to whites. Another result of the abandonment was that whereas the reputations of outstanding providers as ceremonial hosts declined, the influence of Moravian helpers expanded in the villages where they were stationed. Thus becoming Moravians greatly affected economic activities and social statuses as well as religious and moral aspects of the culture. Because of the constant Moravian presence in some villages, their populations underwent far greater and more abrupt cultural changes at this time than they had during the previous period of contact.

GROWTH OF A RELIGIOUS TRIAD

After the United States purchased Alaska, the Orthodox church became in effect a foreign mission. Although it continued to function, it no longer had the support of the Russian-American Company, and in 1870 only four priests remained in Alaska.[53] Upriver Eskimo contacts with Orthodox priests were sporadic from 1866 to around the turn of the century. An indication of what this meant to the local people is conveyed in an 1878 report by Innokentii Shaiashnikov, a priest at Unalaska, after he surveyed church conditions from the Alaska Peninsula north. He quotes an Eskimo as follows:

Russian priests baptized us, they taught us about God and Jesus Christ, for which we are and shall always be grateful. But why did they desert us? Did we offend them? Now the savages (they call their own unbaptized people savages) laugh at us and say that the priests fooled us and deserted us; it is painful to us to hear that. Besides, why did they [priests] take the icons from our churches? We want to have the icons in the places where we gather for prayers; now our chapels are worse than barns. They are full of rubbish and attract only dogs. The savages especially laugh at such conditions at Kolmakovsky Redoubt, where the chapel has neither icons nor roof, and where nobody cares to repair it.[54]

A creole priest, John E. Orlov, finally was transferred from Russian Mission to the Kuskokwim in 1892. He established St. Sergius Church at Little Russian Mission (Chuathbaluk) and remained there until 1896. Orlov traveled widely to tend converts, win new ones, and counteract the Moravian influence. An unbroken sequence of priests followed him until 1926, when the mission was abandoned.[55] Soon after the church was established, Eskimos from nearby had moved to Little Russian Mission, but most of them died in the 1900 influenza epidemic. A few residents remained at the site for a number of years following the mission's abandonment, and the faithful who had moved away continued to return to the church to hold services irregularly and to bury their dead until 1954. At this time some people began to move back permanently.[56]

Unfortunately, next to nothing has been published about Orthodox activities at Little Russian Mission. We know only that the epidemic of 1900 had a negative impact that seems to have been felt by all Christian missionaries in the region. Some Eskimo converts could not understand why God could punish them so severely after they had become faithful Christians, and as a result there was at least a temporary loss of faith. This presumably applied to the remnant population at Little Russian Mission as much as it did elsewhere.

With Moravian dominance extending upriver to Ogavik and Orthodox influence centering at Little Russian Mission, a gap between the two existed; this was filled by Roman Catholic Church workers, who arrived in the area later than the others. They founded a mission on the Yukon in 1888 at Holy Cross and a Kuskokwim mission at Ohagamiut in 1895–96. Although the latter partially was destroyed by fire in 1903 and was abandoned in 1907, it firmly established the Catholic Church along the central Kuskokwim and made Catholicism one of the three faiths that was to most affect the people.[57]

As long as Christian missionaries operated primarily from mission stations, as they did at the beginning of this period, their influence on Eskimos in the region was minimal, despite trips to villages to win converts and minister to congregations. The impact of missionaries did not become intense until after they began living in Eskimo settlements. The Moravians' helper program represented one major change in this direction. Another major change was the establishment of a mission in a village, which was done first by the Roman Catholics at Ohagamiut. Next, the Orthodox established a mission at Little Russian Mission, and when Eskimos began to live there, the same end was achieved. In each instance Christian missionaries increasingly intruded on village life. This change signaled a growth of white control over village life that was tolerated by Eskimos, who applied their customary pattern of accommodation to the new development without realizing the subtle shift in goals that was taking place. Eskimo goals had nothing to do with these expansions of white influence; to the contrary, the purposes being exploited were solely Western in nature. The whites maintained that all changes were intended to benefit the Eskimos, but at no time were the Eskimos given the opportunity to determine for themselves what they preferred. The dominance of Western culture had begun.

6

Expanding Access and Altering Goals

As Westerners exploited Alaska, their goals, and the means to achieve them, typically had a negative impact on the indigenous population. Those Eskimos on Seward Peninsula and near the Yukon River mouth were traumatized at the beginning of the twentieth century by a sudden and vast influx of white gold seekers. The Kuskokwim Eskimos were more fortunate; contacts in their area were more gradual. Initially, few outsiders were interested in the area because local resources were not perceived as of sufficient value to warrant exploitation. Another deterrent before 1900 was the difficulty of access mentioned in previous chapters.

In the mapping of major rivers, explorers typically traveled from a river mouth to the headwaters or from the headwaters to the mouth, yet neither pattern was followed on the Kuskokwim. This helps to account for the geographical obscurity of the Kuskokwim: no one knew until long after its discovery that the river could serve as a major means for transporting goods from the coast deep into the interior. The Russians did not travel the river's length in any single trip, and early American ships off-loaded along Kuskokwim Bay rather than trying to make their way upriver. As long as the volume of imports was small, the latter procedure was satisfactory. An inviting alternative became evident in 1890 when the U.S. Fish Commission steamer *Albatross,* which had a thirteen-foot draft, sailed about forty miles up the river, proving that the lower reaches were navigable.[1] Once discovered, this route does not appear to have been used again until a decade later, when the gold rush made it desirable to transport hundreds of tons of supplies. At this time ships and people gained access to the Kuskokwim and its resources in a magnitude not previously experienced.

The first major influx of outsiders to the Kuskokwim resulted from searches for gold. Following the Nome stampede in 1899– 1900, thousands of unsuccessful prospectors traveled to other areas of western Alaska in their search for gold. Rumors about a strike along the Kuskokwim led some of them in that direction. In the fall of 1900 the first sizable party of prospectors reached the river, and fifteen of them headed for an upper tributary, the Stony River.[2] Also arriving from Nome were traders who came to supply the prospectors; among them were Frank Joaquin and Sam Hubbard, who became mercantile partners with Edward Lind at his Bethel post.[3] Another Nome merchant, Adams H. Twitchell, sailed for the Kuskokwim in 1905 on the *Zenith,* a vessel with a draft of seven feet. Twitchell decided to try making his way upstream and successfully reached Bethel. His arrival was a major achievement and just cause for celebration since no other seagoing vessel had ascended the river this far.[4] However, access from the bay remained dangerous, and during the years around the turn of the century, forty-eight lives were lost in attempts to enter the river.[5]

Kuskokwim River accessibility was more fully realized when seven small seagoing boats made the trip from Nome to Bethel. They arrived in the summer of 1907, and two of them repeated the journey successfully later in the season.[6] In 1908 schooners equipped with auxiliary gasoline engines began sailing from San Francisco to Bethel. That year the *Monterey* carried three hundred tons of goods to this distribution center, and the *Charles Hanson* arrived with several hundred additional tons.[7] However, the channel remained uncharted until 1916, and most ship captains were reluctant to enter the river.[8] The risk of shipwreck in the bay and lower river was sufficient to limit the number of sailings, which kept the freight costs comparatively high.

Freight delivery along the river itself expanded abruptly with the introduction of large stern-wheeled riverboats soon after the turn of the century. Prior to that time, the Americans relied on small seaworthy wooden vessels as a replacement for umiaks. The first of these was the *Bethel Star,* the boat the Moravian mission founders imported to take them upriver in 1885. Over the years the Moravians and others imported or built numerous small riverboats and barges to handle local freight.[9] When white prospectors arrived, they made poling boats and scows, small plank boats useful for hauling comparatively light loads. Their poling boat was narrow, about thirty-three feet in length, pointed at each end, and had a flat bottom. An alternative type was a flat-bottomed scow, square at both ends, and seventeen feet long, with a seven-foot beam and slightly flaring sides.[10] Riverine Eskimos gradually abandoned umiaks and large birch-bark canoes in favor of these forms. Although umiaks were lighter and could carry far more than a typical plank boat, they required greater maintenance and were poorly adapted to fast water streams with rocky bottoms. The same drawbacks applied to large birch-bark canoes. In addition, building a plank boat did not require as much skill as making an umiak or canoe.

The first three large riverboats, the *Nunivak, Quickstep,* and *Victoria,* arrived in 1907 from the Yukon, ready to transport goods to villages and gold camps.[11] In 1910, when it seemed that a major gold strike along the Kuskokwim was imminent, another stern-wheeler, the *Lavelle Young,* arrived from the Yukon.[12] The *Tana,* which began operations in 1916 and continued for many years, became the stern-wheeler most closely identified with the

The Kuskokwim Commercial Company riverboat *Quickstep* docked at Bethel. *Courtesy of the Moravian Archives, Bethlehem, Pa.*

Kuskokwim traffic.[13] The *Wallace Langley* replaced her in 1936 and continued operating until 1952.[14]

Riverboats facilitated the travel and shipment of supplies that were critical to whites now living along the river. To the Eskimos they brought a major change of another order; riverboats provided a source of income for Eskimo men, especially those living along the central river. The early stern-wheelers were numerous and consumed vast quantities of wood. To obtain this fuel steamboat captains contracted with villagers, or possibly more often with village traders, for specific amounts. A trader might contract for five hundred cords and then subcontract with village men, each of whom would supply a portion of the order. Following freezeup the men went out by dog team to cut the wood and haul it to a woodyard along a riverbank, where it would be picked up by a steamer the following summer.[15] Cutting cordwood became profitable employment that fit well into the Eskimo life-style: the men could work independently and whenever they chose during the winter. Because of these factors, cutting cordwood was an important early step in the villagers' shift from barter to a cash economy. By 1911, however, the Eskimo woodcutters who worked either directly for traders or on their own were being replaced in part by whites, who had developed numerous woodyards to supply riverboats.[16]

Oceangoing vessels, stern-wheelers, and smaller boats facilitated the summer transport of freight and passengers, but access to the western interior remained difficult in the winter months. To solve this problem, in 1908 government surveyors plotted a winter trail from Seward to Nome, a distance of 914 miles. During the winter of 1910–11 a small crew cleared and marked the route, which came to be known as the Iditarod Trail after a 185-mile loop of the trail was completed to Iditarod. Once this overland route was opened, travelers from the United States had an acceptable means of reaching western Alaska during most of the year. In the winter months they could take a ship to Seward, proceed to upper Cook Inlet by railroad, and then follow the trail from Susitna northwest through Rainy Pass to the headwaters of the South Fork of the Kuskokwim, going from there to McGrath and Takotna. From Takotna one branch of the trail went to Iditarod,

and another to Nome.[17] From late fall, after most streams froze
over, until just before breakup in April, the trail was open. A man
could walk, use his own dog team, or hire a team. Any man who
hired a team and driver was expected to walk whenever trail conditions were difficult; the only exception was "a fare-paying passenger with a broken leg." [18] Women, however, generally rode on
the sleds.

The trail was popular until the Alaska Railroad was completed
in the winter of 1920–21. This led to a decline in use of the trail,
and with the rise of commercial aviation in the late 1920s, the
trail became neglected, although some segments were maintained
for local travel. During its years of regular use the Iditarod Trail
profited riverine Eskimos, who provided dried salmon to feed the
dogs pulling the many sleds. The opportunity to earn money by
selling dried fish fit well into the life-style of villagers because
they had the capacity to catch far more fish than they were able
to consume. Likewise the timing was opportune: the market for
cordwood had declined, while Eskimo dependence on supplies
provided by traders had expanded.

The commercial aviation that began in 1926, when the first air-
plane landed at Bethel, was popular enough to expand steadily.
By 1932 scheduled air carriers were transporting passengers and
freight to the Kuskokwim from Fairbanks and Anchorage. In addition, charter companies at Bethel flew in and out of the villages
as required. People began to complain that there was not enough
dog sled travel to keep the trails open, a slight exaggeration but
an indication of the growing reliance on airplanes.[19] Before an
airstrip was built at Bethel in 1937, planes landed on sandbars
during the summer and on the frozen river during the winter. The
addition of a military airfield in 1941 brought more and larger
planes to Bethel.[20] World War II produced a lull in nonmilitary air
travel, but soon after the war commercial aviation became more
popular than ever.

AN EPIDEMIC AND ITS CONSEQUENCES

As outsiders came and went to the Kuskokwim area with growing
frequency, particularly after gold seekers arrived in number,
Eskimos inevitably were exposed to exotic diseases. With no
prior immunity and with poor sanitary conditions, the epidemics

were devastating to village populations. A major epidemic in the American period began in July 1900 when influenza and measles reached the Kuskokwim people from an adjacent sector of the Yukon. As they swept together along the river, they dealt a serious blow to Eskimo vitality. Most of the local Eskimos became critically ill. If they survived the diseases themselves, they often contracted pneumonia soon afterward and died. The situation was so severe that at times the living were too weak to bury the dead. In one instance, when the bodies of an entire family were found at a fish camp, they were buried simply by collapsing the tent and shoveling dirt on it.[21]

During the height of the epidemic many of the stricken traveled to Bethel, hoping that the Moravian medical missionary, Joseph Romig, could cure them. Unfortunately, he could do little apart from comforting the ill and burying the dead. Some Eskimos turned to shamans, hoping they could rid the country of these foreign maladies. One shaman from the lower river divined that the dead should be thrown into the river. After this strategy failed to end the sickness, he told the people to throw the dead off housetops, but again the maladies continued. Shamans also suggested burning the Moravian mission or wiping out the missionaries to rid the river of the pestilence, but neither of these alternatives was pursued.

In the aftermath of the 1900 epidemic, some villages, having lost most of their population, were abandoned. Another effect was the people's loss of faith in the curing capacities of both shamans and the medical doctor. About half of the Native population survived the epidemic, but within a few months whooping cough struck this remnant, causing the deaths of many infants and children. About ten years later John Kilbuck noted that "the population now consists of the young generation—like the second growth of timber—with here and there a middle-aged person."[22]

The Moravians' hope that they could direct the changes in Eskimo life seemed especially illusionary after the 1900 epidemic. Nonetheless, the missionaries continued to strive mightily in their effort, working tirelessly to filter out Western influences they considered negative. One of the greatest campaigns was an attempt to shield the people from alcoholic beverages. At the time the Bethel mission was founded, intoxicants were not available to local Eskimos, and for this the Moravians were thankful. The traders imported alcoholic beverages for themselves, however, and in 1893 Edith Kilbuck wrote from Bethel, "I must tell you that I heard for the first time to-day that the Russian trader at the post has been making liquor, and that several of our people have been tempted to take a little." [23] In 1901 some Eskimos became intoxicated on liquor imported by Lind, and in the following years the incidence of drunkenness slowly increased. To the rejoicing of the Moravians, Alaska passed a prohibition law in 1917, to be effective January 1, 1918. That ended the legal importation of intoxicants for a time. [24] Yet ten years later the law was poorly enforced, and drunkenness became a problem that would expand in the coming decades.

It would be valuable to know whether the use of alcohol was due largely to its more ready access or whether other factors, such as the weakening of the people physically and socially after the epidemic plus obvious consumption by whites now living in the area, led to Eskimos' resorting to alcohol as an unsuccessful means of adjusting to their new world. However, no objective information is available from this time period concerning the origins of the excessive consumption of alcoholic beverages that was to prove as hurtful in its way as the epidemic itself.

GOLD

The disruption that gold rushes bring to inhabited areas is characteristically great, and Alaska was no exception. The needs of gold seekers, and the desire of traders to meet these needs, became the next major cause of change in the lives of Upriver People. Gold seekers would change the structure of village social life and would help to modify traditional economic patterns in critical ways; yet these outsiders made no deliberate attempts to affect the peoples' lives in any way. Although prospectors and Eskimos had comparatively little to do with one another in a direct or personal way, changes resulting from gold rush fever were to affect the Eskimos long after rumors of riches brought this influx of whites into the region.

The first report of a strike on a Kuskokwim tributary, called the Yellow River, had reached Nome in the fall of 1900, as mentioned earlier, and the first miners reached the Bethel area by mid-September. They soon were followed by others, who probably numbered in the hundreds. These men, who arrived by boat and later by dog team, did not remain near Bethel but went upriver in their search for the golden river, whose location still was unknown. A few parties set out for the Kuskokwim headwaters, others went up the Stony River, but most thought the Yellow River was a creek near the modern settlement of Aniak. They based their theory on the fact that the water in this creek, which flowed into Whitefish Lake, had a yellowish cast. The same yellow characterized the silt in streams along the upper Aniak River, but despite this coloration, no gold was found in either locality.[25]

John J. Schoechert, a Moravian missionary who was familiar with the Nushagak, Lake Clark, and upper Kuskokwim areas, wrote in a church journal about the Yellow River stampede. He noted, "I can affirm that to the best of my knowledge not $20 worth of gold has been found in the above-mentioned districts." He also observed, "You may still ask, 'Were not good prospects found at the head of the Kuskokwim?' No prospects whatever, to make it pay."[26] Yet no one could deny that Alaska in general was yielding vast quantities of mineral wealth at the time. Placer gold, loose flakes or nuggets deposited in stream beds, valued at about twenty-eight million dollars was mined around Nome from 1897 to 1906, and another sixteen million dollars' worth was recovered near Fairbanks between 1903 and 1906.[27] Despite the failure of the Yellow River rush, it seemed only a matter of time before a major strike would be made in the Kuskokwim drainage. Indeed a major discovery soon would be made nearby, and it deserves mention because of the impact on riverine Eskimos.

In the summer of 1906 prospectors searching Takotna River tributaries of the upper Kuskokwim crossed a low divide to the Innoko River drainage of the Yukon. They found gold colors on bars below the mouth of one stream, and working their way up it, they recovered enough gold to stake a discovery claim on Ganes Creek. Word of the strike spread, and soon after breakup in 1907, more than eight hundred people arrived from Fairbanks, along with several hundred others from Nome. Latecomers located claims on nearly every creek in the mountains of the upper Innoko. A small number of miners dug prospect holes during the winter of 1908, and those on Ophir Creek found some rich gold-bearing gravels. Spring brought hundreds of additional prospectors from Fairbanks to the area.[28] Gold was found the winter of 1909–10 along Moore Creek, a stream flowing into the Tatalina River, a tributary of the Takotna River, and these prospects proved to be comparatively rich.[29] Mining camps established at Moore City and Ophir were more accessible by riverboat from the Kuskokwim than from the Yukon, and supplying them created the first boom in the river economy.

Prospectors continued to search the general area and found placer gold in creeks along another Takotna tributary, Nixon Fork, about 1917. Working their way up these streams, the men found that the amount of gold in the creeks decreased and then disappeared. Returning to the most promising spots, they began to dig prospect holes, and in 1919 they uncovered rich gold-bearing lodes.[30] In contrast with placer gold, recovered as flakes or nuggets from sand or gravel, the gold in lodes, called hardrock gold, is ore that is embedded in rock. The rock must be mined, crushed in a stamp mill, and washed over a copper plate covered with mercury before the gold is freed. Extracting gold from hardrock is a costly process, and most miners who held promising claims sold them to the Alaska Treadwell Gold Mining Company in 1920. The next year the company sank many shafts and built a large stamp mill to process the ore. Work continued on Nixon Fork until 1923; by then it was no longer profitable, and the company withdrew.[31]

One party of stampeders to the Kuskokwim prospected up the Tuluksak River, where the colors they found encouraged them to continue the search. In 1907 they discovered gold in quantity at the head of Bear Creek, where they established a camp.[32] The gold was mixed with gravel in shallow deposits and could be mined by using pick and shovel to open cuts and small sluice boxes to recover the gold. By 1925 the New York-Alaska Gold Dredging Company owned the most productive ground along Bear Creek and named the camp Nyac, based on initials in the company name. To retrieve the gold that lay beneath the shallow deposits required a dredge; the first one was imported in 1925. It began operating the next year, and for a few years the yield was rich. Production fell off abruptly in 1929, and the dredge was not

The only gold rush settlement along the central Kuskokwim River was Georgetown. The large cabin in this photograph, taken in 1910, belonged to George Fredericks, who had lived at the site since 1907. The settlement served as the headquarters for many gold seekers until it virtually was abandoned after a fire in 1911. *Courtesy of the Erskine Collection, #70-28-1047, Archives, University of Alaska, Fairbanks.*

used in 1930. The company imported a smaller, more efficient dredge in 1935, and except for a shutdown because of World War II and as a result of a fire in 1965, the operation continued on a modest scale into the 1980s.[33]

Georgetown, the only settlement that was established along the central Kuskokwim during the gold rushes, was the home of prospectors who had discovered gold along the adjacent George River and nearby Crooked Creek. George Fredericks, after whom the town seems to have been named, was the original white settler there. In the summer of 1909 about three hundred gold seekers arrived at Georgetown, and many built cabins. Companies established stores, and it seemed that the town would become a major base for miners in the vicinity; about four hundred whites wintered there in 1910–11. Nearby gold deposits soon proved to be minor, however, and following a fire in 1911 in which most cabins burned, the community was virtually abandoned.[34] Many of the disappointed prospectors boated down the Kuskokwim from Georgetown, searching tributaries along the way. In 1913 Lapp reindeer herders found a small placer deposit at Canyon Creek on the upper Kwethluk River, and some white prospectors rushed there; this operation continued to have a small output until about 1940.[35]

Once whites were established in an area, they expected to receive mail on a reasonably regular basis, and this meant a new kind of contact with the world beyond the Kuskokwim. Mail was transported to the villages by boat in the summer and by dog team in winter. The extremely large dog teams owned by contract mail carriers required a dependable supply of dried salmon, and this had a significant impact on villagers who earned money by providing food for the teams. In addition, a post office in a settlement brought formal federal recognition to a community, which meant little to Eskimos originally but was to become another means to further their Americanization. The Moravians obtained a post office at Bethel in 1905, and a short-lived one opened at Georgetown in 1912. Aniak acquired its post office in 1914, Akiak in 1916, and Sleetmute in 1923; most others were established considerably later.[36]

As a result of contacts with gold seekers, riverine Eskimos became more thoroughly integrated into the money-based economy that was replacing the barter system to which they were accustomed. Whites paid them for hauling passengers or freight, cutting wood, and supplying them with fish and wild game. This led to a greater expansion of the Eskimo opportunity to purchase goods. Wage labor was seldom available to Eskimos, however. Many whites were seeking work, and the Eskimo work ethic was not compatible with the American boss-employee relationship, nor were Eskimos accustomed to working on a rigid time schedule.

Despite the comparatively large number of prospectors and miners who swept in and out of the Kuskokwim, contacts with Eskimos usually were brief and were limited to economic matters. While the river was a thoroughfare for both, gold seekers spent most of their time at prospects and mines in highlands away from Eskimo villages. Whites and Eskimos typically kept to themselves except to negotiate specific business transactions, and these often were carried out indirectly, with traders serving as middlemen. The social separateness is conveyed by the scarcity of references to Eskimos in books published by white prospectors and miners. Although these works are few and were written about conditions after the major stampedes had peaked, the fact that the authors seldom included meaningful information about contact with Eskimos apart from anecdotal episodes is significant.[37]

Another index to the social separation between white prospectors and miners and local Eskimos or Indians is the material in gold rush newspapers. The earliest and most important papers with information about the Kuskokwim were published at Iditarod, a mining town along the Iditarod River, a tributary of the Yukon. Significant quantities of gold were found in the vicinity in 1909, and a year later the camp had grown sufficiently to support two weekly newspapers. Frequent articles and news briefs covered happenings along the Kuskokwim, especially when it appeared that major deposits of gold were going to be found in the vicinity of Georgetown. Native Alaskans seldom were mentioned in these papers, and the few references that were made tended to be condescending. For instance, when the first dance was held at Georgetown in 1911, all the whites attended, along with "Georgetown natives and a number of up river natives. It was a scene long to be remembered by these simple folk."[38]

The most extensive discussion in these papers about Upriver Eskimos (mistakenly identified as Indians) dates from 1916 when two white men, Bill Lee and John R. MacDonald, traveled from Iditarod to the Sleetmute area in the spring. Lee initially reported in brief that they found the people in dire need of food and living under deplorable conditions. His traveling companion reported, "I have visited very few Indian camps in which filth and hunger did not reign supreme," and he recommended that the government introduce agriculture among them as "the only salvation left for the native." Two white residents of this area objected to the report, responding that there was no hunger and the story "made everybody laugh."[39]

In contrast to the lack of contact indicated in newspapers of the time, missionaries reported that sufficient contact took place to cause concern about the impact of this new group of whites. With respect to the Bethel area the Moravian missionary Arthur F. Butzin wrote, "It is gravely true that many of the white men now here do create serious difficulties in the uplift of the natives. Profanity and basest animal lust are either openly practiced or hidden beneath a much scratched veneer of politeness."[40]

The introduction of American political institutions to the region was one result of the gold rushes that would have a major impact on riverine Eskimos. When a gold camp grew large enough to qualify as a town or city, a U.S. commissioner would be stationed there; his primary responsibility was to record mining claims. Other officials arrived at the same time. A U.S. marshal or his deputy became responsible for making arrests if laws were broken, and a circuit judge or the commissioner heard the cases that resulted. The earliest arrests seem always to have been of whites, but as the laws and regulations were applied to local Eskimos, they too became subject to arrest. At this time their Americanization intensified abruptly, a topic examined further in Chapter 8.

REINDEER

Sheldon Jackson, who was indirectly responsible for the founding of the Moravian mission at Bethel, undertook various projects in his efforts to aid Native Alaskans. Prominent among these was the introduction of reindeer into Alaska. Jackson felt that the walrus and whale harvest by whites was eroding the economy of coastal Eskimos and causing their population to decline. He reasoned that introducing reindeer and teaching the Eskimos to herd them would make their economic future far more secure; in addition, herding would lead to a civilized way of life in contrast to the barbarism Jackson reportedly saw and deplored. This plan, conceived in 1890, was rebuffed initially by federal officials. Undaunted Jackson obtained private funds to launch the project and imported a few animals from Siberia in 1891. The next summer, using the remaining private funds, he arranged for 171 reindeer to be landed at Port Clarence on Seward Peninsula. Soon thereafter the federal government decided to support the project and began by appropriating money for more animals. By 1902, when the Russian government prohibited the further export of reindeer, 1,280 animals had been shipped to Seward Peninsula. The deer multiplied rapidly, and herds were lent to missions so that they could supervise the training of Eskimo herders in an apprenticeship program. The plan was for the offspring of the mission animals to become the nuclei of new herds for successful apprentices. Initially Chukchi from Siberia were brought to Alaska to teach herding, but they proved unsatisfactory and were replaced by herders from Lapland, the first of whom arrived in 1894.[41]

The Moravians requested the loan of a herd in 1896, after deciding that reindeer herding would benefit the Eskimos in a number of ways. The missionaries thought reindeer meat would prevent periodic food stress and skins would be useful for garments. If this proved true, the Eskimo reliance on trapping, a less stable source of these products, would decline. They likewise reasoned that reindeer could replace dogs as draft animals; this would be more economical since the deer were grazers and therefore easier to feed than dogs. Furthermore, the great quantities of fish required as dog food then could be diverted to human consumption. The Moravian appeal was met in 1901 when the mission was loaned 176 animals. The agreement with the U.S. Bureau of Education required the return of a herd of corresponding age, sex, and size in five years. Female deer were not to be butchered, and reports about the herd were to be submitted annually. A proportion of the herd increase was to become mission property at the time the loan was repaid.[42]

Lapp herders and others drove the reindeer from the Norton Sound area to Bethel; when they arrived, the first Eskimos were hired as apprentice herders. Subsequently additional Lapps arrived with more animals to strengthen the herd. By 1908 the mission was responsible for about 2,700 animals in three herds controlled by sixteen owners, including the mission itself. Reindeer management soon proved a complicated and time-consuming process for the Moravians. The ears of each animal had to be marked in a combination of notches unique to its owner and the marks registered; branding reindeer was impractical because of their thick coats and thin skins. Compiling the required records about the animals each herder bought and sold, the number that were born, died, or were butchered, and how far each herd traveled seemed a never-ending task. Furthermore, recruiting good apprentices proved difficult, partially because the program was encumbered with so many regulations.

An Eskimo apprentice could become the owner of a small herd after three or four years under favorable circumstances. He then faced numerous difficulties, most of them unanticipated. The

Reindeer fairs were held annually from 1914 to 1920 as a means of stimulating interest in herding. Kuskokwim Eskimos began herding reindeer in 1901, but their participation in the industry declined during the late 1930s. *Courtesy of the Moravian Archives, Bethlehem, Pa.*

number of deer he received, about fifty, was insufficient to support a family, which meant he still had to fish and trap. While so engaged, he had to hire someone else to herd the animals. Even when the herd had increased sufficiently for the owner to have a few reindeer to sell, it was difficult for him to make a profit because he could be undersold by the owners of large herds.

When John Kilbuck arrived in Akiak in 1911 as a Bureau of Education teacher, he was vitally interested in furthering the reindeer industry among Kuskokwim area Eskimos. For the next ten years he traveled widely and often to visit herders and settle their disputes, attempt to improve poor herding practices, further the apprenticeship program, and help the Eskimos market their animals in the face of competition from Lapps and whites. He introduced the practice of holding annual reindeer fairs as a means of giving visibility and recognition to the industry.[43]

By the early 1930s the reindeer industry seemed well established locally. However, most animals by this time belonged to Lapps and whites, not Eskimos. About 35,000 reindeer reportedly were owned by Akiak residents, 5,000 grazed in the vicinity of Tuluksak, and 3,000 belonged to the Bethel herd. In the late 1930s, the number was reported to be nearly the same although the herds were more widely distributed. Incredible as it may seem, by 1946 only 600 animals remained in a single herd at Akiak, and shortly thereafter they had disappeared.[44]

What caused the demise of the reindeer in the Kuskokwim area, as well as elsewhere in Alaska, has been the subject of a great deal of conjecture and debate. Enmeshed in controversy from its beginnings, the Alaska reindeer industry was the subject of innumerable federally sponsored studies, and the conclusions reached concerning the cause of its failure cover a wide range of possibilities. Initially reindeer fairs, launched in 1914, stimulated interest in herding, but the last one was held in 1920. The end of this form of recognition seems to have had a negative effect on the Eskimo herders in particular. The Eskimos had shown little interest from the beginning in being herders; they became apprentices only after strong encouragement by the Moravian supervisors. A. C. Kinsley, who investigated conditions along the Kuskokwim in 1930, observed that apprentice Eskimo herders no longer were being trained and that those who still owned small herds grazed them adjacent to their settlements and did not tend them closely, which led to the animals becoming increasingly wild. Kinsley observed, "He [an Eskimo] must either become a 'reindeer man' or he must revert into 'dog and fish man.' He cannot be both. That is the big trouble at the present time. The native is trying to ride both hobbies and failing in both."[45]

These difficulties were compounded by an ethnic conflict between the Lapps and Eskimos. The first-generation Lapp migrants were adept herders and increased their holdings to the point of overwhelming their Eskimo competition. The Lapps felt that most Eskimos showed little ability as herders and often looked down on them. Conversely, Eskimos sometimes considered the Lapps unfair in their dealings; this attitude was no doubt partially a reflection of Moravian feelings. The missionaries had worked to obtain reindeer for the benefit of the Eskimos, and they were distressed to see ever-increasing Lapp control over the herds. A Moravian missionary, Adolf Stecker, wrote in an official report, "They [the Lapps] came from a poor country, were greedy, stingy. One cannot reason with them. At or before 1910, they should have been removed, and, at that time, they wanted to go North."[46]

Setting aside the debate about the reasons for the decline of reindeer in general, a major reason that Eskimo ownership of herds never amounted to a great deal was that the Eskimos found reindeer herding to be less satisfactory than, and in many ways incompatible with, their customary economic endeavors. They found salmon to be an abundant and generally predictable staple. Although people sometimes went hungry in the spring, documented instances of people dying from starvation are rare in this century, with the number of deaths always small and localized. Eskimos did not consider this to be a reason to change their economic base. In addition, the introduction of reindeer happened to come at the time of an expanding fur market, and herding conflicted with trapping, which was a long-established economic activity. To obtain reindeer initially the Moravians had argued that the area was trapped out, but this was not the case. The Eskimos themselves felt no need to change their pattern of relying on fish and fur. Apparently most of the Eskimos who became apprentice herders were young men who had attended the Moravian school at Bethel and were strongly influenced by these missionaries to try herding.

Reindeer herding required a pattern of settlement that was different from the one traditional among local Eskimos. Under the prevailing fishing and trapping economy, families moved from their villages to camps along streams or lakes in the spring and fall, and they often spent the summer at salmon-fishing camps along the river. Their lives focused during the winter at their villages, where homes were permanent and had become increasingly comfortable as their owners acquired more wealth and trade goods from whites. Reindeer herding, on the other hand, required moving with the animals throughout the year to control them and search out good grazing grounds. To herd properly a man had to move his family often or leave them for long periods.

Furthermore, close herding was required to protect deer from predators such as wolves. This was extremely important since a wolf could kill many animals in a night. Watching the deer closely also prevented overgrazing and discouraged them from straying to join caribou that might wander nearby. Herd size could be reduced not only by wolves and caribou but by insects; swarms of mosquitoes might cause the deer to flee. Because of these problems and others, good herding meant staying near the animals at all times. For the sociable Eskimo male this daily routine was singularly unappealing.

In retrospect, it would appear that reindeer herding as a viable economic endeavor for local Eskimos was doomed from the beginning. These people did not have the economic problems noted by Jackson when he proposed that coastal Eskimos become herders. With no felt need for the new resource, adult males were unwilling to turn away from their customary subsistence practices. Reindeer herding was the idea of missionaries, and apprentices were most likely to be young men over whom they had considerable influence. By the 1930s this influence had waned, and no new apprentices stepped in to maintain the industry. As mentioned previously, adult men and their wives usually disliked the idea of moving frequently, nor did they willingly accept the tedium of herding. Furthermore, they were not accustomed to the planning required to develop a herd. Fishing and trapping offered the immediate, if short-term, rewards to which they were accustomed, and because the river and land still provided, they felt no strong economic motivation to herd. Using reindeer as draft animals did not appeal to Eskimos, who continued to depend primarily on dog teams. Thus the demand for dog food did not decline. In addition, and of singular importance, Lapps dominated as herders from the beginning of the project to the end. These people had an established cultural focus on reindeer herding, and the ones who migrated to Alaska presumably did so because they were more discontent than most. These factors led to an early and lasting control of herding by the Lapps. Then too, some local whites recognized herding as an unprecedented business opportunity and took part in it as soon as they were allowed to own deer. They had more capital than the Eskimos did and were able to control the sale of reindeer meat to miners. Thus this noble experiment failed to produce a better way of life among the riverine Eskimos. The ultimate inability of reindeer to establish themselves along the Kuskokwim resulted from the factors noted plus the fact that the land was overgrazed by reindeer and caribou in combination.

SALMON

The dependence on salmon and the means for obtaining them underwent little change prior to the arrival of prospectors. The gill nets and traps that had prevailed before continued to be used in the American period. Not until a novel fishing device was introduced by the gold seekers was the nature of fishing altered drastically. This new means of fishing depended on a wheel that operated well in rivers with a moderate current and opaque waters. Although some people believe fish wheels were used by aboriginal Eskimos and others attribute their introduction to the Russians, neither opinion is correct. White prospectors brought the fish wheel to Alaskan waters. In the United States these wheels were set for shad on the Roanoke and Pee Dee rivers in North Carolina by about 1829, and they were used to take salmon along the Columbia River by 1879.[47] In interior Alaska prospectors apparently built and used the first ones on the Tanana River in 1904.[48] Prospectors near Georgetown built the first local fish wheel, possibly in 1910; from that time forward, salmon fishing patterns changed wherever the wheel could be used.[49]

A Kuskokwim fish wheel consists of two wire mesh or wood splint dippers set on arms opposite each other and at right angles to two other arms with paddles attached. The axle is mounted across a log raft set in the river channel and held in place by ropes or cables attached to the bank. Soon after breakup, the owner of a wheel positions it along a bank where he knows salmon will crowd as they swim upstream. The river current propels the wheel by its pressure on the paddles and dippers. Fish swimming within reach of a dipper are caught and lifted from the water; as a dipper moves upward, the fish drop into a chute that leads to a box at one side of the raft.

Fish wheels normally cannot be used below Akiak because the current is slow and may cease during incoming tides. Elsewhere along the river they work well wherever the water is relatively opaque, the current comparatively fast, and the water deep near a bank. A fish wheel does not demand constant attention, although

After its introduction on the Kuskokwim by gold seekers about 1910, the fish wheel soon became popular along the central river. This one was operating above Napamiut in 1953. *Photo by the author.*

it does require a certain number of adjustments and repairs. Once in operation a wheel can take hundreds of salmon daily if the run is strong. Disadvantages are that high water can carry away a wheel and driftwood can destroy or jam it. Consistently high water, abrupt changes in water level, or unusually clear water may result in small harvests. Despite these drawbacks, the overall increase in the catch and the greatly reduced human effort involved during salmon runs led to the ready acceptance of the wheels by riverine Eskimos.

Fish wheels gradually displaced the aboriginal combination of fish traps and weirs to take salmon. The weir-trap form still was used widely in 1912, but it seems to have been replaced soon thereafter by wheels wherever local conditions were appropriate for the use of this new device.[50] The changeover had far-reaching effects on the Eskimo way of life. After a wheel had been built and positioned, it required comparatively little attention, freeing men for other activities. Typically, more salmon were caught than were needed by a family, which meant that the surplus could be sold to the increasing numbers of whites, who bought them for themselves and their dogs. Another consequence was that Eskimos were able to maintain larger dog teams and thus gain greater mobility for subsistence activities and visiting. The most difficult adjustment to the greater harvests was that the women had to work harder preparing fish for sale or storage.

Other technological innovations from the United States brought additional changes in salmon fishing, summer settlement patterns, and river travel. In the early 1900s Eskimos began using plank boats like those introduced by prospectors. By 1914 a few whites owned outboard motors, and after World War I these motors became increasingly popular among Eskimos.[51] Many riverine Eskimos found that with a plank boat and reliable outboard motor a man could tend his nets or fish wheel from his home village; this brought greater residential stability. At the same time store credit or money were required to buy a motor and keep it in working condition, which made the people more dependent on American economic networks. Unlike the Bristol Bay area to the south, commercial fishing along the Kuskokwim did not emerge as important until the early 1960s (*see* Chapter 8).

Fish wheels, more efficient gill nets, and outboard motors on plank boats combined to greatly expand the salmon harvest. Many more fish were taken than the local population could consume, and much of the surplus was dried as dog food, for which the demand was great in the early 1900s. Although the number of gold seekers declined after 1911, they remained numerous enough to be a good market for salmon. In addition, the dog teams of mail carriers, freight haulers, and passenger carriers required vast quantities of fish. However, as noted previously, when the Alaska Railroad was completed from the south to interior Alaska in 1921, the Iditarod Trail abruptly declined in importance, as did the demand for dog food. Furthermore, commercial aviation soon displaced dog sled travel over long distances. It appears that the intensity of salmon fishing for dog food may have peaked around 1930. During that year along the Kuskokwim 343 Eskimos and Indians and two whites used fifty-five fish wheels and about eight hundred gill nets while fishing for salmon.[52] It also appears that by this time imported foods were gaining in popularity among Eskimos, and as a result salmon became somewhat less important in their diet.

FURBEARERS AND TRADING

Furs not only attracted Russians to the Kuskokwim but were the resource most responsible for the presence of American traders until 1900 and were a major trade item into the 1950s. For the early American period we know little about the extent of the harvest until 1884, when trading posts existed at Bethel, Kolmakovskiy, and Vinasale. Of the 9,000 pelts exported, 4,000 were from the Bethel area.[53] Furbearers were becoming scarce around Kolmakovskiy, possibly due to overtrapping, and while valuable species such as beaver, marten, and fox were abundant along the upper river, few Indians and no Eskimos or white trappers lived there.[54] Thus, in the 1880s the center for the fur trade had begun to shift from the central and upper river to the Bethel area Be cause of this change and the decline that American competition had brought to the direct Siberian trade, the importance of Bethel as a trading center expanded.[55]

Before 1900 the fur trade was important but not highly profitable, despite the great markup on imports. For example, for Lind, the principal trader at Bethel, there reportedly was a 400 to 500 percent markup on imports in 1896, whereas fur prices were low.[56] This changed in the early 1900s as fur prices increased and the cost of imports began to decline. Small oceangoing vessels began unloading at Bethel rather than along the upper bay, thus abruptly reducing transportation costs. Fifty pounds of flour that cost $5.00 in 1900 sold for $3.00 in 1906. At the same time fur prices rose abruptly; a mink pelt worth 25¢ in 1900 sold for $4.00 in trade five years later.[57]

Contrary to their original intent, the Moravian missionaries informally and then formally traded with Eskimos in the region. In the early years the missionaries traded largely for fish and firewood to support the mission because they could not obtain supplies as easily by any other means. Trading gradually increased in scope until 1898, when the mission board took a firm stand against these exchanges.[58] As mission expenses soared, the mis-

sion board changed its position; becoming increasingly cost conscious, it allowed stores to open so that its stations might achieve
greater self-sufficiency. The first store may have existed at Ogavik
in 1905; it is certain that it was operating by 1907, as was their
store at Bethel.[59] These missionaries continued to operate stores
into the late 1920s, despite their uneasiness about combining
commercialism with other mission-related activities.[60] They justi-
fied their role as traders by noting that they treated Eskimos more
fairly than did the other merchants.

Access to Bethel by ship and the arrival of gold seekers in the
early 1900s led to the formation of new trading companies and to
the emergence of independent traders at Bethel and elsewhere. In
1906 Frank Joaquin, Adams Twitchell, and Charles A. Fowler
joined to form the Joaquin, Twitchell, and Fowler Company.
They built a store and warehouse at Bethel in 1908, and after re-
organizing the next year as the Kuskokwim Commercial Company, they operated at Bethel until 1916. That year John W. Felder,
who had an interest in the company, joined with Maurice Gale to
buy the Bethel station inventory. Called Felder-Gale & Company,
this operation was sold in turn to the Northern Commercial Company in 1927.[61] The trade at these stores was a combination of
cash transactions, largely with whites, and barter, primarily for
furs, with Eskimos.

Although Bethel was the hub of trading activities, villages
often had traders of their own. The local trader was the most important outsider in an Eskimo village, and the pelts received were
his primary source of income. By the 1920s most sizable settlements had an independent trader; for example, George W. Hoffman founded a store at Napamiut (1906), Frederick Bishop at
Sleetmute (1906), and Denis Parent at Crooked Creek (ca. 1914).[62]
The power of these independent traders during this period cannot
be underestimated. The trader was "king of his village." He
alone decided what merchandise to offer, what prices would be
locally, and the amount of credit a person could receive. A trader
had stock available for what he considered to be a good customer,
but not for a bad one, and he did or did not adulterate what he
sold at his discretion. Gentlemen's agreements between traders
made it difficult for a dissatisfied villager to trade elsewhere on a

regular basis; this was particularly true of any villager chronically or deeply in debt. If a trader was a formal or informal postmaster, he also determined what mail, if any, a villager received. This made it difficult for villagers to sell pelts to an independent fur buyer and almost impossible to ship them to a fur exchange or to purchase goods from a mail-order company. Another way a trader monopolized clients was in the use of trade tokens, or *bingles*. An Eskimo who took his pelts to a trader and did not take their full value in trade items was given tokens to be used later. The pattern was for a trader to accept only his own bingles; this prevented clients from buying at another store, where prices or merchandise might be better. This was an especially popular practice at Bethel, where there were several traders.[63] Villagers obviously were at the mercy of American traders because of these ways the trade was structured and also because they knew so little about the ways of living that existed beyond the confines of their sector of the river.

The first white trappers, or "cat stranglers" as miners called them derisively, began setting their lines in the headwater drainages in 1902–03, or possibly somewhat earlier.[64] Their number expanded as fur prices increased, and in about 1909 eight trappers, all presumably white, harvested $30,000 worth of skins.[65] By the 1910s some of the miners themselves turned to trapping as a useful means of earning a grub stake. However, the rewards were few for most of them; a man typically earned about $500 for his furs, which covered only a winter's expenses.[66] These men seldom represented a competitive threat to Eskimo trappers because they were concentrated upriver, in Indian country.[67] Yet white trappers had a definite influence on Eskimo trapping, particularly as they introduced plank boats and intensified the use of firearms and steel traps.

The Russians did not trade in firearms, although guns were presented to notable men as extraordinary gifts. However, firearms of British origin were traded in the Cook Inlet area by the mid-1830s and possibly were received from Hudson's Bay Company posts. During the Russian period, British guns probably were received by Kuskokwim Eskimos through their contacts with the Tanaina of Cook Inlet.[68] After the American purchase, old army muskets became a popular trade item at Kolmakovskiy.[69] In 1900 the long-standing prohibition against selling breech-loading rifles and ammunition to Native Alaskans was rescinded, and agents of the Alaska Commercial Company were authorized to sell rifles. No such agent existed along the Kuskokwim at that time, but some Upriver Eskimos did obtain guns, probably through illegal trade.[70] Breechloading firearms were desired because of their efficiency for taking big game, such as bears and caribou, but they were used under some circumstances for killing furbearers as well.

The initial effort by the Russians to introduce steel traps in the late 1830s had failed, and they do not seem to have tried again in later years.[71] Based on his observations between 1877 and 1881, Nelson reported that steel traps were popular for taking mink in the lowlands between the Yukon and Kuskokwim rivers and that elsewhere Eskimos used steel traps to take beaver.[72] This was not customary along the central Kuskokwim in 1897, however, which suggests that their use probably did not become common in this region until after the turn of the century.[73]

Fur price fluctuations in the 1910s and 1920s produced an unstable income among Eskimo trappers while nonetheless providing them with more trade goods than ever before. Prices declined by 75 percent at the outbreak of World War I but soon thereafter climbed to unprecedented levels.[74] In 1919 a prime red or white fox pelt brought as much as $45, a prime mink sold for $17, and a muskrat might be worth $3. One immediate result was a temporary increase in the local standard of living; another was a resurgence of exchange feasts similar to those of aboriginal times. According to one account about a particular feast held at Bethel in 1920, an estimated $20,000 worth of goods changed hands.[75] Eskimos had more monetary wealth than ever before, and those who were generous hosts gained personal prestige in this manner. An abrupt decline in fur prices in 1920–21, plus a scarcity of furbearers, made life more difficult, but a few years later successful trappers again were earning as much as $1,000 a year from pelts.[76] With their continued reliance on local resources to meet their basic needs, these Eskimos probably spent most of their money on trade goods.

As long as Eskimo men were able to obtain fish, game, and fur without interference from whites, they could increase their living standards while exploiting the environment in traditional ways. These standards rose as a result of the availability of American technological products and the growing opportunity for the Eskimos to have a higher income. Along with these changes, however, came others that interfered with the freedom of the people to live as they saw fit. Regulations concerning trapping were difficult for the Eskimos to accept, especially when they were enforced in ways that seemed unreasonable to them. For a while after the first regulations were established, Native people continued to hunt out of season and to take young animals. In the early years of this century in particular these furs either could be sold to traders at reduced prices or could be used at home for garments or other purposes. After more regulations regarding the harvest of furbearers were enacted and enforcement became effective in the late 1920s, Eskimos had problems with the new constraints. This led to jail sentences for some of them.[77] In addition to the general regulations now enforced, the Alaska Game Commission prohibited the trapping of beaver whenever their population was considered dangerously low. The intermittent patterning of this prohibition was confusing to Native trappers.

As late as the 1950s some riverine Eskimos remained bitter about the activities of early enforcement agents. They recounted that parkas made of out-of-season skins literally were taken off the bodies of children wearing them. Resentment of enforcement agents remained strong throughout the 1950s, and isolated hunters sometimes shot at the airplanes of these men as they flew over.[78] Federal and territorial government control over hunting, trapping, and fishing, all basic ways to obtain food as well as cash, had a profound impact on the local life-style. Not only were basic subsistence patterns affected, but such control was a critical step by which whites expanded their dominance over the Eskimos.

From 1900 to 1930 trapping regulations were only one aspect of the changes introduced by whites to the Kuskokwim area. The alteration of fishing patterns, the growth of wage labor, the emphasis on Christianity, and the introduction of formal education also began to affect life on the Kuskokwim. No longer could

Eskimos remain untouched while in their villages, as in the past, and no longer was the white population to be as transient as before. The American missionary and trading establishments were more permanent than the Russian ones had been, and they brought a multiplicity of changes that had far-reaching effects on Eskimo culture.

Americanization: I

When access to the Kuskokwim expanded abruptly in 1900 as a result of the search for gold, changes of unparalleled scope and intensity began to affect the local population. Eskimos found their lives increasingly Americanized, especially between 1900 and the early 1920s. In this chapter and the one to follow, these developments are examined. Changes in villages, adult life, Christianity, schools, and health are discussed in this chapter; the following one focuses on economic integration, social welfare, political control, the land, and Bethel.

VILLAGES

One of the major changes at this time affected the Eskimo villages directly. In previous years, most riverine Eskimos had lived in small villages separated by the span of watershed required for their subsistence economies. They were autonomous and were characterized by a diffuse and weak power structure. Villages were relocated not infrequently, although the same families tended to remain together as a new village was established. The Upriver Eskimos had twenty-six major historic settlements, but of this number only Akiak, Kwethluk, and probably Tuluksak had been occupied continuously since the Russian period. Thirteen of the historic villages had been abandoned permanently by about 1900; Little Russian Mission was abandoned but later reoccupied. Villages were deserted most often because of flooding, changes in the river channel, the effects of an epidemic, or a combination of these factors. Of the thirteen larger settlements occupied in 1900, most were newly established, and in some instances the population had made a number of moves before settling in the current locale.[1]

Settlement changes may be illustrated by tracing the movements of one Eskimo group in historic times. Those living in villages named *Kalskag* serve as an example. In Russian times a
number of families lived in a village then called Kalskag, but following the 1900 epidemic, the survivors felt so uncomfortable
surrounded by the many graves of newly deceased relatives that
they gradually moved, family by family, a few miles upriver to
found New Kalskag. The former village, which then came to be
known as Old Kalskag, was abandoned by about 1915. The New
Kalskag residents were Russian Orthodox Church members, and
when some Roman Catholic Eskimos moved from the Yukon to
their village, conflicts began to develop. As religious factionalism
sharpened in the 1930s, some Orthodox families began to live
throughout the year at their summer fish camp a short distance
downstream. After this locale became a permanent settlement, it
was known as Lower Kalskag, whereas the name of New Kalskag
was changed to Upper Kalskag, or simply Kalskag.[2]

An especially notable aspect of village relocation, because it
relates directly to the adaptability of riverine Eskimo culture, is
the steady movement upriver in historic times. This establishment of villages beyond their aboriginal territory has been facilitated by the relatively small number of Indians with whom they
shared a common boundary. In Russian times the farthest inland
settlement that was exclusively Eskimo was Crow Village. In the
following sixty years, Eskimos moved about 120 miles farther up
the river, founding the villages of Napamiut, Crooked Creek, and
Sleetmute. The migration has not ceased; in 1961 they joined
Tanaina Indians from Stony River to found the Kuskokwim village called Stony River. By 1974 the surviving Georgetown Ingalik Indians were living in these villages.[3]

Most modern villages emerged as the people from previously
small and scattered settlements joined to form larger social com-
posites. The populations of long-established villages also have
grown as individuals from a broad area moved into them. For example, Kwethluk had 232 people in 1953; of this number 181 had
been born there. Of the rest, thirteen were born at Bethel, twelve
at villages along Kuskokwim Bay, seven at Akiak, and the remaining ones at various other villages in the area.[4] Attempts to
separate the modern Kuskokwim Eskimo population into the tra-

ditional Upriver and Downriver subgroups are no longer as meaningful as before; furthermore, the Upriver Eskimo population now includes Eskimo migrants from the Yukon as well as Kuskokwim Indians who have become Eskimo in a cultural context.

In the early years of Western contact the Russians did not found permanent posts at these settlements, nor did missionaries establish themselves there. Yet visits by missionaries or traders were reasonably frequent, and either might designate local representatives. As Americanization expanded, some independent traders purposefully built their stores away from village sites to have greater control over what happened at their establishment; as a result they had little direct influence on day-to-day village life. Other American traders built stores in villages, and this sharing of a physical setting led to a far more direct influence of traders over local affairs.

As a store transformed a village into a commercial center, a few whites settled there or nearby. These seem most often to have been prospectors who would not abandon their search for gold; instead of leaving when the area proved marginally productive, as did most of the miners, they stayed on and became long-term local residents. Settling in or near villages with stores, they prospected during the summer months and trapped or cut wood during the winter. These whites and the trader, who were accustomed to postal service, lobbied for a post office. When one was founded, the trader or another white became the postmaster or postmistress, adding a new position of authority held by whites within the village setting. When white miners and traders married Eskimo women, as they usually did, their influence among the local people grew in another way. Sooner or later the whites established a log cabin school for all village children. Eventually a larger structure, made from lumber and having attached or detached quarters for the teacher, replaced the cabin and lent permanent legitimacy to the new institution, again controlled by whites and serving needs they felt were vital. As medical and social services reached a village, most commonly following World War II, the teacher took charge of these programs. Despite their responsibilities for the well-being of community members, individual teachers did not gain lasting influence because they were rotated periodically. The trader, because of his permanence and economic position, was the nonnative exerting the greatest influence on village life by the 1920s.

The precise sequence of American-inspired change in the physical layout of a village varied, but by the 1950s the results usually were much the same. Trading posts were likely to be the first new and different buildings, and they often were set somewhat apart from Eskimo dwellings. As the religious functions of a village qasgiq were assumed by a Christian institution, a church or chapel would be built. Later a school would be added and much later a community hall constructed as a village center. Semisubterranean houses gave way to one-room log cabins, which were in turn replaced by multi-room cabins or frame dwellings. Some families built their own bathhouses and added outhouses nearby. Of the aboriginal structures, only fish drying racks and some caches remained essentially unchanged.

The villages changed most visibly when the federal government set about improving living conditions nationwide. The Great Society programs launched by President Johnson in 1965 had their most profound impact on life in western Alaskan Eskimo settlements. These federal assistance programs began to mushroom in Alaska as vast sums of money became available. This affected even the most remote community. The expanded federal infrastructure and the determination of its administrators made many varied programs accessible to villagers. Among the most important was the one to provide better housing.

Compared with national standards, the housing and sanitary conditions in Kuskokwim villages were deplorable. Previous federal, territorial, and state efforts to upgrade village housing had impacted comparatively few families. With the new federal programs, the living conditions in every village were improved greatly. At Lower Kalskag, for example, about half of the forty households obtained new houses in 1968–69 as the result of a Great Society program. Twenty-three new dwellings were constructed with milled logs, spun glass insulation, and aluminum roofs, and were divided into two or three rooms. As a result of another program, the Alaska Village Electric Cooperative began in 1969 to provide electricity to member households. Other federal programs facilitated the construction of other structures for villagewide use. For example, Lower Kalskag acquired a new school, post office, and town hall, and the people built an Orthodox church on their own.[5] Developments such as these were typical of villages in the late 1960s and were intended to create an environment in which the people could live more comfortably and healthfully.

Although Eskimo villages along the river began to look increasingly like suburban American communities in the late 1960s, the changes generally have not been enduring. Some villages have taken on the appearance of ghettos in more recent years. The government houses, usually poorly built and on unstable foundations, have deteriorated badly. Some wells intended to serve community water needs have proven unreliable, and the same is true of electrical service in some villages. The people and the federal government have not been able to maintain the infrastructure sufficiently to keep the living standard at the level visualized by the program planners.

By the late 1960s other changes were well established in the villages. Canvas-covered kayaks continued to be seen on the riverbanks, but their number declined as men built plank boats and sometimes purchased aluminum craft, ranging from punts to speedboats. All-weather airstrips gradually replaced sandbars and the improvised landing fields first used by aircraft. A more recent innovation affecting the appearance of river villages, one that brings with it a far greater connection with activities elsewhere, is the dish antenna for television reception and for telephone service.

ADULT LIFE

As physical changes brought a new look to villages, altered living arrangements introduced a new life-style as well. The character of adult life changed drastically as men's houses were abandoned and the dwellings of women began to house adult males. Traditionally a men's house had been the residence, workshop, and bathhouse for most males and was the structure with which they most closely identified physically and emotionally. Similarly women had a deep attachment to their matrifocal households, where closely related females lived. Yupik Eskimos living to the west considered the women's houses as symbolic wombs in biological, social, and spiritual contexts, and the same beliefs probably prevailed among Upriver Eskimos.[6] A woman was most likely to have been conceived and to conceive in her dwelling, conditions of primary significance in her life. Furthermore, it was here that she carried out the work characteristic of her adult life, rearing children and transforming food products into edibles and raw materials into artifacts. In aboriginal times it was believed that the activities of women might have a negative effect on the hunting success of adult males if the two sexes lived together; the air women breathed was thought to pollute young hunters. Thus the separate female-male living arrangement played a key role in traditional life. Only during trips to fishing and trapping camps would a couple and their children share a dwelling.

The winter-long residential separation of Eskimo couples conflicted with the Moravians' view of family life, and they were determined to change Eskimo living arrangments. The missionaries sought not only to have couples live together in houses but to insure that they married in an American legal context. By 1896 the Moravians had set a goal that within three years each couple who lived at a village where missionaries were influential would marry in a church service and live together in their own dwelling.[7] Divorce, once both an informal and commonplace means for ending a marriage, became a legal procedure, making it a difficult, even unrealistic, option. Furthermore, a stigma was attached by the Moravians to either informal or formal divorce.

The Eskimos accepted the changes advocated by the Moravians, but in the process they altered much of their traditional culture. For wives to live with their husbands throughout the year destroyed not only the male bonds represented by qasgiq life but the closeness of related females in the households. Likewise, legal marriages, in theory at least, restricted the flexibility in adult female-male relationships and no doubt produced many permanent but unhappy marriages. In the 1950s long-term residents along the river repeatedly stated that early Moravian missionaries had forced couples into formal marriages. A missionary might arrive in a village very early in the morning and marry all those couples he found together in bed. The missionary stressed that these marriages were valid, and numerous step-relationships were traced to such marriages.

The Moravians urged other changes in living arrangements for reasons of health. They viewed Eskimo semisubterranean houses as crowded, dirty, and generally unhealthful residences and urged that they be replaced by log cabins or frame dwellings. Eskimos had already become familiar with log structures during their contacts with Russians. The first Eskimo log house along the river possibly was the one built at Crow Village and occupied by 1843. Excavation of this structure revealed a combination of indigenous and Western construction features. The horizontal wall logs were of Russian inspiration, but they were in a shallow excavation and held upright by stakes, not mortised at the corners in the manner of a log cabin. Also, the roof was supported by four posts in the manner of a traditional Eskimo house.[8] The first log cabin at Ogavik was built in 1904, and during the next year three others were constructed there, along with one at Tuluksak.[9]

Bethel Eskimos were the first group to accept Western style dwellings totally; by 1910 their traditional houses had disappeared. Most people built log cabins, but several families constructed two-room frame houses, sometimes wallpapering the bedrooms.[10] By the 1930s semisubterranean houses had become rare at riverine Moravian-oriented villages. A typical Eskimo house had become either a log cabin, about twelve feet square, or a plank building covered with roofing or tar paper; a storm shed was part of either type. A number of families might share a dwelling, furnishing it most often with a metal cookstove, table and chairs, and sometimes a sewing machine or phonograph.[11] The beds as well as table and chairs were homemade. Although modern houses, usually with several rooms, prevail at present, aboriginal-style dwellings built at ground level still accommodated an occasional poor family in the 1950s or a conservative one in the 1970s.

Log cabin dwellings did not prove to be the housing panacea visualized by the missionaries. Compared to a semisubterranean dwelling the new houses, especially plank ones, were harder to heat, a serious disadvantage during the cold winters, when fuel was difficult to obtain. One solution devised by the people was for several families to live in a single house and share the fuel supply. Body heat too would warm the room when ten to fifteen people occupied a small one-room cabin. For example, at Kwethluk in 1939 fifteen people lived in a cabin measuring twelve by twenty-five feet.[12] Such living conditions became less common over the years but could still be found into the 1960s. Under these circumstances the healthful indoor environment sought by the Moravians was not attained.

As increasing numbers of families lived in log or plank houses and as their traditional religion declined, village social life no longer focused in men's houses. Only old men and youths slept there, but the structure continued to serve as a workshop and bathhouse for males until it fell into disrepair or was destroyed by fire, a common occurrence. The last traditional qasgiq in a riverine village may have been the one at Napaskiak, the first village below Bethel, that burned in about 1950.[13]

The bathing pattern characteristic in aboriginal times underwent significant change when men's houses no longer were used. Whereas only men and boys took hot air baths in these buildings, women began bathing with their husbands or with other women when small, Russian-style bathhouses were used. Thus adults of both sexes were able for the first time to enjoy bathing as a pleasurable escape from the work routine. Small bathhouses belong to the men who build them, and these owners have the right to specify who can use them. Since each bathhouse accommodates relatively few persons at a time, a number of them typically are found in a village.

Village life changed in many of its social aspects as it became influenced by local whites. Abandoning the men's houses meant that storytelling declined and aboriginal ceremonies became far less prominent. These social activities were replaced in part by others learned from whites. One was card playing, which the Moravian and Orthodox missionaries found especially vexing; another of particular concern was social dancing, which the Moravians considered a threat to morality. By 1920 white teachers were organizing dances and card parties, which put the Moravians in the position of disapproving activities that were encouraged by other responsible whites.[14] The Eskimos apparently felt a need for some form of group recreation; the Christian missionaries had little to offer in this respect.

The consumption of alcoholic beverages that had begun earlier grew in importance in the 1930s, but as a socializing activity, it was confined largely to males, judging from drinking patterns in the 1950s. A recreational activity introduced in the years following World War II was the showing of motion pictures. The films were rented by village teachers or traders and shown once or more each week; this was to be a major social outlet in the years to follow. Television was introduced in Bethel when a local station began operating in 1972; as satellite reception became available soon thereafter, watching television became popular among villagers. As the breadth of programming expanded, television served as a major form of entertainment as well as a new source of information. As these new resources combined with radio programs designed for local appeal and with a local newspaper that began publication at Bethel in 1969, villagers became more aware than ever before of local news and life beyond their own locale. In combination, these influences from the world beyond southwestern Alaska had a profound effect, especially among youth. Clothing styles and tastes in music soon reflected those popular elsewhere, and the use of drugs grew from a minor problem to a serious one by the 1980s. A change in attitudes and values accompanied these more apparent manifestations that the Eskimos were absorbing much from their newly expanded environment.

A 1981 study by John Payne and his associates at the villages from Lower Kalskag to Stony River provides special insight into social control, a key aspect of life in small communities.[15] The older people who were interviewed most often expressed a great deal of dissatisfaction about changes in socialization, especially in the nature of family living during recent years. They recalled that as their generation grew up, the life of children centered in units far more concerned with character development. Within the villages and at trapping or fishing camps parents or other adults maintained complete control over children. A "talking to" usually was sufficient to induce conformity in an errant child. Furthermore, in the villages at that time, adults in general helped guide children along approved patterns of behavior. These elders emphasized certain changes; for example, the deference once shown older persons had ceased to exist. They expressed this change in English by saying that children were no longer "bashful" around adults. Not so many years ago in this area young adults often stated that they were bashful in the presence of older persons.[16]

"They know books, that's all" was another way elders expressed discontent about the new conventions. Along with this reference to education, they lamented that children no longer spoke Yupik.[17] Many felt that the school system was not offering good training and that because its scheduling made it impossible for children to learn subsistence activities, the younger generation was being left incapable in many aspects of adult maintenance.

Another dramatic change that was noted was the decline in sharing by villagers during the last twenty years. The elders recalled a time when the meat of the first moose killed in the fall was distributed to every family and the animal might be consumed in one day. Now when someone takes the first moose, "You don't taste it."[18] The increased consumption of alcoholic beverages and its effect on social behavior was another concern expressed. One individual said that the villagers felt unable to do anything about the changes and that "the only way they are going to forget it is by drinking."[19]

This study indicated that the perspective of growing children and young adults differed greatly from that of older people. Youthful individuals viewed the changes as positive ones and felt that the problems resulted from the inability of elders to adjust to new social conditions. The young people realized that by learning English and related subjects they could best earn money and deal with white man's bureaucracy. Since these appeared to be the clearest avenues to economic survival, the younger generation in these villages began to speak English exclusively. This was in part responsible for the widening gulf between the young people and their elders, a gulf made more apparent as the younger generation increased in size and the older one declined.

CHRISTIANITY

Apart from having a local store, the construction of a village chapel or church best symbolized directed Western culture change. Orthodox and Moravian missionaries held services in men's houses until they were established well enough to build their own religious structures. The local impact of Christianity is reflected in the founding dates of chapels and churches in villages, and nearly as important, the dates at which they were replaced by new ones.

In 1925 the first Russian Orthodox church was built at Sleetmute; this photograph of it was taken in 1953. *Photo by the author.*

The earliest Orthodox church in a riverine Eskimo village may have been the one under construction at Kwethluk in 1901. It served until replaced by a new church in 1918, which subsequently gave way to another one built in 1935.[20] The first Orthodox church at Sleetmute was built in 1925 and was replaced by another in 1954–55.[21] Orthodox chapels and churches also were built at Aniak, Crooked Creek, and Lower Kalskag.[22] The only enduring Orthodox station where missionaries lived along the Kuskokwim was founded at Little Russian Mission (Chuathbaluk) in 1891 and continued to operate until the 1920s.[23] After its abandonment a priest from Russian Mission along the Yukon visited the Kuskokwim intermittently, which meant that Orthodoxy was perpetuated largely by the villagers themselves. Despite the absence of resident priests, and possibly as a reaction to Moravian attempts to convert them, the people became more faithful. One Orthodox institution in particular, the Church Brotherhood, has played an important role in village social life over the years. In each village its members assume responsibility for resolving

common social problems, providing economic aid to needy families, and encouraging local support of Orthodoxy. The first two
goals became far less important when government assistance became available following World War II.

The early Moravian missionaries at Bethel held religious services in their homes and later in the school. Once they were well
established, they built an imposing church in 1905.[24] This structure long symbolized the Moravian mission, and when it became
inadequate, it was replaced in 1958.[25] A house at Ogavik was
converted into a chapel in 1893, and one was built at Kwethluk in
1896.[26] In 1911 the Moravians considered the people of Akiak,
Akiachak, and Tuluksak among their "most advanced and faithful
Christians," but these Eskimos still were holding services in the
village men's houses.[27] From 1913 to 1917 a church or chapel was
built in each of these villages.[28]

The initial commitment of the Moravians clearly was to work
among Upriver Eskimos, but their area of interest broadened
when they realized that Eskimos living on the tundra to the west
of Bethel and along Kuskokwim Bay were more numerous and
that, unlike the upriver population, many Eskimos along the
north side of the bay were heathens. Another factor leading Moravians to shift some of their efforts elsewhere was the expansion
during the early 1900s of the influence of other whites on the
riverine Eskimos. As the Moravians began to devote more of
their energies to bayside and tundra settlements, where they
had greater control over outside contacts, they lessened their attention to their converts along the river, especially above Tuluksak. This situation indirectly helped the Orthodox representatives strengthen their position and facilitated Catholic entry into
the area.

To further the understanding of Christianity among converts,
both Orthodox and Moravian missionaries translated and published religious materials into Yupik. The same was true of Roman Catholic priests along the Yukon, but their contribution has
had a lesser impact on Kuskokwim Eskimos. The Moravians
were foremost among Christian missionaries in preparing translations for Alaskan Eskimos. Their traditional emphasis on education plus their goals to teach converts in the vernacular and to
have their missionaries learn the language of the people among

whom they worked provided the stimulus for making translations. Beginning in 1889 and continuing into the present, the production of dictionaries, grammars, hymns, liturgies, and a New Testament translation suggests the scope of their accomplishments. Despite the use of English in schools maintained by the federal Bureau of Education and subsequent Bureau of Indian Affairs, the Moravians emphasized literacy in Yupik. As a result, many Kuskokwim Eskimos learned to read Yupik long before they could read English. Since their Eskimo church workers were not required to learn English to be effective in their teaching, this Moravian policy was important in the development of a Native ministry.[29]

Despite vigorous and persistent Moravian efforts to suppress most aspects of Eskimo ceremonial life, their goal was not achieved until the late 1920s. Attenuated performances of ceremonies dating from aboriginal times were held at numerous, possibly most, villages in the previous decade.[30] One explanation for the cessation may be that few older persons who knew the ceremonies survived the 1900 influenza epidemic, and therefore knowledge of the rituals had declined severely by the 1920s.

Orthodox and Moravian competition for Eskimo bodies and souls has continued, with uneven results, over the years. In addition Roman Catholics entered the region on a long-term basis in the 1930s. Since 1888 Catholics had been active along the lower Yukon, and they soon expanded to the adjacent Bering Sea coast, especially south of the Yukon mouth. As Bethel became the only town in the Yukon-Kuskokwim region, it attracted Eskimos from the surrounding area, and Catholic clergy visited Bethel to serve their members. They built a church at Aniak in 1939 and one at Bethel in 1943.[31] Another denomination, the Assembly of God, built a church at Aniak in 1945, but it did not spread among Eskimos in the manner of the other three.[32] Missionaries of other denominations have worked intermittently at riverine Eskimo villages on a short-term basis but with little success. Thus the people have been exposed to varied Christian religions, particularly in recent years. Although the Catholics have made clear progress, the villagers are predominately Moravian or Russian Orthodox church members.

Over the years the Orthodox have had the greatest vitality at

riverine villages. One reason is that the Orthodox, unlike the
Moravians, accepted members without requiring radical changes
in their way of living. In addition, because Orthodox villages
struggled for many years to maintain their religion without receiving significant outside help, they developed relatively strong
local organizations. The success of the Roman Catholics as they
moved into the area is attributed in part to their comparative toler-
ance of traditional Eskimo ways in the manner of the Orthodox.

In the 1940s the Eskimo helpers for the Moravians began to be
called lay pastors, and their education became increasingly formal, culminating in the 1946 ordination of the first Eskimo pastors. The continuing emphasis on training a Native ministry resulted in the establishment of the Alaska Moravian Bible School
in 1948; by 1955 it had evolved into the Moravian Bible Seminary. Through these and other efforts, the Moravians carefully
nurtured a group of Eskimo church leaders. In 1978 a major
change was made in the administration of their mission in Alaska;
the Moravian Church delegates to a General Church Conference
voted to form the Alaska Provincial Board, which was composed
solely of Natives and served to formulate and implement local
church policy.[33]

The last heathen Upriver Eskimos probably were converted to
Christianity or died in the 1930s, and in the following decade
membership in the local Christian churches became relatively
stable. By 1986 Upriver Eskimo communities with Moravian
churches were Bethel, Kwethluk, Akiachak, Akiak, and Tuluksak. The strongest Catholic churches were at Aniak, Bethel, and
Kalskag, while Orthodox strength was greatest at Chuathbaluk,
Kwethluk, Lower Kalskag, and Sleetmute.

SCHOOLS

Soon after founding the Bethel mission, the Moravians realized
that few adults could be transformed into their idealized version
of unwavering Christians. Those who became early members of
the church, some of whom were shamans, had little understanding of Christianity and tended to revert to their old ways. In addition, some Eskimos became converts for economic reasons. The
mission intermittently provided its members with food and material goods; this attracted some persons, who became known

as "tea converts." The religious dedication of these individuals was not what the Moravians had sought. They soon concluded that true conversions would come largely from their work with children.

The traditional Moravian stress on education and the goal of casting Eskimo lives into a Moravian mold led logically to an emphasis on formal education. In 1886 the missionaries opened their first school at Bethel; this was to be the only lasting one they founded along the river.[34] Since the Moravians could not staff schools in other villages on a reliable basis, they lobbied the federal government to found schools, but the response was slow. The first step was the contracting by the U.S. Bureau of Education (BE) to pay teachers at the Bethel mission school. The BE also hired John Kilbuck, who had resigned from the Bethel mission in 1898, to teach at Wainwright. He taught also at Douglas before returning to the Kuskokwim to teach at Akiak in 1911. That year his wife Edith supervised the construction of the Akiak school while John traveled widely on government business. John taught at the school, but much of his time was consumed by managing government reindeer herds. In 1916 he became the Assistant Superintendent of the Western (Kuskokwim) District for the BE. The same year he was reinstated as a Moravian missionary, but he did not give up his post with the BE to become an active missionary until 1921. Unfortunately he soon was taken ill with pneumonia and typhoid fever and died in 1922.[35]

One of John Kilbuck's last campaigns was to establish an orphanage in conjunction with a school. In 1919 he described the plight of orphans in poignant terms, pointing out that they often were maltreated by guardians and lived almost like "slaves." As Kilbuck wrote, "Such children not only become timid, like a wild animal, always ready to dodge an unexpected blow, but with advancing years become vicious and incorrigible."[36] His efforts led to the 1925 founding of an orphanage and school at Nunapitsinghak, a site along the lower Kwethluk River.[37] This institution operated until 1973, when it was phased out as a result of state regulations, rising costs, and changing attitudes toward the care of orphans.[38]

Although the first lasting school was established by the Moravians, the earliest educational system along the Kuskokwim was

Edith and John Henry Kilbuck, possibly taken at Akiak in the 1910s.
Courtesy of the Moravian Archives, Bethlehem, Pa.

under BE control. The bureau's schools admitted all children but were designed for Native instruction and concentrated on the basic skills of reading, writing, and arithmetic, plus homemaking for girls and industrial arts for boys. The BE schools in Alaska and the medical services they provided were transferred in 1931 to the Office of Indian Affairs, which subsequently became the Bureau of Indian Affairs (BIA). As the number of white children and those of mixed blood who were leading a "civilized life" (e.g., the children of white men and Native Alaskan women) increased in villages throughout Alaska, whites pressured the federal government to create a separate school system for their children, whom they felt were receiving an inferior education in the existing schools. In 1905 a congressional act established a separate school system for white children; this was the basis for the Territorial Department of Education (TDE) school system in 1917, which in turn became the Alaska Department of Education established at the time of statehood in 1959. While in theory the TDE schools were exclusively for white children, in practice whites attended Native schools and vice versa, depending on which school system operated in a village.[39] The first territorial school along the Kuskokwim reportedly was opened at Napamiut in 1920. Of the thirty students about twelve of them were children of the trader George W. Hoffman. At Crooked Creek a TDE school was established in 1928, probably because some white miners had settled there, and the same was true at Aniak, where a territorial school was established in 1936. As the number of whites at Bethel grew, the TDE built a school in 1923 for white children and those of mixed blood; a BE school continued to be operated for Native children. The BE built a school at the Eskimo village of Sleetmute in 1920, and another one opened at Akiachak in 1930.[40]

The Americanization of Native Alaskans was a long-established federal policy, and education was considered the most effective means to achieve this goal. In any assessment of Kuskokwim village schools before the 1960s, it must be emphasized that the curriculum was designed for Americanizing the pupils. Instruction was in English, and since an Eskimo child typically knew no English when entering school, much instructional time was spent teaching English. By the time most students were sixteen years old and could leave school, they probably had reached about a third-grade level of comprehension in most subjects. Thus their formal education may have exposed them to subjects taught throughout America, but it left them with too little training to be competitive with white Americans as adults.

The attitude of Eskimo parents had a profound effect on the school attendance of their children and on their responsiveness to the school curriculum. Some wanted a formal education for their children and willingly moved to a village where a school was to be opened. Far more often, it seems, they sent their children to school because of pressures from whites. Parents typically placed no great value on formal education because they could see no far-reaching benefits. It hardly need be noted that during the first half of this century, and beyond, the villagers had no control over the school curriculum and little control over the teachers. Many parents considered schooling a negative influence on their children, both because of its American emphasis and because attending school during formative years meant that a child did not learn the cultural skills required to succeed in village life. This attitude, coupled with the traditional pattern of parental permissiveness toward children, provided little incentive for children to attend school regularly and little motivation for them to learn well.

A village boy might attend school until he was sixteen years old and after that might seldom speak English again or put most of his education to practical use, and the same was true of girls.[41] Most Upriver Eskimo children did not enter junior high, partially because they were incapable of handling the material and partially because they had to be sent to boarding schools far from home if they sought a secondary school education. Most parents preferred to keep their children at home. If students went away to school, they most often traveled to Sitka, where they attended Mt. Edgecombe, a secondary boarding school for Natives established in 1947. Children who went to boarding school tended to be of two types: those who had created problems for their parents and those who had learned well because their parents valued an American education. In sum, the goal of the federal and territorial school systems, as well as the original state system that followed, was to train riverine Eskimo children to function in

American culture; through education the next generation would become "civilized."

High salaries, freedom from close classroom supervision, and the frontier setting attracted teachers despite the drawbacks of comparatively difficult living conditions and the limited likelihood of success in the classroom. Most village teachers were not Alaskans, and their familiarity with peoples of different cultures was limited or nonexistent. Most but not all teachers were reasonably fair-minded. Those who came from the southern states or from eastern states bordering on the South were likely to transfer their attitudes of superiority over blacks to the local people, with obviously negative consequences. In the 1950s Native Alaskan teachers were rare in rural schools.

Teachers in the TDE schools often, perhaps typically, instructed their students and had no other major job-related duties, whereas the extra-curricular obligations of their counterparts in the BIA schools were great. Although they might be, and most often were, totally inexperienced at the varied jobs they were expected to handle, the BIA teachers served as informal postmasters or postmistresses, provided emergency medical aid, were often the local welfare agents, and had considerable control over the dispersal of BIA relief funds. In other ways as well, a teacher had an important impact on the village; he or she strongly influenced which children went to boarding school and selected the person to be the school janitor, often the only local full-time job available to a villager. What is most important, however, is that the arrival of schools in villages, whether BIA, territorial, or state, meant that dealings with the outside world would increase and would be directed to a large extent by teachers, not by the villagers themselves.

After Alaska became a state in 1959, the public schools in urban settings were opened to all children, but no immediate effort was made to reorganize the rural school system. The state and the BIA agreed that the state eventually would control all schools, but the change-over was slow because the BIA had a long-established power base and was reluctant to relinquish its control over village schools. The special needs of village children began to be addressed as the social activism of the 1960s grew and as pressure from Native leaders increased. The Alaska State Operated School System that was created in 1970 was independent of the Alaska Department of Education and was designed to help meet Native desires and needs. Native representatives took part in decision-making, but the system failed because of organizational defects and political pressures. To replace it the state legislature created the Regional Educational Attendance Areas (REAA) in 1976. This plan established twenty-one administrative units in rural areas; each area was controlled by a regional board supplemented by a local board, in much the same pattern as American school districts.[42] The REAA is still in existence, but realistic local control seldom prevails. The Upriver Eskimo villages are in the Lower Kuskokwim and Kuspuk attendance areas, where the last BIA schools (Akiachak, Akiak, and Tuluksak) were turned over to regional control in 1985.[43]

One factor that has complicated the emergence of local control over schools is the proliferation of village boards and committees related to education. A community with a few hundred people, most of whom are children or young adults, might have had a BIA advisory school board, a bilingual education Community Advisory Group, and an REAA community school committee, among others. In many villages the latter committee afforded input in school decisions that residents felt was especially valuable, but these committees were abolished in 1979.[44] Each organization that remains is meant to serve a specific function, but their number has placed a strain on the few persons capable of serving well on boards and committees.

A burning issue faced by REAA decision-makers is whether they can develop programs culturally relevant for particular localities. As Frank Darnell notes, a repeated question is, "Can the education system create the means for acquisition of improved economic opportunities by northern natives without destroying their rights to be culturally different?"[45] This issue produces highly emotional responses, making its resolution all the more difficult. The curricula now being introduced allow children to learn about varied aspects of their traditional life, recognizing that the value of such knowledge is related to their ethnic identity; meaningful training in other areas is also stressed. As yet no consensus prevails about whether a productive balance can be attained. Darnell suggests that village schools will not become relevant until their curricula are reflective of modern community life, and it appears that a tendency to move in this direction is growing as greater control is exerted locally over educational policies and practices.

Another major issue is bilingual education. Established by Congress in 1968, bilingual programs were designed to ensure that those students who did not speak English when entering school could learn their other subjects while also becoming proficient in English. However, Congress later expanded the law in such a way that the student's Native language and culture became emphasized, which led to less stress on training in English. Alaska law, which predates federal bilingual programs, dictates that students be instructed in their strongest language.[46] The goal was to give Native children the opportunity to begin their education by using their own language in school. By the 1970s the strongest language of small children in many Upriver Eskimo villages was English, not Yupik, but this was not true in others. At Akiachak nearly all children spoke Yupik as their first language, and here a BIA bilingual program, the Rural School Project, that included instructional material in this language was begun in 1970. Villagers have been pleased with the results of the program, and it was introduced at Kwethluk in 1975.[47] This *language transfer method,* meaning that Yupik serves as a vehicle to introduce children to English, had been introduced previously in some BIA schools, where it was well received. In those villages where English is now the dominant language of children, *language maintenance programs* have been introduced to help perpetuate Yupik. The first such program, which teaches Yupik as a second language, began at Bethel in 1970, and because of the success there, it has since been introduced in other schools in the area.[48]

In recent years education has become big business along the river, especially as a decline in Eskimo infant mortality rates has led to a larger school population and as the opportunity to have more local institutions has grown. Although most villages had long had grade schools, nearly a third of Native Alaskan youths lived in communities without high schools as late as 1970.[49] These students either dropped out of school, were sent to distant boarding schools, or lived with friends or relatives in settlements with high schools. One new approach to this problem was the construction of housing for students wanting to attend the high school in Bethel. The Bethel Regional High School Dormitory was opened in 1972 and accommodated 175 students; state approved boarding homes provided housing for 125 others. However, the program did not work out as smoothly as anticipated. Many students moving to Bethel were away from home for the first time, and their adjustment problems were great. The most serious was that, while under limited supervision, they were exposed to alcohol and drugs that previously had not been so available to them. This had a negative effect on their socialization, and following objections by parents and others, the dormitory was closed in 1980.[50]

Another approach was represented by the "Molly Hootch case." This case was launched in 1972 to require that secondary schools be provided in all villages requesting them. The case did not go to trial because in 1976 the state agreed to build local high schools as requested. In 1979 one was completed at Sleetmute for fifteen students, another at Chuathbaluk for twelve enrollees, while yet a third was constructed at Crooked Creek. The same year Red Devil acquired a two-classroom school in which twenty-one students in grades one through twelve were taught by two teachers and a teacher aid.[51] Considering the specialized needs of high schools with respect to equipment and teacher training, it remains to be demonstrated that students in these schools receive an effective education. Furthermore, many parents still prefer to send their children to boarding school for their secondary education. Mt. Edgecombe High School at Sitka, which had been the traditional school for many Eskimos, continues to attract many students from villages. When the Kwethluk High School opened in 1980, an estimated seventy students were eligible to attend, but fifty chose to go to the Mt. Edgecombe school.[52]

The impact of public education on village young people has grown steadily. In 1970 the percent of Native Alaskans who graduated from high school was 37; in 1980 it was 59. Even with this increase, however, in the latter year about one high school student in four dropped out, whereas among non-Native Alaskans the 1980 high school drop-out rate was half as great.[53] The trend for more education has continued in the 1980s. The REAA system is destined to guide the immediate future in education along the Kuskokwim. Its goal of providing a better learning environment for children is clear, and it has enabled localized Native control to begin. Yet precisely how current ideas about being a Kuskokwim Eskimo can be integrated with traditional goals in American education remains to be seen. The problem of retaining the sense of Eskimoness while adequately preparing students to compete effectively with other Alaskans for jobs has not yet been solved. For example, it appears that some Eskimos graduating from high school in the mid-1980s cannot read or write adequately, despite annual education costs per pupil reaching as high as $17,000 a year, compared with an average of $2,600 a year in California.[54] The results of establishing village high schools as one means of providing a better learning environment suggest that this may only perpetuate the inferior quality of Kuskokwim secondary education. It appears that although progress has been made, there is yet to be developed an amalgam that will lead to a viable sense of being Eskimo at the same time it produces individuals who can succeed socially and economically in contemporary Alaska.

HEALTH

Early Moravian missionaries as well as later public health service workers and teachers all were distressed by Kuskokwim Eskimo living standards. The sanitary conditions that whites considered vital to good health were nonexistent. One dramatic example will suffice. Eskimos might use the same wooden bowl as a chamber pot at night, a washbasin in the morning, and a dishpan for washing cups during the day.[55] Even the most avid cultural relativist presumably would concede the merit of introducing Western concepts of health and sanitation.

The earliest attempts to improve Eskimo health were hampered by the negative effects of diseases new to the area and by the state of Western medical knowledge. Mention has been made of the smallpox and influenza epidemics that killed so many people and weakened others. Added to these epidemics were other less severe ones, plus the constantly negative impact of tuberculosis, which had become endemic. The early Moravians did their utmost to introduce sanitary practices and to treat those who were ill. Yet as helpful as this was to the people, the missionaries fully recognized the pressing need to add health professionals to their ranks, and they urged the home mission to send such persons.

Finally a nurse, Philippine King, was stationed at Bethel from 1893 to 1896, and she was succeeded by the medical doctor Joseph H. Romig, who practiced there from 1896 to 1905.[56] As important as their contributions were, their capacity to meet the needs of so many people in poor health was limited. The first person to have a strong personal impact on local Eskimo health and sanitation practices was John Kilbuck's wife, Edith. Unlike her husband, who was an inveterate traveler, Edith had many years of day-to-day contact with the residents of Bethel and later with those of Akiak. Edith not only spoke fluent Yupik but was a forceful individual who was absolutely devoted to Eskimo welfare. The people unquestionably trusted and respected her more than any of her white contemporaries, and she deserves the greatest credit for early efforts to improve the quality of family life.[57]

The first public health nurse to work in the area was Lulu Evans Heron, who arrived at Akiak in 1916. She traveled widely in the region working among villagers into the late 1940s. Heron began her program with a campaign against lice, and once this parasite was under control, she concentrated on encouraging weekly housecleanings, regular baths, and the use of clean drinking water. Before the people actually understood the benefits of sanitation, they did as she asked because they wanted to please her and because they knew she was the best person to seek out when they were ill. After 1924 Mrs. Heron worked out of Bethel, and the vigorous program of health care she developed, especially after village schools became numerous and teachers could help maintain the program between her visits, was a major positive contribution.[58]

A good indication that serious attention is being paid to health problems in any area is the construction of a local hospital. Along the Kuskokwim an eleven-bed facility was opened at Akiak in 1918 by the Alaska Native Medical Service.[59] The first physician was Frank Lamb, but his time in the area was very short. When the 1918 influenza epidemic struck western Alaska, Dr. Lamb traveled to the Yukon to treat patients, only to die himself from the disease.[60] In some sectors of Alaska, such as the Nushagak region, the death rate from this historic epidemic was greater than from any other.[61] As influenza spread, the people of the Kuskokwim were forewarned, and a strict quarantine was imposed successfully.[62] The replacement for Dr. Lamb at the Akiak hospital proved to be a bigoted person, and his successor was even less suited for his appointment.[63] Recruiting competent physicians compounded the difficulties in providing even minimal health care. The Akiak hospital closed in fiscal 1933–34, but a physician remained there to serve the area.[64] A new hospital was built at Bethel by the Alaska Indian Service in 1940. It burned in 1950 and was replaced in 1954; another replacement was built in 1980.[65]

In villages with BIA schools the teachers were expected to provide a limited amount of health care. They had medical supplies but little training, and they treated routine cases as well as emergencies with an understandable reluctance. In the 1930s some teachers and traders began operating two-way radios, which meant that they could contact trained medical personnel, and the expansion of charter air services enabled desperately ill patients to be flown to the nearest medical facility. A continuing expansion of charter airlines and the addition of scheduled flights facilitated the movement of patients to hospitals even more. After World War II the BIA teachers began using their radios for scheduled medical consultations with a doctor at the Bethel hospital, and a twenty-four hour emergency radio service was introduced in 1968.[66] Another major development in village health service was the introduction of the village health aid program in the 1940s. This was expanded, and in 1967 a community health program was introduced in which villagers were trained by medical professionals to handle routine and also emergency cases.[67]

As severe as the 1838–39 smallpox and 1900 influenza epidemics had been among riverine Eskimos, deaths from tuberculosis have probably been more extensive over the years. This disease arrived with the Russians and presumably had spread to the Kuskokwim by the 1840s. By 1880 tuberculosis was reported to be the most common disease among Native Alaskans.[68] When the first comprehensive study of Alaskan death rates was made in 1930, it was found that one of every three Native Alaskans died of tuberculosis.[69] In the mid-1940s, 4,000 active cases had been

identified, but there were only enough beds in the territory for
seventy patients.[70] By 1950 the Native Alaskan death rate from
this disease was about 673 per 100,000 compared to about 18 per
100,000 for whites in the United States.[71]

During the period when the incidence of tuberculosis was so
high, the personal trauma it caused among Kuskokwim Eskimos
is barely conceivable. Far more babies and small children died
than lived in the early 1950s. For a woman to give birth a dozen
times and have two children reach maturity was not unusual. Ex-
actly how many of these offspring were victims of tuberculosis is
not known, but it was without doubt the most common killer.
Death was not the only result of tubercular infection. Tuberculosis of the bone was reasonably common in children, and the
resulting deformities often were piteous. Equally pathetic was the
effect on a family if parents became diseased. A mother who was
wasting away was unable to care for her children, and when a
father fell victim, the standard of living for his entire family
dropped precipitously.

The prevalence of tuberculosis may well have contributed to
the reputation of riverine Eskimos as a docile and phlegmatic
people by the 1950s. Reports in earlier years of the century suggest that they had been more assertive and self-confident in the
past. By the time white missionaries, traders, and teachers began
directing the Eskimos' lives, sometimes in a dictatorial way, tuberculosis already had sapped their energy. Eskimos usually
complied without overt protest, perhaps lacking the strength and
will to do otherwise. Their poor state of health also may have led
to their acceptance, without protest, of the ways whites treated
them as possible carriers of a highly contagious disease. Many
whites, especially teachers, had an almost pathological fear of
contracting tuberculosis and therefore refused to have any close
contact with the people or their belongings. Numerous teachers
avoided any physical contact with their pupils in the classroom
and refused to enter Eskimo homes or permit Eskimos in their
quarters. Their caution had a reasonable basis, and yet the dis-
crimination that resulted made Eskimos second-class citizens in
their own villages.

In 1954 a radical new method of tuberculosis treatment, chemotherapy, was introduced. The next year the health service admin-

istration of the BIA and the Alaska Native Medical Service became a part of the U.S. Public Health Service, which meant far greater resources for health care delivery. The Public Health Service launched an extensive treatment program of chemotherapy for ambulatory cases of tuberculosis, making it possible for most patients to remain at home and take the required drugs rather than go to a distant hospital for years. Soon a program of preventive treatment by means of drugs also was implemented, and the combination was so successful that by 1970 tuberculosis was not the primary cause of death of any Native Alaskan. Such an achievement in less than twenty years was truly remarkable.[72]

Despite the virtual elimination of serious tuberculosis cases among riverine Eskimos by the 1970s, the previous effects of the disease remained, and coupled with other diseases and disabilities common to the area, they resulted in an assortment of distressing health conditions. In a 1970 study of Lower Kalskag a medical anthropologist, Lynn D. Mason, examined the health records of thirty-five male heads of households.[73] He found that twenty-nine had spent an average of nearly a year in a hospital. In most cases these men were being treated for tuberculosis before the chemotherapy program began, and about a third underwent pulmonary surgery. The records showed that thirty of the thirty-five suffered from chronic or acute illnesses such as hypertension, polio, rheumatic heart disease, stroke, and a severe form of hepatitis. (Of the 180 people in the village, over 50 had contracted hepatitis in the previous 15 years.) Eight were visibly crippled, and seven jeopardized their health by consuming excessive amounts of alcohol. The health of women was slightly better; twenty-three of the thirty-two sampled had been hospitalized for reasons other than childbirth, and their average stay was for six months.

In a discussion of the effects of health problems on family life, Mason points out that men with disabilities seldom could compete successfully for jobs, nor was welfare aid sufficient to maintain their families. The normal subsistence routine was arduous in the winter, and numerous men who had been ill found they had a diminished capacity to withstand cold. Trapping and moose hunting were largely beyond their strength, and hauling firewood was difficult. Some of the handicapped gravitated toward government construction projects, such as building village houses, but this was temporary work at best. Men with impaired health could still fish locally for salmon, and this was their primary means of supporting their families. The food yield from salmon fishing was high, and fishing from wooden boats equipped with outboard motors and using nylon gill nets was less strenuous than hunting and trapping.

The psychological factor of disability, a topic seldom considered in studies of Eskimos, plays an important role in cases such as these. Mason noted that Eskimos traditionally placed great emphasis on physical well-being because in their environment it is essential if one is to be a successful provider and complete person. With this cultural image, a man who contracted a debilitating disease, even though he survived, was nonetheless considered less than competent and therefore suffered a loss of respect.

By the 1970s most of the widespread and pressing problems affecting health had been resolved, with one major exception: alcoholism had become pandemic and was causing serious health problems among both men and women. With the repeal of prohibition in 1933 most Bethel stores began to sell intoxicants to anyone old enough to purchase them.[74] Homebrew also was made, and its use increased when the sale of intoxicants intensified during World War II. Following the war, liquor could not be bought in Bethel but could be ordered by airfreight from Anchorage and Fairbanks. This made intoxicants more expensive and also created a time lag between ordering and receiving a shipment, which prevented the spontaneous drinking sprees that often created social problems.

Moravian missionaries, other whites, and some Eskimos deplored the amount of drinking by Eskimos in the early part of the Americanization period, yet problem drinking existed for many years more in the minds of prohibitionists than in fact. For instance, records about Kwethluk show that between 1934 and 1939 only two villagers were arrested in Bethel for being drunk and disorderly; each received a thirty-day jail sentence.[75] In 1955 only one man in the village of Napaskiak was considered a heavy drinker. He spent about $150 a year for intoxicants and could go on only short sprees because the price of intoxicants was relatively high, and like most villagers, he had little cash.[76]

The volume of intoxicants imported to Bethel mounted steadily in the 1950s, and by 1960 many persons felt the community should own a liquor store. They argued that since people already bought large quantities of intoxicants, the profit from its sale should go to the town of Bethel rather than to Anchorage or Fairbanks merchants and airlines. The matter was put on a ballot in 1960 and was defeated narrowly. It was approved in 1963, but following the summer of 1965, in which thirteen drownings were attributed to drinking, the town again voted to be dry. The next year the decision was reversed, only to be changed again in 1973.[77] The Ekaiyurvik (Sleep-off Center) was founded at Bethel in 1971 and was open on a twenty-four hour basis until it closed in 1974. During that period, when the regional population was about 15,000, the facility accommodated 200 to 1,000 cases each month.[78] It was succeeded by the Bethel Alcoholic Treatment Center opened in 1975 and then by the Phillips Alcohol Treatment Center.[79]

Bethel was the only place along the lower Kuskokwim where intoxicants were sold legally after 1933. Along the upper river at McGrath liquor has been sold by the bottle continuously since 1933. A liquor store also was opened at the central river settlement of Red Devil in 1955, and it has operated since then. When charter air service expanded abruptly following World War II, villagers began going by plane to the nearest liquor store to make their purchases. Intoxicants have been available to persons with money from that time forward. By the 1970s drunkenness had become common along the river, and many persons were identified as chronic alcoholics. The fights, murders, rapes, and cases of child and spouse abuse that accompanied the drinking resulted in increasing stress in the lives of most villagers. By 1979 there were occasions when most of the adults and many of the youths in a particular village would be drunk at the same time. In one central river village drinking to excess became common for all adults except the members of two families that had been affected by recent deaths resulting from drunkenness.[80]

A comparative study of alcoholic beverage consumption in two unidentified Eskimo villages, one along the lower Kuskokwim and the other on the adjacent seacoast, was made in 1980. It suggests that about 24 percent of the adults were problem drinkers at the coastal village as opposed to 7.5 percent at the riverine village. In the latter village alcohol abuse was considered a major problem, and the comparatively lower incidence was attributed to an alcohol control program that was well integrated into community life. There was no similar program at the coastal settlement.[81] Of the programs to reduce the rate of alcoholism that were launched in 1970, most failed or met with only temporary success. However, in the early 1980s, an expanded alcohol treatment program, and an increased presence of Alaska state troopers in villages, led to a dramatic decline in alcohol-related incidents.[82]

The most radical legal change in recent years was passage of a local option law by the state in 1981. As amended, this law prohibited the importation and sale of alcoholic beverages, except for sacramental wine, in villages that voted for local prohibition.[83] By early 1986 villagers in Kwethluk, Sleetmute, and Tuluksak had voted to ban the import and sale of alcoholic beverages. Local prohibition was voted down at Aniak and Red Devil; other villages voted to be dry and then wet or did not hold elections.[84] Many people came to feel that a major flaw in the 1981 law was that intoxicants could still be imported for personal use into a community that had voted to be dry. As a result a new local option law was passed by the state in 1986. Under it a village could ban the personal possession of intoxicants; the law was passed overwhelmingly despite questions about its constitutionality.[85]

Local option laws enable voters to reduce drunkenness in their villages dramatically if they so desire. Although the alcoholism of Kuskokwim Eskimos has lessened somewhat since the 1970s, it remains a serious problem. Its existence is attributed to the relatively recent availability of intoxicants to Eskimos, increased opportunity to earn money to purchase them, and perhaps most important, a lessened chance to pursue a personally satisfactory way of life.

Riverine Eskimos departed from their old ways as their environment was altered dramatically by others and, in consequence, by themselves. The changes occurring during the early American contact period involved accommodations to a new life-style the Eskimos found more favorable in some respects than their own.

They were willing to adopt a new form of family living and religion, and they accepted a new approach to training for their children, although they had reservations about the value of its end result. In general, they were able to follow the ways of the newcomers without suffering losses that were apparent to them at the time. That the effect on their own culture was to be profound did not become evident until later.

Americanization: II

As the dominance of Americans grew along the Kuskokwim, their economic impact and political power affected nearly all aspects of Eskimo life. By establishing their basic institutions, whites transformed village life, especially for the generations growing up in the altered cultural setting. However, as the impact of whites on Eskimo culture expanded, especially during the mid-1900s, we see another change occurring. As Eskimos became more knowledgeable about the white world, they expressed an increasing concern about the loss of their own culture. This Eskimo awareness arose primarily because of developments described in this chapter.

ECONOMIC INTEGRATION

The gold rushes, especially those occurring between 1905 and 1916, introduced unprecedented opportunities for riverine Eskimos to enter a new economic network. The early Western trade that had relied on Native Alaskans as the exclusive customers was replaced by a trade focusing largely on the far greater needs and resources of whites new to the area. At the same time fur prices generally were higher than ever before, making trapping more profitable. The market for fish expanded, and men in many villages cut wood for riverboats. These developments enabled Eskimos to obtain considerable amounts of cash, and with traders importing unprecedented quantities and varieties of American products, they had the opportunity to buy far more than ever before. At this point riverine Eskimos became dependent on outsiders for the fulfillment of many fundamental needs. Their dependence led the Eskimos to accept the authority of whites as an accompaniment of the changes they viewed as desirable. Not until later were the Eskimos to become aware of the overall effect this acceptance was to have on their lives.

As increases in the inventories of exotic goods and foods at the trading posts made more desirable products available, most Eskimos expanded their trapping, which had become a source of considerable income by the 1940s (*see* Chapter 6). As their material possessions grew, however, adults found village life increasingly comfortable, and the women in particular disliked giving it up, even temporarily, for the crowded and primitive conditions of trapping camps. Furthermore, villages now had schools, and children were expected to attend classes from September to June. Uncooperative parents were threatened with jail, which meant that village families with school-aged children could go to spring and fall camps only briefly if at all. Because of this change, young males no longer had the opportunity to learn trapping skills; a father often went to camp alone or with one or two other men. In addition, men disliked being away from their families for extended periods, and so they tended to stay only a short time at trapping camps, which reduced their fur take.

By the 1950s trapping decreased as an important source of income. Not only had fur prices declined, but trapping was deemphasized by traders and Eskimos alike as other sources of income became better established. Along the lower river, trapping was relatively unimportant by the late 1960s. For instance, only one man at Tuluksak trapped in 1969, and at Kwethluk by 1977 only four families went to spring camp.[1] However, among the Eskimos at Sleetmute in the early 1980s, trapping, especially for beaver and marten, remained a primary source of cash. Sixty-one percent of the households included trappers whose income from furbearers ranged from $2,000 to $3,500 in the winter of 1982–83. It appears that Sleetmute had become a major center for riverine Eskimo trapping primarily because of the accessibility of good trapping areas and the absence of alternative sources of cash.[2]

Long before trapping began to decline in most of the riverine Eskimo area, much of a man's attention centered on the most reliable resource, salmon. As mentioned, fish wheels and a new market brought profits from the sale of salmon by the second decade of the 1900s. Another kind of salmon fishing, commercial fishing in the Bering Sea area, affected the riverine fishermen in subse-

Chuathbaluk (Little Russian Mission) was founded as a Russian Orthodox mission center in 1891. Abandoned in the 1920s, the site was reoccupied in 1954 by Sam A. Phillips (Crow Village Sam) and his sons,
with their families. By 1979, when this photograph was taken, about
140 people lived there. *Photo by the author.*

quent years. Commercial fishing effectively began along Bristol
Bay when the first salmon cannery opened in 1884 at Kanulik
near Nushagak. However, this had no effect on the Kuskokwim
Eskimos at the time.[3] To protect subsistence fishermen in the
Kuskokwim region, where the salmon runs were not nearly as
great as in the Bristol Bay area, the federal government severely
limited or prohibited commercial operations in Kuskokwim Bay
until 1913. Commercial fishing began in Kuskokwim Bay that
year, but for the first few years the number of salmon harvested
was small. The area was closed in 1926 but was reopened in
1930, after which commercial operators processed small numbers
of salmon for many years.[4]
    The first real impact of commercial operations on these
Eskimos came with employment opportunities at stations along
the southern Bering Sea. Kuskokwim Eskimos were transported
to a cannery at Port Heiden in 1917, but they were poorly treated
and earned little money.[5] As the canneries expanded, they soon
began to import Asian laborers seasonally for menial jobs, but

this became impossible during World War II. At that time Eskimos became their replacement.[6] Eskimos living in the Bristol Bay area were employed first, but since they were comparatively few, labor was recruited from adjacent regions, including the Kuskokwim. In 1943 about two hundred men and women from the river were hired and sent by boat to Bristol Bay canneries, where they worked for about six weeks and earned $500 or more.[7] Following the war, employment of Native Alaskans, especially Eskimos, intensified, particularly after new airfields built at numerous settlements made it possible to fly large numbers of workers to and from the canneries. Cannery work now provided many riverine Eskimos with a dependable annual income, and this brought new life to the local economy.

Cannery work helped displace trapping, which was less reliable, as the primary means to obtain cash. However, it sometimes affected local salmon takes in a negative way. A male cannery worker necessarily missed the best opportunity to fish for salmon along the Kuskokwim. Therefore, unless one man in a family remained at home to fish for the winter staple, much of the economic advantage of this seasonal employment was lost. Cannery work was significant not only for the income earned but because it exposed many men and some women to wage labor employment, a clock-regulated work routine, and an employer-employee relationship, two key steps in the process of Americanization.

Soon after World War II, other short-term summer employment became available. There was more lightering and freighting to be done, especially at Bethel. Men were hired to fight forest fires in the general area and found increasing employment on construction projects. Wage labor opportunities beyond the Kuskokwim grew to include more than cannery work as dependable air service lent greater mobility to the work force. A few men contracted to work at gold dredges near Fairbanks; others worked on government defense projects in western Alaska, harvesting fur seals on the Pribilof Islands, and for the Alaska Railroad. Employment of this nature, although limited, provided work experience and monetary gain and also exposed participants to the different life-styles found elsewhere.

The greatest stimulus to the local economy in recent years has been the expansion of commercial salmon fishing that began along the river in the 1960s. Such fishing first became legal along the lower Kuskokwim in 1935, but few persons undertook commercial operations until after World War II. In 1954 a chinook salmon season became legal, but no one took advantage of it until a means of profiting from such fishing came into being in 1959.[8] During that year the major airline serving the area, Northern Consolidated, introduced turboprop aircraft and reduced its airfreight rates, thus making it profitable to ship fresh salmon to Anchorage and Seattle.[9] Most of the Kuskokwim catch has come from the fishing subdistrict extending from the upper bay to just below Tuluksak. From there to the Kolmakov River was another subdistrict, with a low salmon quota; the upriver stretch from the Kolmakov River to the headwaters was closed to commercial operations in 1966.[10]

To better control the commercial salmon harvest and thereby protect the breeding stock, the state introduced limited entry permits in 1973. These permits, designed to restrict the number of fishermen, were issued to ten thousand persons, enabling them to fish for salmon commercially. A permit is for the lifetime of an individual and can be passed on to an heir, presented as a gift, traded, or sold. The major problems with the system are that a man with a permit may have more than one heir and that purchasing a permit requires thousands of dollars, a cost beyond the means of most younger Natives. The greatest concentration of limited entry permits along the Kuskokwim is among persons in the Bethel area.[11] Profits fluctuate annually as a result of changing market demand and strength of the runs. In 1982 the commercial salmon harvest was worth about 4.2 million dollars to riverine and bayside fishermen; this fell to about 2.6 million dollars in 1983. The average yearly income for an individual fisherman was between three and five thousand dollars. Since commercial salmon fishing is not expected to expand, it can be seen that its benefits to riverine Eskimos are limited, but it nonetheless has become a significant local source of cash.[12]

One might assume that as the price of gold rose in the 1970s a revival of gold mining along the Kuskokwim would benefit Eskimos and whites alike. Yet local gold deposits never have been vast, and with few exceptions, they nearly were exhausted before World War II. In 1984 a small but productive mine operated along upper Crooked Creek as a family-focused enterprise; a dredge at Nyac also had continued operating on a relatively small scale. Despite the high price of gold, unless labor and other operating costs can be kept to a minimum, the likelihood of significant ongoing production being profitable is remote. This especially is true now that state and federal legislation require that miners protect the environment from serious damage by their operations, which raises costs. Gold mining, once responsible for major changes in riverine Eskimo life, currently has little impact on the local economy, and this situation seems unlikely to change.

In the aboriginal subsistence round and during the early transitional years, mobility in the winter months was a key economic factor. If a man had few or no dogs, he was severely handicapped in his capacity to fish, hunt, or trap. As subsistence patterns changed and new equipment became available, Eskimos turned increasingly from dogs, who consume large quantities of salmon and other fish as food, to mechanical vehicles that now could be purchased with the money they earned. Vehicles with engines slowly emerged as an alternative to dog sleds for winter travel, but they were expensive to build and sometimes unreliable. The earliest ones were homemade machines with propeller-driven engines and with skis. In 1932 a Moravian missionary, Augustus B. Martin, built one of the first snow machines used locally.[13]

By 1960 commercially manufactured snowmobiles were becoming popular along the river. Figures for the following years reflect their increasingly intense use. By 1967 families in the Kuskokwim area owned about 2,250 dogs; 14 percent of them also owned snowmobiles. By 1978 families in the same area owned about 2,500 dogs, and 85 percent also had snowmobiles.[14] Dog teams persisted in part because it was not especially difficult to harvest fish for dog food and they provided good back-up transportation. Most snowmobiles were produced for the recreational market in the northern states and Canada and were not designed for hard use under subarctic conditions. Furthermore, they were expensive and lasted comparatively few years. In villages the clutter of broken-down snowmobiles saved for parts attests to their low rate of survival under strenuous conditions.

The Eskimos soon recognized that snowmobiles did not compare favorably with dog teams as a reliable means of travel under certain conditions. The breakdown of a snowmobile far from a settlement can be dangerous, if not fatal, whereas such total immobility is unlikely with a dog team. Furthermore, dogs have a good sense of direction, and the dog sled traveler is less likely to become lost in a storm. Unlike machines, well-trained dogs can recognize dangerous trail conditions and will veer off as they approach thin but snow-covered ice. Equally or more important, a drunken Eskimo traveling by dog sled can be rather certain that the dogs will take him or her home safely, whereas accidents and deaths have become commonplace for drunken snowmobile drivers.

Despite these drawbacks, snowmobiles have numerous advantages over dog teams. As the people commonly observe, the "iron" dog eats only when it works. Because snowmobiles are much faster, their owners are able to trap, hunt, or fish at greater distances in shorter time periods than when traveling by dog sled. This is especially important as more people live in fewer settlements and exhaust nearby resources; men with good snowmobiles can exploit distant areas readily. In addition, the use of snowmobiles further integrates local Eskimos into the American life-style.

Imports apart from snowmobiles likewise have made the people more dependent on the outside world. Major purchases include outboard motors and aluminum boats. These have become an important part of the fishing equipment of many families, again producing greater mobility and leading to larger harvests in a shorter time. As cash incomes have grown, people have invested also in items that are less vital but lead to greater comfort. Home furnishings, including television sets, are purchased if there is cash available for them. Most clothing now is bought in stores, as are many edibles. The supermarkets in Bethel and Aniak have become comparable to those providing goods to citizens in other parts of the United States. The regular purchasing of food and clothing has increased the amount of money required to maintain a household, especially since shipping costs are high for products brought in from other states. In 1986 food costs at Bethel were nearly double the U.S. average.[15]

The modern economic picture is one of Eskimos highly dependent on the greater American economy. No longer do riverine people feed and clothe themselves solely from the local setting. They rely on many American products, including technological forms in particular, and can obtain them reasonably well by combining their use of local resources with their considerable government aid. Their reliance on national markets, products, and financial support has raised their standard of living, but at the same time it has eroded their autonomy.

SOCIAL WELFARE

The Americanization of riverine Eskimos underwent profound changes as federal programs were established for the social benefit of various segments of the population. At the end of World War II the scope and intensity of these programs, some of which had been initiated earlier, increased dramatically. Many people began to receive Social Security benefits, special relief funds distributed by the BIA to the needy, benefits from Old Age Assistance, Aid to Families with Dependent Children, Aid to the Blind, and unemployment benefits. Furthermore, the free health services introduced earlier began providing greater coverage. These developments led to decided changes in the life-style and economic status of many villagers. At Kwethluk, for instance, the total village income for the 250 people who lived there in 1957 was about $94,000. Unearned income accounted for nearly $34,000, with $25,000 received as Aid to Families with Dependent Children.[16]

Other programs intended to upgrade the quality of village life began in the 1960s as the pangs of social conscience gnawed increasingly at the greater American public and as the poor and politically impotent received national attention. Blacks were in the forefront as they stridently fought for full rights as citizens, but Indians, Eskimos, and other minorities profited from the wave of activism and broader social concern that arose. The standard of living among many blacks, although deplorable, was not nearly as low as that of some reservation Indians, and even worse conditions prevailed among Native Alaskans along the Kuskokwim and lower Yukon rivers. At this time the Yukon-Kuskokwim area reportedly had the highest poverty level in the United States.

As federal programs proliferated, the poverty of Kuskokwim Eskimos came under attack. The Food Stamp Program introduced in 1968 soon made a meaningful contribution to a better diet and improved health for many families. Although the government-sponsored housing, which replaced the substandard homes in every community, usually was of poor design and construction, it was meant to be an improvement. Drilled wells provided safe and abundant water, and sewage systems were installed in some villages. New generators provided electricity, and old school buildings were replaced by larger, more modern ones. Within a comparatively few years these federally inspired changes made the villages more pleasant and healthful places in which to live.

By the mid-1970s dozens of government agencies were represented in Bethel, and most were involved in programs offering something to Native Alaskans. The pattern has been for the government to provide a great deal and require little or nothing in return. As a result, Eskimos and the many whites who benefited indirectly from these programs have come to depend on them. In some instances the administrators of federal programs, who usually have been white, have acted in direct self-interest, seeing in the programs a means to continue their employment. Others are working with the primary purpose of "improving" the quality of life among their clients. Whites not directly associated with the various federal or state programs usually are cynical about the likelihood of positive results being attained and also are resentful of such largess being distributed selectively to the local population. They sometimes say, "The Natives get everything for nothing and don't appreciate it," or they cite the failure of one program after another to produce positive or long-lasting results.[17]

If we seek one expression of attitudes Kuskokwim Eskimos hold currently concerning whites, it is that since whites have so much, they should share more freely with the local people. Sharing, especially in times of stress, has had a high positive value in historic Eskimo culture. Furthermore, white traders shared with the people in times of extreme need, as did missionaries. Because the Eskimos were well aware that the assets of traders and missionaries were limited, expectations were not high; however, in the early 1900s villagers began to rely on government subsidies.[18] To them the government logically held the role of the primary institution for sharing because of its vast resource base. They most clearly were exposed to government generosity in 1918 when the Alaska Native Medical Service hospital that opened at Akiak treated people from along the river free of charge. Village schools became another indication of government largess. If the federal government could spend all this money, why not more? By the mid-1930s Otto George, a traveling physician who worked for the federal government and was stationed at Akiak, wrote of the Native attitude, " 'The government,' it seemed, was a vague somebody with an inexhaustible money supply and one that I could call on at will." [19] Once the aid programs of the 1960s and 1970s began providing so many kinds of fiscal help, the Kuskokwim Eskimos not surprisingly assumed that the benefits would continue to expand. The concept that one could expect benefits only until becoming able to function independently was indeed part of their early historic culture; however, they have found themselves unable to reach that self-sufficient point in this new world of which they are now a part.

POLITICAL CONTROL

Upriver Eskimo political autonomy declined as Americans imposed and enforced their own political norms on everyone living along the river. In the earliest years of contact, Eskimos had maintained political control in their villages by continuing to rely on their traditional means of achieving justice. This meant gossiping about, then ridiculing, and finally socially ostracizing a nonconforming individual. A village conflict might be solved by negotiation, or on rare occasions, it might lead to homicides and feuds. If conflict spread beyond a community, it might result in warfare. As the Russians and Moravians settled into the area, they followed their own legal norms, but they exerted little direct control over the Eskimos. The Russians were concerned mainly about keeping peace between the villages, and that they arranged with little interference into the daily lives of the people. The Moravians made more active efforts to control aspects of Eskimo life that they considered wrong, but they lacked any legal authority and sought to influence behavior by persuasion.

When the gold rushes began, many more Americans came to the river, and with them came their legal system. The U.S. commissioner who arrived to register the claims of prospectors also fulfilled other legal functions, serving as a lesser court judge, ex officio justice of the peace, probate judge, and notary public. A U.S. deputy marshal generally arrived at about the same time to serve as an executive officer of the court responsible for the care of prisoners and insane persons.[20] The earliest commissioner for the Kuskokwim area, who possibly was appointed in 1902, stayed at Komakovskiy.[21] While early commissioners and deputy marshals represented the law with respect to all residents, they made few Eskimo arrests. Their primary responsibility was to maintain law and order among the new arrivals, and they had little contact with village Eskimos.

Federal regulations regarding the harvest of furbearers typically were the first white man's laws to affect riverine Eskimos. By 1911 trapping seasons had been established for many local furbearers, the use of poisons was prohibited, and the shipment of furs was monitored by the U.S. Bureau of Fisheries.[22] At that time out-of-season pelts commonly were being taken by Eskimo trappers, who did not know about or comprehend the new laws, and the keen competition among traders led some of them to accept such skins.[23] It appears that hunting and trapping regulations were not stringently enforced until the Alaska Game Commission, part of the U.S. Biological Survey, was established in 1925. In 1926 a game warden was stationed at Bethel, and in 1927 the game commission had a small cabin cruiser patrolling the Kuskokwim.[24] According to the Moravians, the local presence of a game warden led to the jailing for a month of several Eskimos who broke laws of which they were unaware.[25] In other areas of Alaska, major conflicts that developed between Eskimos and enforcement agents have involved migratory waterfowl or big game such as caribou or moose. Along the Kuskokwim, these concerns have not loomed large, possibly because comparatively few migratory birds nest in the area and the Upriver Eskimos depend on fish as a primary staple.[26]

The first major involvement of Upriver Eskimos with the formalities of law may have followed an incident occurring in the summer of 1911. At that time Eskimo witnesses were required to testify at the trial of a white man accused of murdering two other white men near Tuluksak. One Eskimo heard the shots and saw the murderer at a distance, and others had information bearing on the case. A deputy marshal went to Tuluksak and subpoenaed two Eskimos, whom he took with him as he started to the trial site at Iditarod. On the trip one Eskimo ran off because he was afraid, causing the marshal to return to Tuluksak for two additional witnesses. After being kept at Iditarod three months, these three men testified through an interpreter at the trial.[27] Although they were not directly involved in the incident, the Eskimos had their rights restricted for a considerable length of time. This was a new experience for them, and although they cooperated, they did so reluctantly. A few years later the erratic behavior of an Eskimo man at Akiak threatened other villagers, and the authorities were called, no doubt by John Kilbuck. A deputy marshal took the man to Iditarod, where he was declared insane and sent to a mental institution in Oregon.[28] This apparently had not occurred before to an Upriver Eskimo, but the people accepted Kilbuck's handling of the matter because they respected his judgment.

The role of John Kilbuck in introducing American political institutions to villagers in the 1910s cannot be underestimated. He returned to the Kuskokwim in 1911 as a Bureau of Education representative and as the federal employee who most often visited the many villages. He was highly respected by villagers as a result of his prior missionary service at Bethel, and his ability to speak fluent Yupik was invaluable to them. Although Kilbuck did not formally represent the law, his judgments were accepted widely. In his new position of authority he could advocate Christian morality more effectively than ever before. For instance, while at Tuluksak in 1916, he pointed out to a couple that their common-law marriage was legally and morally wrong.[29] Kilbuck also was able to defend the local people against exploitation by whites, and he did this more often and more effectively than anyone else along the river.[30]

Traditionally villagers were unaccustomed to having outsiders make decisions concerning them. The consensus leader in a riverine Eskimo village, called by them *a man indeed*, was their informal leader. In situations affecting village social stability, this man, after consulting others, sought to resolve the difficulty. This means of social control that had been satisfactory in the past probably was weakened after many of these leaders perished in the 1900 influenza epidemic and its aftermath. Nonetheless, villagers did their best to settle internal differences on their own and sought to avoid intervention by outsiders. However, by about 1930 it had become increasingly necessary for Eskimos to accept the decisions of outsiders as their own means of social control weakened from disuse. In some cases white traders informally settled minor disputes. If more serious confrontations arose, teachers and traders might encourage one Eskimo to file a legal complaint against another with the U.S. deputy marshal. Game wardens, marshals, and commissioners told the people what was right or wrong according to the American legal system. Among the people themselves, independent traders who were of mixed Eskimo and white ancestry usually held informal positions of authority, and they most often modeled their behavior after whites. This was true also of those Eskimos who were influential because of their association with a Christian religion; these included the Moravian helpers and the heads of Orthodox church brotherhoods.

In 1934 Congress enacted a New Deal for Native Americans comparable in scope to the dramatic social changes being proposed for other Americans. The Indian Reorganization Act passed in that year was designed to revitalize the traditional life-styles of Indians and Eskimos as well as to stimulate the economies of reservation Indians. A key provision was that a tribe could organize as a corporate entity and thereby exert far greater control over local affairs. The act was amended and extended to Alaska in 1936 to afford Native Alaskans the same rights given Indians in the states.[31] BIA teachers encouraged villagers to form local corporations under the act, but the only riverine communities to comply were Kwethluk (in 1940), Akiachak (in 1948), and Akiak (in 1949).[32] At this time and later, other villages established elected councils, but they did not seek formal federal recognition. Over the years these councils have come to be identified as traditional village councils.

Little has been published about the workings of Kuskokwim village councils, but there seems to have been a consistent effort to resolve conflicts locally and thus avoid the intervention of whites. The usual pattern was to attempt to reintegrate rather than punish an offender. For example, at Napaskiak one man who was a heavy drinker was elected as village marshal, and another was elected to the council when his consumption of intoxicants became a major issue.[33] Here as elsewhere, whenever a council had difficulty implementing a decision, it turned to representatives of the BIA at the Bethel field office for help. For instance, in the early 1950s the Tuluksak council asked the BIA supervisor at Bethel to take action against a man who repeatedly beat his wife. The man had been fined by the council but refused to pay, and the villagers sought BIA intervention. In another instance the council requested advice from the same source because it did not know what action to take about a person who was acting in an apparently insane manner.[34] These and other examples show villagers beginning to apply laws and regulations imposed by whites, although they seem to have made decisions in keeping with their traditional concepts whenever that was possible.[35] If a council found itself helpless to enforce a decision, it turned as a body to the local deputy marshal by filing a complaint against the offender. The most novel office within the council organization was that of village marshal, which was without precedent. As noted in the Napaskiak example, the marshal himself could be an offender; this was not in keeping with the ideals of the American legal system but was compatible with the Eskimo one.

When Alaska became a state in 1959, the U.S. commissioners serving in rural areas were replaced by state magistrates. A magistrate, as a lay judge, was appointed by a superior court and empowered to hear cases arising from violation of village council ordinances and state misdemeanors under certain circumstances. Magistrates also held preliminary hearings in felony cases. Although no study has been made of this system as it functioned in Kuskokwim villages, in all likelihood it undermined the power of village councils as it reportedly did in northern Alaskan Eskimo communities.[36]

The changes in power structure within villages moved gradually from the decision-making of a consensus leader to that of white law enforcement agents acting together with elected councils and then to the emergence of control by state magistrates. Another political change occurring within the same time frame was far more rapid and disruptive. When World War II brought the Japanese occupation of Attu and Kiska in the Aleutian Islands, there was widespread turmoil in the territory; many Americans expected an all-out invasion of the Alaskan mainland. Local Eskimos became eligible for the draft, but few were inducted because they could not pass the physical examination or the English literacy test. However, many joined the Alaska Territorial Guard (ATG), which was formed as a voluntary military organization and an extension of the U.S. Army. Village units were organized, and their members were trained in guerrilla warfare.[37] Upriver Eskimo units were founded at Akiak, Akiachak, Bethel, and Kwethluk. In each community older men were appointed as officers, and others served as enlisted men. The ATG officials were lax in their dealings with village units, and there was comparatively little formal military discipline. The greatest advantage of belonging to the ATG, apart from the money, was that members were issued vast quantities of military equipment, including clothing, sleeping bags, rifles, and ammunition. They were permitted to wear the uniforms whenever they wished and could use or lend their equipment. These material advantages of membership were alluring enough to bring many villagers into the units.

In 1948 the Alaska National Guard (ANG), which had been placed under federal jurisdiction in 1941, replaced the ATG and established its Second Scout Battalion for the area, with headquarters at Bethel.[38] Village units from the former ATG came under its jurisdiction, and their importance increased during the Cold War. The units were administered differently under the ANG than they had been formerly. Clothing and equipment could not be loaned, and members were to use them only during training and on special occasions. Furthermore, most older villagers who had been unit leaders were replaced by young, aggressive, English-speaking villagers. These men, who became sergeants, received special training and subsequently introduced rigid military drill in the training sessions. In the new organization respected elders often were privates, and other villagers were amazed to see that the government encouraged young men to reprove, even ridicule, their elders in public. Many men were members because of the money they could earn and because of the yearly two-week encampment near Anchorage, which they considered a wonderful vacation. In the mid-1950s Oswalt observed the ANG unit in the village of Napaskiak and found it to be the American institution with the most negative influence on traditional community life.[39]

Until the draft ended in 1973, villagers typically served in the

ANG as an alternative to be drafted. The effectiveness of their military training apparently increased as they were sent to Fort Ord, California, and elsewhere for instruction. Although no study has been made of the impact membership in U.S. military organizations has had on Eskimo life since 1941, one would suspect that it has been deep and lasting on most of the persons involved.

Another way Eskimos were embraced by American political institutions was through the Alaska Department of Public Safety. In 1968 it established a program for training men to police their own communities. The first class began in 1971, and the program has continued since that time.[40] One of its goals is to reduce the caseload of state troopers. Village police, together with village councils, can handle misdeameanors that do not require referral to the local magistrate or district court. Delegating authority to local police and village councils has the potential of providing greater justice because of the familiarity of these individuals with the general cultural background of offenders. Yet the village police officers usually are young, and they may lack legitimate authority in the eyes of villagers. In this sense, they resemble the young leaders in the National Guard, who are vested with authority reluctantly accepted by the older villagers.

In 1966 a major step was taken to provide Native Alaskans with trained assistance as they attempted to deal with the complicated American legal system. Under the auspices of the federal Office of Economic Opportunity, a legal services program was launched for those villagers who could not afford an attorney. Alaska Legal Services, as it was called, had representatives in Bethel.[41] One of its major cases, which it pursued successfully, was to force the state to build high schools in those villages requesting them. Legal services personnel also have been active in helping people receive food stamps, getting poorly constructed public housing renovated, and preventing villagers who are debtors from being forced to go to urban centers to defend themselves against small claims actions. More than any other program this one has brought justice to villagers affected by American laws. However, cutbacks in financing diminished the activities of Alaska Legal Services in the early 1980s, which has handicapped Eskimos faced with legal dilemmas they cannot solve on their own.

Following statehood, a new option became available for the organization of villages. Rather than functioning as local tribal corporations, as Akiachak, Akiak, and Kwethluk had chosen to do, or as an entity controlled by an elected council, a village now could organize a second-class city under provisions established by the state. Governments of second-class cities have elected councils, and council members select one of their number as mayor. Second-class cities may not provide educational services, and they are limited in their capacity to impose property taxes. They have the authority to build roads and sidewalks, control loose dogs, and regulate some aspects of public behavior. A second-class city receives from the state revenue-sharing funds that are to be used to support bureaucratic positions and city services. More important, however, are funds received for capital improvements and discretionary monies for projects such as bulk fuel storage.[42] Because of the monetary advantages most villages along the river have become second-class cities.[43] In addition to state funds, they qualify for federal revenue sharing, and even though these funds have been reduced in recent years, they have remained significant considering the size of most villages. Just as federal funds have diminished, the same is true of state funding.

Another significant development resulted from the Indian Self-Determination and Education Assistance Act passed by Congress in 1975. This act provided federal financial assistance to those villages having formal or traditional village councils. Such villages became eligible to draw on federal monies to contract services, such as school management and health clinics, formerly controlled by federal agencies. State monies usually have not been available to unincorporated villages or those having traditional councils because the state has not recognized these governments. It is clear, as will be considered later in the discussion about Akiachak, that the state continues to question the legitimacy of federally recognized village councils. At present, the federal funds are enabling these villages to upgrade their community services.

THE LAND

As long as Eskimos were the principal inhabitants along the river, local resources were open to exploitation by all, and it never occurred to anyone to ask who owned the land. Village houses, trapping and fishing camps, and hunting or fishing sites belonged to their users until abandoned. The Russian claim to Alaskan land was of course meaningless to Kuskokwim Eskimos, and at the time Russia sold the territory to the United States, it expressed little concern about the future status of Native Alaskans. According to the 1867 Treaty of Cession, in practical terms the American government considered the Kuskokwim Eskimos among the "uncivilized tribes" who "will be subject to such laws and regulations as the United States may from time to time adopt in regard to aboriginal tribes of that country."[44] At the time of the Alaskan purchase, treaties were being made with various Indian groups in the United States; as one result, many were being confined to reservations. It seemed reasonable to expect that the same procedures would be followed in Alaska. However, Congress discontinued treaty-making with Indians in 1871, and no immediate effort was made to clarify the political status of Native Alaskans.

The Organic Act of 1884 was the first attempt by Congress to govern Alaska as a political entity. Acknowledging the unique position of Native Alaskans, the act stated that they "shall not be disturbed in the possession of any lands actually in their use or occupation or now claimed by them."[45] Homestead laws were extended to Alaska in 1898, but Natives could not thereby acquire title to homesteads because technically they were not citizens of the United States. Subsequently Congress passed the Native Allotment Act of 1906, which made it possible for Natives to obtain 160-acre plots from unreserved federal land. However, few such allotments were made, perhaps because in general, Alaskan Natives did not feel threatened in their use of land at that time and had no real awareness of the implications of legal ownership.[46] The allotment act made no real impact on Native Alaskans until shortly before the Alaska Native Claims Settlement Act was passed in 1971. At that time Native Alaskans were encouraged by BIA representatives and others to apply for allotments under the terms of the 1906 act so that they could in essence own a homestead before receiving other land from the 1971 act. Thousands did so, but most applications were not correctly prepared, did not reach the proper office before the deadline, or were not processed immediately by the Department of the Interior. If they had not been recorded before passage of the settlement act, they were considered invalid. This has since led to legal action by applicants who claimed that bureaucratic problems made their claims unacceptable. It now appears that hundreds of these people will receive the allotments for which they had filed.[47]

When statehood was proclaimed in 1959, the rights of Native Alaskans to their land had not been resolved. Before statehood the federal government had removed millions of acres from the public domain to establish national forests, monuments, parks, and wildlife protection areas as well as to create a few reservations for Eskimos and Indians. In addition, innumerable small parcels of land had been set aside for missions, schools, and government installations. The Upriver Eskimos largely were unaffected by these actions since none of their area was included in major federal withdrawals or reservations.

Under the terms of statehood, Alaska was to receive title to 103 million acres of land from the public domain. Some of the state's selections were from areas where Native Alaskans lived, and after organizing, they protested this action. The result was the first serious attempt to resolve the long-lingering issue of aboriginal rights and land occupancy in most of Alaska. Native Alaskans had been poorly organized before the early 1960s and had exerted no direct influence on land policy decisions, but now that they realized their lands would be taken from them, their attitude and actions changed. In 1962 an Eskimo, Howard Rock, launched and began editing a Fairbanks newspaper called *Tundra Times*. The paper became the voice of Aleuts, Eskimos, and Indians wanting to lobby for land rights and influence other issues affecting Natives. As an indirect result regional organizations were created to press particular claims, and in 1966 a statewide organization, the Alaska Federation of Natives, was founded to coordinate mutual interests. The land dispute peaked in 1966 when the Secretary of the Interior, Stewart Udall, refused to grant the state title to its land selections because of unresolved aboriginal claims.[48]

Nineteen sixty-six was a critical year in another respect as well. Native Alaskans protested the federal sale of oil and gas leases along the Arctic Ocean, and Udall responded by temporarily suspending the sales. This, coupled with the more general land freeze, produced a situation that led to a strange alliance among Native Alaskans, the State of Alaska, and major oil companies, each of whom sought an end to the stalemate.[49] After lengthy evaluations of land use and intense lobbying, the Alaska Native Claims Settlement Act (ANCSA) was passed by Congress in 1971.

The act extinguished any individual aboriginal Native Alaskan claims based on local land use and occupancy, including hunting and fishing rights; homestead claims lie outside this ruling. The people as a group were to receive clear title to forty-four million acres of land, the mineral rights to this land, and 962.5 million dollars over a number of years. One of the first steps in settling the claims was to compile an enrollment comprising all eligible persons, meaning any person with one-quarter or more Aleut, Eskimo, or Indian blood who was living at the time the act became law and sought to participate in the settlement.[50] The act established twelve regions and a corporation in control of each; all qualified enrollees were to be members of the corporation established in the area with which they were identified. Each corporation was to manage a region's assets and make a profit for its members. (In 1975 a thirteenth corporation was formed of persons eligible by birth but not living in Alaska.) The act also provided for the creation of village corporations within each regional corporation. The qualified enrollees were to be members and shareholders in both types of corporations and elected the managements. When the enrollment was nearly complete, the corporations were organized and began receiving funds paid from the U.S. Treasury to the Alaska Native Fund. The village corporations received 45 percent of the distribution (50 percent after 1977) to regional corporations.[51]

Most of the Kuskokwim River system and all of the Upriver Eskimo section is in the Calista Corporation (CC); the name was chosen because *calista* means "worker" in Yupik. CC manages the area from Cape Newenham on the south, north to just beyond the north mouth of the Yukon River, west to the coast including adjacent islands, and east up the Yukon River to near Russian Mission and along the Kuskokwim to Stony River. Of all the corporations, Calista had the largest number of resident shareholders in 1974. The 13,500 members originally lived in fifty-six villages, and the land area specified encompassed about 56,000 square miles or 6.8 million acres.[52] However, legal problems long prevented title transfers on much of the land. By 1982 CC had received title to only 2.4 million acres, and thirty-two village corporations had not received their major land entitlements.[53]

The goals of the ANCSA are forthright, but the charters under which the regional and village corporations were established have proven immensely complicated. They are, in fact, a nightmare of complexity, partially because so many agencies are involved in implementation of the act. It was the intent of Congress to convey land titles to the regional and village corporations promptly, but each agency has its jurisdiction to protect and its own regulations. For example, federal regulations concerning easements along major waterways have contributed to years of delay in conveying land titles. The agency most responsible, the Bureau of Land Management, is still attempting to work out a means of permitting public access that is acceptable to the state, federal government, and Natives. Without title to the land the regional and village corporations have found it difficult to launch programs of economic development effectively. The long delay is all the more critical because tax immunities and other stipulations designed to aid the corporations were to expire in 1991.

Another type of difficulty that has impeded satisfactory implementation of the act is the legal interpretation of some provisions. For instance, one provision requires that 70 percent of the revenues each regional corporation derives from timber and mineral rights be shared by all regional corporations based on per capita enrollments. *Revenue* was not precisely defined in the act, and the question of how it shall be determined as well as what deductions and depreciations are legitimate have resulted in lawsuits among the corporations for what they consider their fair proportion of monies under this provision. The net result has been the spending of an extraordinary amount of corporation money for legal fees and management costs.

When the ANCSA became law, most Native Alaskans and interested outsiders expected it to assure the economic security of all the people involved rather quickly. The terms of the act seemed generous to an extreme considering the small number of beneficiaries and the large amounts of land and money at stake.

The money allotted to corporations was indeed a great amount, but the recipients were ill-prepared to administer multi-million dollar corporations. No training in business management had been provided prior to the settlement. Of the Native Alaskans who were twenty-five years of age or older in 1970, about 20 percent had completed four or more years of high school, and only 2.2 percent had completed four or more years of college.[54] Despite their generally poor educational background and limited experience as businesspersons or administrators, the people understandably wanted to take direct charge of their own corporations. The corporation members who have profited most handsomely from the act are part-Natives in middle-management positions. Sometimes referred to as "Brooks Brothers Eskimos," these individuals typically are those who have had the most training and background experience in dealing with the ways of whites. Their management practices and those of their advisors have led to disastrous results, however. By 1985 the CC had lost nearly forty-three million dollars; total assets at that time were about seventy-nine million dollars.[55]

Contrary to the general pattern, some middle-management employees of CC have been highly effective. One such person is Glenn Fredericks, who was hired soon after the settlement act was passed to manage an office at Sleetmute. In 1973 he helped individual villages in the region draw up articles of incorporation, elect governing boards, and open their own offices, each with a small operating budget. Fredericks realized that with comparatively little money and limited business expertise, the village corporations would find it difficult to operate effectively, and he urged the formation of a cover organization to help each village deal with land problems, investments, accounting procedures, and legal questions common to all. For this purpose the Kuskokwim Management Corporation (KMC) was created in 1975.[56] Working with representatives from the ten villages from Lower Kalskag to Stony River Village, plus Lime Village along the Stony River, the new corporation helped villagers resolve common problems. It also made a major investment in an apartment and office complex built at Aniak, and each village shared in the profits on a per capita basis. The KMC gained a clearer sense of direction when Janet A. Fredericks, the wife of Glenn Fredericks, became the manager in 1975. Her background and administrative experience with other Native corporations brought the first day-to-day effectiveness to the corporation.

In 1976 the settlement act was amended to permit consolidation of the corporation assets of villages. With this enabling legislation the idea of a multi-village merger grew; the creation of such a unit would eliminate the need for each village to prepare a separate audit and other reports and hold its own annual meetings. The question that loomed largest in the minds of all villagers was how a merger would affect ownership of the land. It was realized that establishing a multi-village unit would require individual villages to relinquish control over their particular land allotments. Although there also was money involved, it never became an issue comparable to that of keeping village lands under Eskimo control. The merger proposal was put to a vote in 1976, and most villages unanimously favored it. The exception was Lime Village, which elected to retain its autonomy as a village corporation.

The ten settlements that voted to merge formed the Kuskokwim Corporation (KC) in 1977. It had about 1,200 enrolled members and assets amounting to about three million dollars. The money had been invested previously by the CC but now was withdrawn so that it could be reinvested on behalf of the consolidated village corporation. The KC board retained the Aniak apartment and office complex and also purchased mortgages, corporate bonds, and property in Anchorage. Initially professional advisors handled the money, but in 1979 the board began making its own investments. A nonprofit arm of the KC, the Kuskokwim Native Association (KNA), was established to originate and implement projects with direct local socioeconomic impact. One of the KNA programs provides technical assistance to the member villages for setting up training programs and obtaining grants for local projects. Another administers supplemental educational programs under federal grants. The association operates a clinic, helps organize recreational activities in villages, and has developed a mental health program concerned especially with the prevention of alcoholism. It also has established an experimental agricultural project at Aniak.[57]

Because of the aforementioned plethora of stipulations in the claims settlement act, the KC and KNA necessarily include a complex maze of institutional networks that villagers often find difficult to deal with effectively. Furthermore, a large number of federal and state agencies or programs operating in the area at the present time impinge directly on them. They must cooperate with federal agencies such as the BIA, Forest Service, and Bureau of Land Management, each with its own subdivisions. At the state level the Department of Fish and Game and the Department of Community and Regional Affairs are important in their lives. Much decision-making is appropriately at the village level, and innumerable boards, board representatives, councils, or committees have been organized to facilitate participation in many varied programs. Village education committees decide how to spend certain federal monies, land committees make decisions about the future utilization of local resources, and city or traditional councils make political decisions.

When considering federal, state, and corporation involvements, it must be kept in mind that the settlements from Kwethluk to Stony River Village are small. In 1980 the total year-round resident native population of these villages was 2,159; the smallest one was Napamiut, with a population of 4, and the largest was Kwethluk, with 441 persons.[58] About half of the residents are youthful, and thus there are comparatively few adults to assume the many responsibilities and fewer still with an interest or capacity for participating effectively in the diverse organizations represented.

Contrary to the expectations of many outsiders, passage of the settlement act did not intensify the process of Americanization among village Eskimos along the river. Quite to the contrary, the act united them as never before and led to a new search for an Eskimo cultural identity. The Americanization that became increasingly prominent at Bethel during the 1970s was a result of socioeconomic forces that had begun to affect the Eskimos before the settlement act. A reversal of Americanization is now underway in some aspects of village life.

BETHEL

When the Moravians founded Bethel in 1885, they intended to create a House of God, and for about fifteen years they succeeded eminently well. Their mission work grew both in intensity and geographical scope during this time. However, the gold rushes of the early 1900s ended Bethel's isolation and led to a decline in their monopolistic control of the community. Bethel became not only a mission center but the major port of entry for gold seekers and their supplies. The world view and material goods of the prospectors brought a new life-style to compete with that of the Moravians. The missionaries understandably disapproved of the card playing, intoxicants, dancing—calling it "the devil's frolic"—profanity, and "basest animal lust" now introduced to Bethel.[59] However, this way of life had a greater appeal to some Eskimos than did the Moravian one. In 1916 the mission superintendent, Arthur F. Butzin, wrote of the Eskimos, "The great difficulty with Bethel is its shifting population. There is no village spirit. People drift in here from the most backward villages. These newcomers are backward in morals and foremost in superstitions. Added to this already heterogenous native population there has been a coterie of the 'Bowery' type of roughs about Bethel, during the past winter."[60] It soon became apparent that Eskimos visiting Bethel carried non-Moravian ways back to their villages. While at Akiak in 1921 Edith Kilbuck wrote her husband, "Bethel is a vice center and I fear our young people here are not untouched by such things. Sure it is, I have never known in years past of so much slander, backbiting, lying, and deviltry of all kinds. I don't know who to trust any more."[61] Edith Kilbuck's remarks are one indication of the changing world view of local Eskimos and their departure from traditional values.

Presumably those Eskimos who settled in Bethel in its early years were so dissatisfied with social and economic conditions, or both, in their home villages that they were willing to leave when an alternative was established nearby. It is not surprising that they found American ways appealing, and because some of them probably were nonconformists by nature, they could be expected to sample this new life-style, whether it was approved by the missionaries or not.

The population characteristics of Bethel began to change as it became the dominant Eskimo-white contact community in the lower Yukon and Kuskokwim basins. When the Moravians first had arrived, the only Bethel residents were the trader, his Eskimo employees, and their families. After the mission was established, nearby Eskimos, especially those living across and up the river a short distance at Mumtrekhlagamute, began moving to Bethel as they found advantages in living at the new settlement. In 1890 the population included 14 Native Alaskans and 6 whites; the Eskimo population grew to 110 by 1910 and to 651 by 1950.[62] By 1960 there were 1,132 Natives and 126 non-Natives; in 1982 an increase in both groups had led to a total of 1,757 Natives and 1,735 non-Natives.[63] It can be seen that as the population grew, the percentages changed. In 1960 the population was 90 percent Native; this had diminished to 50 percent Native by 1982.

By the late 1930s Bethel had become the major sea, river, and air hub for the general region and as such attracted both transient and resident workers. The Alaska Native Service hospital completed in 1954 became the major health service facility for the people of seventy villages in the area. Since health care was poor in villages at the time, many Eskimos traveled to Bethel for treatment. Bethel also was becoming an increasingly important center for governmental activities by the mid-1950s. An Alaska Communication System telegraph office existed there as did a large Civil Aeronautics Authority airport, the BIA field office, the Second Scout Battalion of the U.S. National Guard, and the regional jail under the jurisdiction of the resident U.S. deputy marshal. The stores, which had grown to five, were better stocked than others in the region and drew customers from hundreds of miles distant. Two roadhouses, four restaurants, two pool halls, and two theaters added to the local facilities. A city government was formed in 1957 as residents took an increasing interest in the political status of their community within the territory.[64]

Bethel's rise to prominence fed on itself. Expanding airport facilities led to rapid and reliable air service by jet aircraft. In 1971 there were daily flights from Anchorage, and by 1980 the number of flights to and from Anchorage had nearly tripled, with larger aircraft generally used.[65] This expanded accessibility contributed greatly to the vitality of the town. Bethel became an even more important center for the redistribution of imported food and goods and now also served air passengers going to outlying vil-

By 1979, when this photograph was taken, Bethel had become a town with a population of about 3,000. *Courtesy of George S. Young,* Tundra Drums.

lages. Because of its importance as a regional transportation hub, state and federal agencies founded or enlarged their offices at Bethel, which likewise fueled the local economy.

Beginning in the 1960s the Great Society programs, the "War on Poverty," and increased state involvement in rural areas brought new forms of assistance to the local population. A federal job corps program began in 1965, and in the same year the first Volunteers in the Service to America (VISTA) were assigned to Bethel and surrounding villages.[66] Unlike the VISTA programs in other states, the Alaskan one was sponsored by the state itself. VISTA workers were to help local people develop leadership skills and resolve community-wide problems, but they were not accepted wholeheartedly. In 1970 the Association of Village Council Presidents, the largest Native nonprofit organization serving the fifty-six villages in the Calista region, objected to its lack of control over the volunteers, who usually were young, white, and naive. The program was suspended temporarily and later was reopened under greater local regulation.[67] This action taken by the village council presidents was a clear indicator that local leaders were becoming more assertive than in the past. Although VISTA workers often caused problems for their supervisors, the early volunteers seem to have conveyed to the Bethel people and villagers alike a useful awareness of how to gain control over economic and political changes.

The Alaska Legal Services, funded by the Office of Economic Opportunity, opened an office at Bethel in 1966. As mentioned earlier, these lawyers were dedicated to fostering local Native interests in such varied matters as adoptions, divorces, voting rights, food stamps, and the use of native languages in public meetings. Within a short time they also became involved with issues centering about education and the ownership or use of land.[68]

A major project was undertaken at Bethel to replace the woefully inadequate housing of poor Natives. Funded by the U.S. Department of Housing and Urban Development, the Turnkey or Bethel Housing Project provided two hundred low-cost houses. The first units were completed in 1968, but the results of the project were far less satisfactory than had been hoped. Not only were the houses poorly designed and constructed, but they were clustered far from the center of town. This set the poor apart from the general population, which further compounded their problems.[69]

By the mid-1970s forty-three government agencies had representatives at Bethel. Eight million dollars came to the community through the BIA annually, and a half million dollars came from the state. Much of this money was used for administrative costs, but the needs of government agencies, the hospital, and schools, were primarily for skilled personnel, which generally meant whites. The unemployment rate for unskilled workers, the category most Natives fit into, was about 40 percent.[70] By 1984 the income for the 3,300 Bethel residents totaled about fifty-one million dollars a year. Transfer or subsidy payments from the government, including general assistance, Aid to Families with Dependent Children, Social Security, and educational assistance, went primarily to Eskimos and accounted for about 15 percent of the total community income. Fifty percent of local employment was by state, federal, and local governments, in that order. About 22 percent of the other employment came from trade, services, and transportation. Unemployment in all categories for whites and Natives combined was then estimated at about 13 percent.[71]

The negative side of Bethel living cannot be ignored. In the 1950s Bethel was known as the "sin city" of Alaska or by even less flattering terms, and its unsettled social atmosphere has not improved. In the mid-1970s drunkenness had become a major concern, and the same was true of crime. At that time Bethel had the highest per capita homicide rate in the United States. By 1979 the gonorrhea rate was twenty-five times the national average. The incidence of reported rape cases in 1981 was 812 per 100,000 (compared to 96 per 100,000 in Anchorage); the unreported cases were estimated to be 50 percent greater than the reported ones.[72]

Two singular demographic characteristics of the Bethel population at about this time were the large proportion of young people and the number of transient residents. According to 1982 statistics, 40 percent of the people were under twenty years of age; 30 percent of the Natives and 46 percent of the non-Natives had lived in Bethel for less than three years.[73] As Ann Fienup-Riordan has noted, Bethel is more a crossroad than a melting pot. The Native population functions separately from the non-Native one by and large, although there is a mixture in most of the residential areas.[74]

Despite the decidedly urban nature of living in Bethel, one solid link with the village life-style has continued with unexpected vigor. It is the strong reliance of residents on local food resources. Seventy percent of the households in 1979 reported that they utilized locally available edibles. Nearly one third of them relied on local subsistence activities for one half or more of their food. Considering that grocery prices at Bethel are high, it is obvious that harvesting local products saved these households thousands of dollars.[75] In addition, some Eskimo residents probably preferred the traditional diet, and thus it became a major aspect of their continuing Eskimo life-style. Other select aspects of their culture have been retained as well. Most Bethel Eskimos speak Yupik, and although a survey indicates that about half of the Bethel residents own cars, more than half own a fishing boat.[76]

One of the nicest aspects of living at Bethel, according to two thirds of its residents, is the people.[77] Another advantage is that

Bethel is a step away from village life for those Eskimos seeking an alternative. Some villagers move to Bethel but find living there unattractive and return to their home villages, sometimes repeating this pattern time and again. Others become permanent residents, and still others move from villages to Bethel and then on to major Alaskan cities, especially Anchorage, or less often to cities in other states. Although Bethel is an unsettled and sometimes unsettling place in which to live, it is the most prominent way-station to Americanization for those Kuskokwim Eskimos seeking to change in that direction.[78]

9

Bashful No Longer

Upriver Eskimos could neither establish nor systematically pursue their own distinct cultural goals until they were in a position to deal effectively with Americans on largely American terms. While the goals of Americans shifted periodically, their assertive and domineering behavior toward these Eskimos changed comparatively little. Under these circumstances it obviously was Eskimos who would have to change the most if they were to become able to attain their own goals.

Before 1900, when scattered trading posts and the fur trade dominated white interests, economic accommodations between Eskimos and Westerners seemed satisfactory. The Eskimos found some of the new ways useful and felt no compelling reasons to return to their former way of life. Two factors above all others disrupted this relative stability in their relationships with whites. The gold rushes introduced Eskimos to different kinds of Americans who provided access to novel artifacts and foods, offered intermittent economic opportunities to obtain them, and introduced social customs far different from those to which Eskimos had been exposed earlier. The epidemic of 1900 was the second factor. It halved the Eskimo population, with devastating effects. In its aftermath some villages were abandoned, and others were characterized by a new, younger configuration of residents. Youthful Eskimos, the principal survivors of the 1900 epidemic, lived a village life greatly altered from that of their parents. They could not sustain traditional ceremonies because they lacked the knowledge to do so; furthermore, they lived such changed economic and social lives that there seemed to be no place for such traditions. Aboriginal artifacts diminished as adults no longer had the craft skills to produce them and found imported substitutes readily available. These rather abrupt changes soon were followed by others, such as the introduction of nuclear family dwelling units, American political institutions, village schools, trading posts, and post offices, which more gradually, but perhaps also more conclusively, altered the Eskimo life-style.

CONTINUITIES FROM PAST TO PRESENT

Some Western introductions prior to about 1920 have become so deeply embedded in modern Kuskokwim Eskimo culture that for most intents and purposes they are considered Eskimo. This is true particularly of select traits established during the Russian period. Nearly two hundred Russian loanwords were integrated into Yupik; these include words for edibles such as *bread, butter,* and *flour,* for items of material culture such as *ax, cup,* and *drinking glass,* and for *cross* or *icon* as important religious objects.[1] Likewise the Russian Orthodox Church itself, although obviously Western, is in some contexts regarded as an indigenous church along the Kuskokwim in contrast to the denominations introduced more recently. Celebration of Russian Christmas, or *slaviq,* is in many respects regarded as Eskimo. It is the focal point of the Orthodox ceremonial cycle and one in which participation by non-Orthodox is increasingly common. The Russian-style steam bath is another complex considered by most people to be Eskimo. Americans introduced about sixty English terms that have been incorporated fully into Yupik. These include words for manufactures, such as *bicycle* and *sewing machine,* and for consumables, such as *bacon, cookies,* and *milk.*[2] Some Western-style manufactures that have been made locally long enough to be considered an intimate part of Kuskokwim Eskimo living include log cabins, plank boats, and many home furnishings.

More important as continuities linking the past and present are the traditional aspects of riverine Eskimo life that have retained at least a certain degree of vitality. These especially are significant because they embody the ongoing cultural heritage of these people. Included are salmon fishing, fur trapping, Yupik language, aboriginal manufactures, social patterns, religious beliefs, and expressive culture manifestations. The degree of vitality is greater in some aspects than in others, but all represent meaningful retention of their Eskimo heritage.

Salmon   The gold rushes were responsible for introducing the fish wheel, which increased the salmon catch, and for the emergence of a commercial fish market, which proved a major stimulus for expansion of salmon harvesting. Salmon remained the primary Eskimo staple, and still there were enough to sell vast quantities to whites for themselves and their dogs into the 1930s. Money obtained in this way enabled Eskimos to participate in a cash economy until most miners left the region and airplanes replaced dog sleds for long distance travel. Then wage labor opportunities at the Bristol Bay canneries became an important source of cash; employment at the canneries increased steadily from 1943 through the 1960s.

Commercial salmon fishing along the Kuskokwim became economically feasible in 1959, when new jet aircraft brought an expanded capacity to export fresh fish. Local Eskimos comfortably and opportunistically exploited this change. By the late 1980s, however, commercial salmon fishing most profited lower river Eskimos because of harvest restrictions in other sectors of the river, and, equally important, restrictions on the number of commercial fishers.

For most Kuskokwim Eskimos salmon has remained the primary staple for varied reasons. Most significant are the high prices of imported foods, the comparatively low incomes of most Eskimos, the availability of salmon, and its traditional importance in their diet. The key role of local resources in the diet is well documented for Lower Kalskag. The protein produced by the harvest of edibles, especially salmon, was calculated for 1983. When fixed costs such as boats, outboard motors, and nets are considered along with variable costs such as gasoline and oil and these are divided by food output, the cost per pound of protein was 69¢ by dry weight. (At that time pork chops cost $5.49 per pound at a local store.) The replacement cost of the amount of protein obtained locally, if it were purchased at a local store, would average about $108,000 for each of the fifty-five families. This is overwhelming evidence for the value of local food products.[3] As a basic food and as a basic subsistence activity, salmon and salmon fishing represent critical continuities with cultural life in the past.

Fur   The emphasis on furbearers to provide food and pelts, which represented a primary means to obtain trade goods, remained strong until the late 1950s. In the following twenty years, however, many villagers abandoned trapping as other ways to obtain cash, and thereby store merchandise, proved more profitable. Trapping continued to decline until the early 1980s. One factor that led to its resurgence at that time, despite low fur prices and a continuing dependence on wage labor and welfare aid, was the mobility provided by snow machines. Another factor, of equal or greater importance, was the way in which trapping had become associated with modern ideas about traditional Eskimo life. Numerous persons felt that being a weekend or intermittent trapper enabled them to better retain their identity as Eskimos and reassert their capacity to live off the land. In 1983 trapping accounted for nearly a quarter of family income at Lower Kalskag.[4]

Language   Yupik, the language originally spoken by all Eskimos of southwestern Alaska, remained the exclusive or primary means of communication in most Kuskokwim villages until the 1920s or later. After religious texts were published in Yupik by missionaries beginning in 1896, an unknown number of Eskimos learned to read this language as well as to speak it.[5] When village schools were founded in the 1920s and 1930s (except for Bethel in 1886 and Akiak in 1911), they were intended to Americanize Eskimos, and therefore they required the use of English. However, children, like their parents, spoke primarily Yupik at this time, and its prohibition made the classroom a poor learning environment for them. They seldom became proficient enough in English for their formal education to cover subject matter beyond that of the primary grades. Despite the emphasis on English in the schools, Kuskokwim Eskimo children continued to use Yupik as their primary language through the early 1960s. Along the lower river and in the area to the west, bilingual education programs date from the late 1960s and persist into the present. These have enabled Eskimo children to acquire a better education while still retaining the Yupik-speaking ability their elders favored. Along the central river, however, Yupik is no longer the first language used by children, nor is it being taught in the schools.[6]

Technology   As would be expected, most items of aboriginal technology disappeared years ago, although a few types persisted into the comparatively recent past. Records of fully aboriginal

forms still made and used at Napaskiak in 1970 include such
items as wooden dippers, mauls, boat paddles, and bird-wing
brooms.[7] Not only are these types few in number, but they are of
simple design and serve humble purposes. A useful technological
shift has been toward making forms inspired by American products. They are created by villagers who want the American types
but are unable to afford the factory-made products. Included are
home furnishings such as beds, cupboards, tables, and wash-
stands. Eskimos also have learned to make larger Western forms
they find functional. These include log cabins and plank boats.
Ironically, Kuskokwim Eskimo technological skills have endured
partially through the crafting of American, not Eskimo, artifact types.

The technologically innovative capacity of these Eskimos has
remained strong and is evidenced by their use of industrial products in novel ways. Fuel containers serve as an example. An intact one-gallon plastic container for oil might be used as a net
float or a five-gallon gasoline can might be remade into a stove.
Furthermore, Eskimos have recognized the value of substituting
imported materials for those formerly used in numerous aboriginal tool types. For example, they have replaced stone with metal
for the blades of such basic tools as adzes, skin scrapers, and
ulus. Yet, in general, local manufactures are declining in importance and quality.

Social life   Until the 1980s Eskimo social behavior contrasted
with that of local whites in innumerable and significant ways.
Among Eskimos gossip persisted as a major means of social control, followed by ridicule and sometimes by social ostracism. Another aspect of interpersonal relations, the Eskimo sense of kind-
ness and courtesy in dealing with others, has endured into the
1980s. This behavioral characteristic bears special emphasis, particularly in light of the way these people have been treated by
others. In face-to-face dealings with each other and outsiders,
Eskimos remain inordinately considerate. One of their courtesies
is to feed and if need be to shelter guests with no remuneration or
gratitude expected. Such behavior is but one expression of the
high positive value placed on sharing with family, guests, and
others who have a need.

Villages remain insular as in the past, and residents tend to be distrustful of strangers, especially those without local connections. Also as in the past, Eskimos are wary of outsiders, particularly non-Eskimos, who marry into a village. Many of these marriages do not last, and one reason is that outsiders do not have kin ties in the community to buffer them through any problems that arise. In particular, newcomers who do not participate successfully in subsistence activities have difficulty becoming integrated since these activities form a key aspect of village life.[8]

Another singular social feature is the attachment of many villagers to their settlement as the only proper place in which to live. Although individuals or families may move temporarily to Bethel, Aniak, or other Alaskan population centers, they often return to their home villages. Extended family ties remain strong irrespective of where members live because it is close relatives on whom one may most rely. In general, the extended family remains the most important broad social group. This pattern is an extension of that in the past, although in former times it was less apparent to outsiders because of the customary residence pattern.

Religion   Christian missionaries and cultural discontinuities resulting from the 1900 epidemic led riverine Eskimos to abandon their traditional annual ceremonial round by 1930. Despite this change, significant aspects of the old religious life have endured. These include the continuing reliance on male and female shamans, whose special relationship with spirit beings reportedly leads to their inordinate ability to cure illness and foretell the future. Myths that encapsulate pre-Christian ideology and concern the origins of people, animal species, and geographical configurations also are widely recounted. Individuals practice numerous taboos that have no basis in Christian belief systems and presumably have survived from aboriginal times. A belief in ghosts, giants, and dwarfs with supernatural qualities likewise probably prevails more widely than generally is acknowledged.

We also find recent reports of people thought to have supernatural powers. One such person, an Eskimo man named Klutuk, was born at Tikchik about 1893. He lived as a recluse and became feared by residents of the area when he killed two other Eskimos in 1919. He later reportedly murdered at least six whites on four different occasions and killed at least one other Eskimo. Klutuk is associated with the Kuskokwim because he is known to have visited his wife and sister, who lived at Sleetmute. Despite intermittently intense efforts by whites to apprehend him, Klutuk reportedly died a natural death in 1931.[9] However, some Eskimos, perhaps many, believe that Klutuk is alive, living in isolated areas, and that he is responsible for events that otherwise cannot be explained.[10]

Expressive culture   In nonreligious contexts, the expressive culture of Kuskokwim Eskimos exhibits considerable vitality, possibly more than any other aspect of their culture apart from subsistence. Along the Kuskokwim proper this is most evident in Eskimo oral traditions. Legends that focus on events in the past as viewed with historical license possibly are most prominent. These often are war stories or relate the adventures of culture heroes. Other stories, such as accounts about relations with the Russians, are meant to be purely historical. A final but not insignificant block of oral traditions centers on family histories and individual remembrances.

Making craft items, such as grass baskets and masks, for sale to others as well as performing Eskimo music and dance have undergone a revival in recent years. The same is true to a lesser extent of Eskimo sporting events, such as wrestling and headpulling. Some of these aspects of expressive culture have become popular in riverine villages, but the main activity center for them is Bethel. The outstanding performers are primarily Yukon-Kuskokwim delta area Eskimos, but riverine Eskimos are participating with increasing frequency.

CULTURAL RENAISSANCE

A singular hallmark of Eskimo culture in its five thousand years of recognized existence has been the capacity of these people to adapt to changing environmental circumstances while strengthening their own distinct identity. In prehistoric times their adaptations hinged to a great extent on devising new means to exploit changes in the resource base. Throughout the early historic era in Alaska, and more particularly on the Kuskokwim, Eskimos continued to adjust, this time to contacts with Westerners. Initially their cultural separateness remained strong as a result of the limited access of Russians and their modest goals. After about 1900, with expanding American cultural presence and the growing intensity of these contacts, distinctive Eskimo cultural identity diminished.

By the time of Alaskan statehood in 1959, three generations of riverine Eskimos had had expanding exposure to American institutions. Schooling had taught most of them English and the essence of the American knowledge system. These and other contacts of an economic and political nature had combined to give them an ability to deal with whites in a reasonably effective manner. At the same time, they became increasingly aware of what they were giving up as they became integrated into their new world. Although many objected to being Americanized, they remained true to their own backgrounds by being nonassertive in their dissatisfaction.

However, since the mid-1960s Native Alaskans in general, and these riverine Eskimos in particular, have reassessed their position, and this has led to a cultural renaissance. They now are less willing to acquiesce wholeheartedly in the many changes imposed on them by whites. They have developed a clear awareness of their past and are regaining an identity with their Native heritage. As a result of the ANCSA at least a temporary cultural renewal was predictable. *It could not have been otherwise.* For individuals and groups to be recognized under the act's terms, they were *required* to prove their Native heritage in overlapping biological, historical, and legal contexts. They further were *required* to identify the geographical areas they traditionally had occupied and used. These involvements forced each person to look carefully into his or her past to establish a claim. Successful claims conferred membership in a regional and village corporation plus rights to land and money. Because of these advantages a personal identity as a Native Alaskan became a favorable status for the first time in this century. The settlement act not only had a great deal to do with the new cultural awareness of Kuskokwim Eskimos, it also placed them in an unprecedented positive position and enhanced their economic power. With their new respect for the value of the past in the present, they have attempted to preserve, continue, and revive select aspects of their former life-style.

In many ways Eskimo efforts along these lines constitute a *revitalization movement,* meaning a deliberate, organized, conscious effort by members of a society to create a more satisfying culture.[11] Many of the recent attempts to revive aspects of earlier Eskimo lifeways have been made through whites locally active in the field of education. For example, as a result of strong Native pressures, the Kuskokwim Community College founded at Bethel in 1972 agreed to provide formal training in business, trade, and academic subjects. Yupik language courses and classes about Native Alaskan anthropology, history, and politics soon were added. College courses were taught in numerous villages by traveling instructors, and villagers also might obtain such instruction by television and two-way radio communication. Although the administration of the community college system recently was reorganized, the Bethel college offerings are being expanded to help meet local Eskimo needs.

When outsiders ask Kuskokwim Eskimos how their own culture can be strengthened, they commonly say that this goal can be achieved if they are left alone. This response reflects a deep-seated and often bitter resentment of American intrusion on all aspects of their lives. Yet on further inquiry one soon learns that to be left alone does *not* mean that they seek an end to most social and economic support programs, health services, or wage-earning opportunities; on the contrary, their felt needs along these lines are expanding. To many Eskimos being left alone means the capacity to live by their own values if they so desire, including a return to their spiritual life of old, to exploit local resources free from outside intrusion, and above all else to have full and lasting control over their land. They are tired of being told by outsiders what to do and how to do it. They are weary of the ethnocentric Americanism of many whites and resent being the victims of subtle or blatant racism.

As today's Upriver Eskimos express the desire to return to their old ways, they most often seem to mean pre-World War II conditions. That was the time they remember best as their former way of life. Most white-inspired changes had been launched by then, and yet these Eskimos remained comparatively independent and were able to hunt and fish as they had in the past. Their lives still centered in their villages, and most of them, including the young people, still spoke Yupik.

In the public schools Yupik language transfer and language

maintenance programs now are offered in the lower grades, but these courses are not nearly as prominent at riverine villages as in those of the Yukon-Kuskokwim delta area. Other select aspects of Eskimo culture have gained increasing emphasis in rural classrooms. These include Eskimo music and dance, Eskimo craft skills, and wilderness survival training. At the Bethel Regional High School one federally funded project that has affected the entire area is especially noteworthy. Hundreds of students were sent to villages in the region to record ethnographic and ethnohistorical information. In 1974 they launched a journal, *Kalikag Yugnek* (Book of the Yupik People), to publish their findings, and from 1974 to 1978 eight issues appeared. These are a rich source of data about the past and include some material about the present as well. Collecting the information unquestionably was a rewarding experience for the students, and the published results have been a source of gratification to the villagers involved. The journal, one of the few local publications by Eskimos for Eskimos, was a useful contribution to the ethnohistorical writings about the area.

Since more riverine Eskimos live in and near Bethel than in other upriver communities, Bethel understandably has become the center for Upriver Eskimo institutional activity. The Yugtarvik Regional Museum was founded in 1967 to collect and preserve Eskimo artifacts and art from the area. A weekly newspaper, the *Kuskokwim Kronicle,* began publication at Bethel in 1969 and was succeeded in 1974 by the *Tundra Drums.* These papers have recorded current and past Eskimo life through the printing of articles and photographs pertaining to the region, local history, biographical sketches of important persons, and present village conditions. In addition, the Yukon-Kuskokwim State Fair now well established at Bethel stresses local Eskimo activities, emphasizing especially crafts and sports. Special programs devoted to traditional and contemporary Yupik life, such as Ellangutnek Yugcetun Nitiliq (Yupik Awareness Week), also are offered at Bethel. Finally, the Bethel television and radio stations present programs in Yupik on a regular basis.

These developments, while deliberate, are diffuse; while individually organized, are poorly coordinated; and while conscious, are sometimes superficial. They contribute to local Eskimoness but are insufficient to satisfy the definition of a revitalization movement. This is because the goal of sustaining Eskimo culture is not their avowed purpose. Revitalization must be motivated by a strong desire for renewal of economic, political, social, or other aspects of a culture, and it must be led by members of the culture involved. The institution with the greatest potential for leading such a revitalization is the regional corporation, Calista, described previously (*see* Chapter 8), but it has not done so, possibly because it sees its primary function in a different light. Organized to administer local aspects of the settlement act, it does not view itself as an institution to perpetuate Eskimo culture.

Calista, the regional corporation established by ANCSA, includes in its membership all Kuskokwim Eskimos. Bringing village Eskimos together in an integrated business enterprise has been difficult because there has been no precedent, and Calista has struggled from the time of its inception. Over the years the incompetent and ineffective leaders of this corporation caused millions of dollars to be lost, and in the process they alienated the stockholders. The corporation likewise has been responsible for the emergence of a two-tiered social structure; for the first time, the people are divided into managers at one level and members at another.

Upriver Eskimos represent thirteen of the fifty-six original communities in Calista and about one-sixth of the membership, yet in many ways their interests have been subordinated to those of the Yukon-Kuskokwim delta Eskimos. In particular, the riverine Eskimos living in villages upstream from Bethel have found the corporation unresponsive to their needs. They feel that the corporation caters to delta Eskimos, who have been subject to fewer disruptive Western influences and have had a shorter period of contact than those along the Kuskokwim. These people remain more isolated, more dependent on local resources, and, as a partial result, more conservative.

Because of their dissatisfaction and desire to be part of a smaller group, the villagers from Lower Kalskag to Stony River Village organized as the Kuskokwim Corporation in 1977. With its small membership of about 2,200, this corporation of villagers living in a consolidated area has a sense of common ethnic and local identity, has been much better able to keep in touch with its shareholders, and has served members' needs more directly. Furthermore, the membership has profited from the many years of positive leadership provided by Nick Mellick, Jr., and Glenn Fredericks. The Kuskokwim Corporation, as an independent institution within the Calista Corporation area, controls the assets of member villages through the Kuskokwim Corporation itself and its subsidiaries. It has paid modest but rather frequent dividends and represents an example of a thus far successful organization created as a result of the ANCSA.

FUTURE PROSPECTS

The cultural future of Kuskokwim Eskimos defies prediction despite studies about the past and about present realities. Too many variables are involved to forecast long-term changes accurately. We can see that if the trends of the past are maintained, the distinctive riverine Eskimo way of living will most likely be lost. If, however, present-day Eskimo efforts to establish a political base are integrated into comprehensive revitalization programs, the Eskimo culture that has survived to this point could become the basis of a viable permanent one. In any event, we might well consider the economic basis for riverine Eskimo life as one of the factors certain to affect the future.

Local resources, such as fish, fur, minerals, and timber, represent a key component of the economic lives of these Eskimos. Trapping seldom is a primary activity, but fishing remains dominant. Despite considerable variability in the size of the annual salmon harvest, these fish are a reliable staple and a salable item. However, subsistence fishing has been affected in recent years by commercial salmon-fishing operations, which are profitable for relatively few individuals. Both cannot be maintained satisfactorily if the local population continues to increase and if the people continue to depend on salmon as a major item in their diet. The other major resources, minerals and timber, are not expected to become important because of extraction costs and environmental issues. Thus the riverine resource base currently utilized is narrow, and its economic value apparently will remain limited in the near future.

As dependence on local resources has diminished, the economy has been buttressed by expanding reliance on state and federal monies. Present indications are that external aid will continue, but at declining rates. State of Alaska oil revenues, which account for 85 percent of state funds, declined in the late 1980s, as did the oil revenues shared by the regional corporations according to terms of the settlement act. Calista's share of the latter monies is expected to be reduced by about one fourth.[12] Furthermore, the allotment of federal monies for social and other programs for Native Alaskans appears to have peaked. With increased concern over the federal deficit, fewer funds are available. Thus the outside support that has caused subsistence activities, a key aspect of Eskimo culture, to become less necessary may decline to the point that Eskimoness will become stronger by default.

The social factor most likely to affect the continuity of riverine Eskimo culture is population stability. It clearly is the villages, not the towns of Bethel and Aniak, that most emphatically sustain the Eskimo life-style. If villages continue to lose much of their core population, as they have in recent years, the effect on Eskimo cultural vitality will be decidedly negative. In 1986 a third of all the Upriver Eskimos who were members of the Kuskokwim Corporation did not live along the river.[13] Resident losses of this magnitude suggest that being a riverine Eskimo in the present environment is not a high priority for a significant portion of the population.

With respect to the people themselves, there is another factor of singular importance—the capacity of individuals to adjust to contemporary conditions. Problems of this nature are evidenced by suicide statistics, which are a widely accepted index to serious social stresses. For the Yukon-Kuskokwim area in 1985 the suicide rate was 55.5 per 100,000, five times the national rate; in nearly all cases alcohol was a contributing factor.[14] Other statistics that are equally alarming indicate the stressful conditions under which Native Alaskans live. In 1980 the arrest rate for Natives was more than three times that of non-Natives. The murder rate for Natives was twelve times higher than that for non-Natives, and rape statistics were seven times higher for Natives than for non-Natives. Furthermore, although Natives represented only 16 percent of the Alaskan population in 1980, they accounted for 30 percent of admissions to the Alaska Psychiatric

Institute.[15] In a recent study of drug use by Alaskan school children from the ages of ten to thirteen, including those at Bethel, it was found that nearly 50 percent had at least experimented with marijuana and about 18 percent with cocaine. In comparison a somewhat similar national survey yielded 27 and 7 percent respectively.[16] Finally, in the Lower Kuskokwim School District there were 17 reported cases of sexual assault on children in 1980 and over 140 cases in 1985, with many additional cases said to have gone unreported.[17] When these figures are combined, they indicate the severe stress many Eskimos undergo as they attempt to fit into their current cultural environment.

The "Akiachak Revolt"   Any successful revitalization movement characteristically originates within the culture involved and requires an unambiguous theme around which to emerge. Among riverine Eskimos control of the land clearly is the rallying point with the greatest potential to articulate Eskimoness. In this case the words *the land* identify far more than a physical entity; they encapsulate feelings about living along the river, pride in the past, and comfort in a unique cultural heritage. In short, to these people their relationship to the land symbolizes their ethnic identity. Therefore, their greatest hope for a future as Eskimos lies in a grassroots effort to gain control of the land and to use this control as the basis for reviving and sustaining other aspects of their culture. A land-based movement led to the formation of the Kuskokwim Corporation in 1977. A more recent organizational approach of a distinctly different nature has emerged at Akiachak, and because of its broader implications, it merits detailed review.

Akiachak was one of the three riverine villages to organize what was called a *tribal* government under the Indian Reorganization Act when it was extended to Alaska. Its first formal government, technically a village one, was recognized in 1948 by the Bureau of Indian Affairs and continued until 1974, when the residents elected to become a second-class city with a city council. The change was made because state and federal funds could be obtained as a result. However, the white population began growing, and by 1980 the Akiachak Eskimos realized this government structure would not be in their best interest if they became a minority. Because the tribal type of government by definition is controlled by the "Native Community," a return to it would insure complete Eskimo control. The Akiachak Eskimos also feared that they might lose their village lands if they did not make a concerted effort to protect them. Under the terms of the ANCSA, members of a village corporation could sell their stock to anyone after 1991. This meant that whites could then buy shares from stockholders and thereby gain ownership of the land. By transferring the ownership of stock, i.e., land titles, to a tribal government, the Eskimos hoped to retain full control over the land after 1991.

School administration had become another issue of concern to Akiachak Eskimos. When the BIA school was turned over to the state in 1985, it came under the jurisdiction of the Lower Kuskokwim Rural Attendance Area. Villagers knew, from the earlier experiences of other communities, that being within a regional school district meant comparatively little local control over the education process. They hoped that by establishing a tribal council government again, they could contract directly with the state to manage the local school.[18]

Law enforcement was another area of dissatisfaction for Akiachak Eskimos, who resented the power of the Alaska state troopers as well as their unannounced arrivals in the village. The Eskimos maintained that with a tribal government they should have full authority over local affairs. Furthermore, although Akiachak accepted a villager hired by the state in 1983 as a policeman (village public safety officer), he was terminated in 1985 by the IRA council as it sought to regain control over law enforcement.[19]

For these several reasons, in 1983, while the Eskimos were still a majority, the city council members resigned their posts, a special election was held, and Akiachak unilaterally withdrew from the status of a second-class city.[20] However, by mid-1986 the State of Alaska Local Boundary Commission, the body responsible for Alaskan municipalities, still declined to recognize Akiachak's tribal government. One result was that the villagers did not receive revenue-sharing funds from the state.[21] The status of Akiachak vis-à-vis the state has become less important than other aspects of the issue in more recent years.

The youthful leader of the Akiachak Revolt, Willie Kasayulie, who originally advocated local self-government, soon realized that a multi-village confederation would better accomplish his major goal of establishing Eskimo political power. Under his leadership, the Yupiit Nation, with its charter villages of Akiachak, Akiak, and Tuluksak, was founded in 1984. By late 1987 sixteen additional villages within the Calista Corporation, none of them members of the Kuskokwim Corporation, had joined the new nation.[22] Kasayulie envisions this confederation as ultimately controlling one or more quasi-reservations. To achieve legitimate authority over the land and its people, the Yupiit Nation is seeking congressional passage of a Yupiit Restoration Act to accomplish its purposes.[23]

Quite obviously the Yupiit Nation is on a collision course with the Calista Corporation.[24] Managers of the latter have a well-established vested interest in furthering regional priorities at the expense of village corporations or groups of villages such as the Kuskokwim Corporation and the Yupiit Nation. To date Calista management has resisted the efforts of some board members to challenge the Yupiit Nation by developing a parallel organization. However, the sovereignty movement must affect Calista in the long run since both cannot have control over the same region.[25]

The sovereignty movement in Alaska, best characterized by the Yupiit Nation, is in essence an attempt to ignore, at least for political purposes, the settlement act. It is an effort to retain control of the land, revitalize village government, and return to the basic goals of the IRA as it was extended to Alaska in 1936. Presently the most influential group of community leaders in the lower Yukon-Kuskokwim region is the Association of Village Council Presidents, which represents all fifty-six villages of the Calista Corporation. In 1986 the association elected Willie Kasayulie, the founder of the Yupiit Nation, chairman of its executive board.[26] This recognition of Kasayulie by the village council presidents was clear acknowledgment that his sovereignty movement had gained acceptance and momentum among leaders of the Eskimos throughout the region.

Just as the leaders of the sovereignty movement have attempted to ignore the settlement act, so have the Alaskan members of Congress attempted to ignore the sovereignty movement. When they are forced to consider it, they contend that sovereignty goals can be achieved within the terms of the settlement act.[27] However,

Kasayulie and his supporters reject this position. They seem to suspect that the congressional delegates are covering the situation with a smoke screen in the hope that the movement will dissipate.

Alaska Native Claims Settlement Act   The recent sovereignty movement is not alone in affecting the political future of people along the Kuskokwim. The other major factor is the ANCSA, with its well-established institutional basis. At the request of the international Eskimo organization the Inuit Circumpolar Conference, this act has been examined carefully in recent years by a Canadian justice, Thomas R. Berger. Berger visited sixty villages and held extensive meetings to solicit opinions about the act. He concluded that the framework of the act itself was badly flawed if it was meant to provide the land and reimbursement the Alaskan Natives rightfully deserved as original landowners. He notes that the corporations involved were not formed as a result of economic opportunities, as is the typical pattern, but were instead thrust on the Natives by Congress. In most settings and cases they cannot succeed because they were not established on a viable institutional foundation. He faults the act for weakening tribal governments, which he would strengthen by granting them ownership of much of the corporation land. Finally, Berger recommends strengthening the subsistence rights of the Native population since so much of their identity is based on this aspect of their lives.[28]

In 1986 many Native leaders, working through the major statewide organization, the Alaska Federation of Natives, urged the Alaskan delegates to Congress to seek revisions in the ANCSA to rectify what they consider to be unfairness in the original act. Proposed changes include the issuance of new stock to Natives born after the act was passed in 1971, an extension beyond 1991 of the protection from taxation afforded the corporations, and the right of shareholders to vote on whether stock would be offered to the public after 1991. Congress did not act on the proposals in 1986.[29]

By late 1987, Congress had again not acted on proposals to change the terms of the 1971 settlement act in a 1991 bill. The proposed changes were essentially the same as those considered the previous year, but in 1987 at the annual meeting of the Alaska Federation of Natives a major split developed. A proposal was made that the 1991 bill include a provision for "qualified transferee entities"; it would allow corporate assets to be transferred from Native corporations to local traditional councils, IRA councils, or nonprofit cooperatives. The proposal was rejected by the Alaska Federation of Natives. However, the Association of Village Council Presidents and the Tanana Chiefs Conference (representing forty-three interior Native villages) supported the provision and subsequently withdrew from the federation so that they could launch a new cover organization (the Alaska Native Coalition) to represent their particular interest. The membership of this new group comprises about half of the Native Alaskans covered by the settlement act. In essence, the split is between those who support the existing structure of the Native corporations and those who support more control of assets by local populations. To many, this means favoring the sovereignty movement.[30]

In 1988 Congress passed the Alaska Native Claims Settlement Act Amendments of 1987. One major amendment was to prohibit the sale of corporation stock to outsiders without approval by a majority of the stockholders in any particular corporation. Another was that underdeveloped corporation lands could neither be taxed or seized in the event of bankruptcy proceedings. The latter provision is designed to insure that subsistence activities on such land cannot be threatened. Furthermore, corporation shareholders now are permitted to issue new stock to eligible persons born after passage of the 1971 settlement act.[31]

Future Possibilities Passage of the 1988 amendments by Congress seems to insure continued Native ownership of corporation lands if the stockholders so desire. However, judgments made by the officers of the regional corporations soon after they were established have placed most of the shareholders in a difficult financial position. In general, decisions of the Calista Corporation board, advisors, and managers have brought this corporation to the brink of bankruptcy. The major Calista asset, the forty-five-million-dollar Sheraton Anchorage Hotel, was threatened with foreclosure in 1987 and sold for twenty million dollars, a substantial loss, in 1988.[32] As a result of this development and other indications of continuing mismanagement, at the 1987 annual meeting disgruntled stockholders attempted, unsuccessfully, to unseat virtually the entire board.[33]

Present indications are that many non-Native Alaskans who have been sympathetic to the special needs of Natives feel the original settlement act was sufficiently generous and additional concessions are either unnecessary or undesirable. Furthermore, non-Natives often resent the special treatment of natives with respect to their exploitation of fish and game. One result of this attitude is that state regulations have been encroaching steadily on what the Natives have regarded as their traditional right to fish and hunt. This may have become more possible as the proportion of Natives to the local Alaskan population has declined; the Native count is about 14 percent of the total. The fact that Alaskan delegates to Congress do not support many major changes in the settlement act, and adamantly oppose any sovereignty clauses, may reflect the minority position of Natives in the political decision-making process within the state.

Some Natives and non-Natives alike long have contended that the original settlement act was first and foremost an effort to assimilate Native Alaskans and that any other purported goals were in fact designed to fail. They point out that to expect villagers to be transformed overnight from subsistence hunters and fishermen and housewives into corporate managers and effective corporate members was a cruel hoax. However, while this pessimistic interpretation of the act seems valid in some respects, the results have not been consistently negative. Although some regional corporations are in deep financial trouble, others are reasonably successful. With respect to the Kuskokwim River Eskimos, the Kuskokwim Corporation is an example of how sound management practices by fishermen and housewives can have positive results. The success of this corporation thus far explains why the sovereignty movement has not appealed to the population of the central river as much as it has to those people farther downriver and beyond the Kuskokwim Corporation boundaries.

Two political institutions Eskimos along the Kuskokwim have created to pursue their own goals seem to provide alternative keys to the future. The way each institution remains viable under the settlement act may determine which has the opportunity to influence the Eskimos' future. The Kuskokwim Corporation (for villagers living from Lower Kalskag to Stony River Village) and the Yupiit Nation (for those from Bethel to Tuluksak) both have lasting control of the land as their primary goal. However, beyond that there are differences of critical importance to the perpetuation of Eskimo culture.

The most fundamental goal of the Kuskokwim Corporation has been to keep control over the land for the mutual benefit of members. Since the land gives these people their primary sense of identity, its importance is paramount. However, there are no strong indications that identification with the land has resulted automatically in the reviving of other aspects of traditional riverine Eskimo life. Instead, strong evidence exists to the contrary. As detailed previously, these Eskimos have become Christians, have adopted Western material culture, and are active participants in such government programs as health care, welfare, unemployment benefits, and social security. Numerous residents also are wage laborers and business persons. Village living no longer satisfies most of these Eskimos. In fact, by 1988 most villagers had either moved to Bethel or Aniak or had settled at places distant from the Kuskokwim. The Yupik language is not being taught to most Eskimo children, extended family ties are giving way to a focus on the nuclear family, young people often find the behavior of their elders irrelevant to the present, and alcoholism is a serious concern. Thus, despite its firm commitment to land control, the Kuskokwim Corporation has not developed effective and integrated institutional means to foster the identity of members as Eskimos. It is always possible, however, that continued Eskimo association with the land, if it remains strong enough, may become sufficient to perpetuate the Eskimo heritage.

For the Yupiit Nation members, control over the land for their benefit also is an overriding goal. Judging from the efforts by Akiachak Eskimos to gain control over their schools, law enforcement, local resources, and external funding, theirs is a reasonably well integrated effort to assert their cultural identity in varied positive ways. This clearly is the beginning of a revitalization movement.

When we consider the resistance to the Yupiit Nation by the Calista Corporation and by the Alaskan delegates to Congress, it is difficult to imagine how the goals of the nation's leaders can be achieved. Contrary to their present strategy, their best hope may be to work within the framework of the settlement act, despite the difficulties involved. Even if they are able to institute the changes they propose, many of the negative factors influencing the lives of Kuskokwim Eskimos as a whole apply to their membership. Although statistics for particular problems in specific villages are not readily available, information about Eskimos in this general area indicates that spouse abuse and especially child abuse are commonplace, the incidence of rapes is alarming, and rates of suicide and homicide are high. If the Yupiit Nation can succeed in fostering its current efforts to reassert Eskimo cultural identity and can at the same time reduce the problems of social disorganization currently affecting the population so adversely, it may indeed be able to point with pride to a renewed Eskimo culture along the Kuskokwim.

Commentary and Comparisons

The documentary sources on which this Upriver Eskimo ethno-history has focused are comprehensive in the sense that collectively they span the chronological period with no major gaps. Because of this, it has been possible to discuss each major development even though some sources are richer in detail than others. Accounts about these Eskimos early in their history are not nearly as full as might be hoped, and particulars about the fur trade in the nineteenth century are far from comprehensive. An Eskimo perspective could not be fully developed from the source material, despite a conscientious effort to supplement written records with data obtained orally. As a major documentary source, the Russian-American Company records are limited compared with those of the Hudson's Bay Company. Likewise information about the local variability in Kuskokwim Eskimo culture is uneven. These factors have defined the parameters of this study.

As a framework was sought for presenting the findings, two approaches focusing on lasting contacts between indigenous peoples and Westerners appeared useful and were considered carefully before being set aside. One of these, especially favored in studies about subarctic Indians, involves an identification of *eras* as major markers of far-reaching changes.[1] In the American subarctic the eras identified have been those of the fur trade, mission, and welfare-dependency. Each era is regarded as a largely self-contained stage covering a particular time span with respect to a specific population. As the Kuskokwim Eskimo findings were examined, an era approach proved inappropriate. A *fur trade era* among these Eskimos posed more problems than it solved. The fur trade dominated from proto-Russian times until after World War II, faded temporarily, and reemerged in some villages to become a significant, but not dominant, factor to this day. On the other hand, a *mission era* did not occur among Upriver Eskimos as a coherent temporal marker. The Russian Orthodox Church gained its greatest strength in *post*-Russian times, and Orthodox mission workers were never a dominant force, except perhaps from 1892 to the 1920s in the vicinity of Little Russian Mission. An era of Moravian mission dominance can be identifed readily for such lower river villages as Bethel and Akiak, but it existed only as far upriver as Tuluksak. Roman Catholics maintained a mission briefly at Ohagamiut and later established themselves elsewhere, but theirs always was a limited presence. Each of these Christianizing efforts was of unquestioned importance, yet it is difficult to isolate a mission era as a unified timespan. Likewise, a *welfare-dependency era* would vary widely by timespan and locality. That welfare dependency has been a major economic condition since World War II is undeniable, but the label does not, to my way of thinking, encapsulate the essence of what was happening at the time.

A second possible model for the presentation of contacts between indigenous peoples and Westerners is based on a *dependence theory,* with its emphasis on the collapse of the subsistence system supporting indigenous populations and their subsequent entry into the world market economy at the dependency level. This theory has been applied often to Third World peoples and to a lesser extent has provided a framework for American Indian ethnohistories.[2] It is not considered a very desirable basis from which to interpret the Kuskokwim Eskimo data for several reasons. The Eskimo subsistence system of old has retained a great deal of vitality into the present, especially with respect to fishing and hunting. These people have not been displaced from their homeland, been inundated by white settlers, nor had their traditional resource base destroyed. Although they have come to depend heavily on federal and state aid, this represents only one aspect of their lives and livelihoods. The economic and political situation that exacerbated dependency since the 1920s seemingly was resolved by the Alaska Native Claims Settlement Act of 1971, despite the many failings of this act. The Indian Self-

Determination and Education Assistance Act of 1975 was legislated specifically to reduce dependency on the federal government, and among Kuskokwim Eskimos it has been moderately successful. In recent years legal cases involving Indian sovereignty have been upheld often by the U.S. Supreme Court; these findings contribute to nondependency and a new sense of purpose among numerous Indian groups. The sovereignty movement emerging in Alaska during the early 1980s has been led by Kuskokwim Eskimos who hope to attain far greater control over their lives than they have had at any time in their historic past. A final objection concerns the dependency theory in general. It is becoming, or more realistically has become, a self-fulfilling prophesy as whites, especially some politicians and administrators, view Native Americans in its terms. Numerous groups, including some Kuskokwim Eskimos, devoutly seek an alternative way of life, but while they do so, the dependency model emphasizes their disadvantaged position.

As a means was sought to analyze the Kuskokwim findings and to compare them with ethnohistorical developments elsewhere, it became obvious that the identification of a single dominant and ongoing process to accommodate major changes was imperative. As noted in the introduction, my own observations, plus the study by James R. Gibson about supplying the Russian-American Company in Alaska, suggest the usefulness of *access* as an effective means by which to view culture change in this general region.[1]

Access, as used here, means the capacity to reach and subsequently frequent a locality. It is proposed that the comparative ease of access by Westerners to an area and their intensity in frequenting it establish the character of change occurring in the indigenous population. Without dependable access there obviously would be no lasting contacts with such peoples in their homelands. Intermittent and low intensity historic access leads to an environment in which changes of external inspiration probably will be superficial, whereas frequent and high intensity access creates one conducive to potentially far-reaching changes. The time frame, degree, and intensity of access by Westerners is, except as limited by unalterable geographical conditions, dependent on Western *goals*. Goals represent the singular or multiple purposes, or motivation, behind the presence of Westerners, whereas access is a factor affecting the ease or difficulty with which these goals can be attained.

Access is fundamentally dependent on regional and local geographical conditions, but other factors affect it as well. The farther an area is from the nearest established Western center, the greater the probable difficulty in gaining access to it. The means of travel available and other cultural conditions, such as the receptivity of an indigenous population to outsiders, are additional but secondary factors. Access changes by degree through time, typically becoming less difficult, which in turn facilitates culture change.

The nature of Western access to the Kuskokwim molded ethnohistorical developments among riverine Eskimos. Since 1830 the scope and intensity of access has changed dramatically, and this has led to major shifts in all aspects of Kuskokwim Eskimo life. Furthermore, the differential accessibility of particular localities within the region created a mulifarious pattern of change. In examining access to the Kuskokwim, my major focus is on habitual and normal access from a distance, not on unusual or trial trips or entry from nearby localities. The stages of access identified for the Kuskokwim are the following: *Exploratory access:* Geographical discovery and mapping of an area by Westerners. *Transient access:* Seasonal trips by Westerners into the region to launch the fur trade, during which temporary stations were founded. *Summer access:* The utilization of waterways to transport trade goods and supplies on an annual basis once, or more often, each year after year-round trading stations had been established. Only under temporary or extraordinary circumstances were trade items imported during the winter months. *Year-round surface access:* Travel by boat, ship, dog sled, or other surface means to facilitate trade, mining, mission, and other activities. Such access was restricted during breakup and freezeup periods, when travel for long distances was difficult if not impossible. *Year-round air access:* Scheduled air transportation throughout the year, as a highly reliable and rapid means of personal travel and for the shipment of mail and supplies.[4]

Major changes in Western goals appear to have introduced each new stage of access. *Exploratory access* was launched with Russian probes northward and most clearly began with the arrival of Cook's ships in Kuskokwim Bay (1778). It continued with the overland trip by the Ivanov party (early 1790s) and concluded with the inland journey to the Kuskokwim by Vasilev (1830). Geographical discovery was the goal of Cook, but for Ivanov, Vasilev, and other Russians their explorations were made to expand the fur trade. Vasilev's journey was especially notable because it established a route for reaching the Kuskokwim from the south. *Transient access* is represented by the fur-buying trips of Fedor Kolmakov and Semen Lukin, the founding of Kolmakovs and Lukins odinochkas, and the arrival of fur hunting parties (1832–40). The first phase of *summer access* began with the founding of Kolmakovskiy Redoubt (1841) and the supplying of this and secondary stations by kayaks and then by umiaks in the Russian period (1832–66) and by ships and umiaks in the American period (ca. 1870–1909).[3] A second phase of *summer access* came with the influx of gold seekers (1900–16), whose numbers led oceangoing vessels to sail as far as Bethel. Before long, riverboats began to transport freight along the river, a pattern that continues into the present. *Year-round surface access* began with the opening of the Iditarod Trail (1910–11) and the completion of the Alaska Railroad to the interior (1920–21); from the railroad a relatively short winter trail led to the upper Kuskokwim region. *Year-round air access* commenced when charter airlines began operations in the area on a regular basis (early 1930s) to serve traders, miners, and other travelers. Air transport expanded abruptly following World War II (ca. 1946), and since then reliable air cargo and passenger transport have combined to make the Kuskokwim readily accessible by air on a year-round basis.

Throughout these expanding stages of access, riverine Eskimos have continued to identify as Eskimos, albeit with less clarity over the years. For many, emotional bonds with their villages remain strong, and they continue to rely on the surrounding areas as a source of much of their livelihood. The insular nature of village life has continued and contributes to this retention of Eskimoness. The American educational system, despite its relative ineffectiveness in imparting Western knowledge, has taught these people how to deal with whites, especially administrators, while at the same time retaining primary identity with their own culture. The cultural renaissance introduced by the settlement act, the formation of the Kuskokwim Corporation and the Yupiit Nation, and a continuing emphasis on local resources are among the factors sustaining Eskimoness along the Kuskokwim despite expanded access and strong influences in the opposite direction.

To place the scope of what has occurred along the Kuskokwim among the Upriver People in a broader context, ethnohistorical developments among other Native Americans in the region need to be considered. Comparisons are preferably limited to people whose ethnohistorical data are most closely parallel, but in this case, reviewing accounts about other Eskimos and Indians indicated two major difficulties in selecting comparable studies. Foremost is the timespan involved. While the Kuskokwim study includes information from the earliest contact to the late 1980s, no other account covers as long a span nor deals as broadly with contemporary conditions. Second is the emphasis on access and goals in the Kuskokwim Eskimo presentation; these were not the focus in other studies. After examining varied accounts, those dealing with the Eastern Kutchin Indians, Nushagak Eskimos, and Anvik-Shageluk Ingalik Indians were chosen as providing the best comparative material.

Eastern Kutchin   Shepard Krech III examined the emergence of the fur trade among these Indians, especially between 1847 and 1853, but extending to 1860, and his findings have many parallels with early historical developments along the Kuskokwim.[6] Because of the limited time frame considered by Krech, it is not possible to make comparisons with respect to the varied stages of access, but the material is invaluable for comparisons about early access to a distant region and the establishment of trading stations.

Like the Kuskokwim Eskimos, the Eastern Kutchin received Russian goods along aboriginal trade networks before a local trading station was founded. The Peel River Post, which the Hudson's Bay Company established in their area in 1840, was the company's most remote station. This parallels the situation when Kolmakovskiy Redoubt was founded in 1841, becoming the most distant Russian-American Company redoubt. Each company held a monopoly on the local trade, and access to their stations posed major logistical problems for each. In general, the environmental settings were similar; the Peel and Kuskokwim rivers flow through coniferous forests and adjacent upland tundra areas exploited by the local people. In contrast, the Eastern Kutchin were more mobile than Kuskokwim Eskimos during most of the year, and they placed greater emphasis on hunting than on fishing.

Many of the similar developments at the post and redoubt can best be attributed to the inaccessibility of the respective stations. Each had few employees, and these men were isolated from contacts with other company employees for most of the year. As a result they were not in a position to dominate their clients because to do so might place their lives in jeopardy. The prolonged isolation made it difficult for some employees to remain obedient to company administrators; one response was the insubordination of workers to the local managers. The Russians soon resolved this difficulty by replacing Russian workers with creoles and Aglurmiut Eskimos, but the English did not make a similar adjustment. Food scarcity was commonplace at both stations. Neither company could import enough food to feed its employees adequately. Since the employees were unable to harvest enough fish and game locally to fully supplement their rations, they relied partially on their clients to provide food. Clients were helpful in maintaining the stations in another respect as well. Because of the distances involved from both stations to their supply centers, the agents depended on their customers to help transport goods. At the post credit for clients against future fur harvests is well documented, and it may have been available to customers at the redoubt. Finally, both stations were profitable operations, despite their remoteness.

Certain differences between redoubt and post activities had an effect on the trade. These may have been less dependent on access than on the particular situation in which the company found itself. The English relied on Indians as interpreters, whereas creole and Native employees at the redoubt fulfilled this function. Among the Eastern Kutchin, middlemen played an important role in the trade at the post, and interband hostilities influenced the trade. Neither factor was prominent in the redoubt trade at the time. Bloodshed between Eastern Kutchin and other ethnic groups was not common but did occur, whereas among Kuskokwim Eskimos, physical conflict with other Eskimos, the Aglurmiut, had been settled before the redoubt's establishment. Furthermore, guns were traded by the Hudson's Bay Company but not by the Russian-American Company. Finally, an exchange of local products was an intimate aspect of trade at the redoubt but does not appear to have taken place at the post.

Overall, certain parallels especially are notable. In his discussion of the early Eastern Kutchin trade, Krech emphasizes the innovative role of Indians at the Peel River Post; the same quality prevailed at Kolmakovskiy Redoubt with respect to Kuskokwim Eskimos. The Russian-American Company's reliance on a trade in local products to integrate its customers and increase the scope of its transactions may have been balanced at the English post by the use of Indians as interpreters and as middlemen in the trade. Because the supply problem was great for both stations, company agents at each had to devise means for provisioning and maintaining their stations, and clients had to devise ways to further their ability to trade. For both establishments during the years reported, accessibility was a key factor in the success or failure of the trade. This presumably was also true in later years.

Nushagak Eskimos The comprehensive ethnohistory about these Eskimos by James VanStone spans the period from European discovery to 1965.[7] In geographical outline the Nushagak and Kuskokwim riverine areas are similar. In both instances the bayside terrain is a flat, funnel-shaped alluvial deposit with shifting channels and tides that enter the lower rivers. Tundra vegetation extends up the lower rivers and gives way to spruce forests. Both rivers are navigable along their length by shallow-draft vessels, but the Nushagak is much shorter, being about 110 miles long. In both river systems tributary drainages provided valuable hunting and trapping grounds for local residents in the time period being considered. The flora and fauna are much the same with one major exception: the number of salmon spawning in the Nushagak drainage is far greater than in the Kuskokwim area.

Exploratory access began with Russian probes and most emphatically with the arrival of Cook's ships (1778). More directly pertinent to the fur trade were the overland explorations of the Korsakovskiy party (1818) sent to reconnoiter and select a station site for Russians seeking to expand their fur trade northward. As a result Alexandrovskiy Redoubt (modern Nushagak) was established by the Russian-American Company as its local center (1819). The absence of a *transient access* stage is explained by the relative ease with which the Korsakovskiy party reached the Nushagak area, the marginally acceptable anchorage found, and the ability of ships to supply the Nushagak post from Sitka or Kodiak directly, without cargo transfer. *Summer access* began when the redoubt was supplied by ship (1819) during its first year. Unlike conditions along Kuskokwim Bay, upper Nushagak Bay provided relatively safe anchorage near the shore. Summer access intensified after the first commercial salmon cannery was founded near Nushagak by Americans (1884). Since salmon runs are confined to the summer months, this was the season in which most outsiders sought access to the region. Unlike the Kuskokwim area, *year-round surface access* to the Nushagak never emerged because Western goals in the Nushagak region did not lead to its development. Gold seekers were drawn to the Kuskokwim throughout the year because placer mining operations require working during the winter months; in contrast, gold never has been found in significant quantities along the Nushagak drainage. The final stage, *year-round air access,* a much more recent development, began in the 1930s. As can be seen, the stages of access are fewer and more straightforward for the Nushagak than for the Kuskokwim. In brief, the Russian-American Company goal to establish its first Bering Sea drainage redoubt posed rela tively minor access problems compared with its later expansion into the Kuskokwim drainage. This might be expected to lead to a more successful trade venture in the Nushagak region, but as in dicated subsequently, the results were not that favorable.

As Nushagak and Kuskokwim Eskimo ethnohistorical developments are compared, numerous parallels reflect similar responses to Western influences. This is not surprising since the initial agent of change in both instances was the Russian-American Company. Major parallels include the peaceful launching of the fur trade and the emergence of the Orthodox religion as a dominant institution. The epidemics of smallpox in 1838–39 and influenza in 1900 had devastating biological and cultural impacts on both groups. A second outside influence in both areas was the Moravian Church; however, its missionaries withdrew from the Nushagak after a brief period (1886–1906), returning only much later (1950). Reindeer herding was introduced to both areas, but it was far less important in the Nushagak drainage. As along the Kuskokwim, the herding experiment in the Nushagak area had failed by the early 1940s. Whereas Bethel became the major urban and administrative center for the Kuskokwim region, the Dillingham-Kanakanak area emerged as the Nushagak center. Bethel and Dillingham-Kanakanak each had a hospital, numerous well-stocked stores, missions, a major airport, and many administrative offices. Both attracted Eskimos from adjoining villages as temporary or relatively permanent residents. Each similarity between the two was a direct or indirect product of Westerners seeking to achieve their goals.

Since the 1880s the external factor with the most far-reaching impact on Nushagak Eskimo life unquestionably has been the commercial salmon fishing industry; its influence on Kuskokwim Eskimos has been minor by comparison. Commercial fishermen were attracted to Bristol Bay because the adjacent watershed had the greatest red salmon runs in the world, along with significant runs of other salmon species. The first cannery opened at Kanulik, near Nushagak, in 1884. The commercial fishing season rapidly became the major focal point of each economic year. In the early 1900s ten canneries operated along upper Nushagak Bay, and by 1920 twenty-five canneries functioned along Bristol Bay. The latter number probably was the maximum since catches declined in the following years, but commercial salmon fishing has remained a major focus in the lives of Nushagak Eskimos into the present.

From their inception the canneries had a great impact on local Eskimos, but the direct involvement of these people evolved slowly. Initially the fishermen were white, and nearly all cannery workers were imported Chinese laborers supervised by whites. Eskimos were not considered to be dependable employees and were hired only under extenuating conditions. Despite the absence of long-term employment opportunities during the earliest years, Eskimos camped near the canneries each summer. They were attracted to the cannery sites during the fishing season to work at odd jobs and to obtain the fish wasted by the processors; this they prepared as winter food. By 1905 Eskimos were being hired in increasing numbers to supplement the Chinese labor force when salmon catches peaked and the regular workers could not process all the fish.

The labor-intense process of canning salmon by hand changed in the 1910s when a machine, the "Iron Chink" was introduced to behead, clean, and split the fish; this reduced the demand for labor by about three-quarters. The workers continued to be primarily imported contract laborers until World War II, when these employees were unavailable and were replaced by Eskimos living in southwestern Alaska. A few Eskimos were employed as fishermen by canneries by about 1930, but it was not until the early 1960s that they commonly worked on fishing boats. By this latter date the vast majority of Nushagak Eskimos were employed by the canneries either as workers or as fishermen. This was in marked contrast with the commercial exploitation of salmon along the Kuskokwim, which was just beginning at that time and has never approached the intensity of Nushagak operations.

Other major differences separating developments of Western origin in the Nushagak and Kuskokwim areas are primarily the product of differential accessibility to the respective regions. For example, oceangoing vessels sailed to the Nushagak post in 1819, whereas it was not until 1905 that they began to anchor at Bethel. The effect of the influenza epidemic of 1918–19 on the two regions was directly related to access. When influenza spread to the Nushagak region, it killed more local Eskimos than did any other historic epidemic. This epidemic did not reach the Kuskokwim since there was time enough, because of the distances involved, to impose an effective quarantine on the region.

Major differences in Western goals for exploiting the respective regions centered about gold and salmon. Because prospectors searching the Nushagak drainage did not find gold in any quantity, their influence was both minor and fleeting. However, gold seekers in the Kuskokwim region made a great impact on local Eskimo life, albeit it indirect, from 1900 to 1916. Cannery jobs introduced Nushagak Eskimos to wage labor by the early 1900s on an ever-expanding basis, whereas for Kuskokwim Eskimos wage labor did not become a realistic possibility for most persons until the 1940s, when they began to work in the Bristol Bay area canneries. Most Kuskokwim Eskimos earned comparatively little money from cannery work, an average of $450 a sea-

son in the mid-1950s, becuase they usually held low-paying jobs.
By comparison, at that time some Nushagak Eskimos were commercial fishermen and were earning far more. In 1964 most
Nushagak Eskimo fishermen averaged about $3,250 for a season,
and an exceptional individual might earn as much as $15,000. In
addition, Nushagak Eskimos, especially those along the bay, had
long before undergone a major shift in residence as they moved to
cannery sites, where they lived throughout the year.

By the 1960s eight generations of Nushagak Eskimos had been
exposed to direct Western influences, and cannery operations
dominated the lives of the three most recent ones. The major historic epidemics, especially the 1918 one, likewise had disrupted
their cultural identity as Eskimos and favored cultural discontinuities. By the 1960s most of these people did not look like
Eskimos, and the majority of middle-aged and younger persons
spoke English, not Yupik. Eskimo material culture had disappeared long before, as had their customary political institutions
and religious ceremonies. Apart from subsistence activities, traditional Nushagak Eskimo culture was gone.[8] In comparative
terms, by the 1960s Nushagak Eskimo culture had become far
more Americanized than had Kuskokwim Eskimo culture.

In the early 1980s two studies were made about the people of
the Bristol Bay region as "Alaska Outer Continental Shelf Region" reports for the federal government.[9] These works, which
focus largely on contemporary socioeconomic life, emphasize
that among Nushagak Eskimos traditional subsistence activities
continue to make a substantial and stable contribution to the
economy. They are supplemented, to a greater or lesser extent depending on the community involved, by commercial fishing,
other cash-producing labor, and various forms of state and federal aid. Furthermore, the authors note that extended kinship ties
remain the most important socially integrative factor. Yet it does
not appear that a cultural renaissance has occurred in the Nushagak area in the aftermath of the settlement act, as was found
among Kuskokwim Eskimos, nor has the sovereignty movement
had a clear or compelling impact on the Nushagak area Eskimos.
Thus the two aspects of Kuskokwim Eskimo culture that hold the
greatest promise for their lasting identity as Eskimos are not evidenced in the Nushagak sector.

Anvik-Shageluk Ingalik Indians   The study about these people by VanStone covers the period from before their discovery by the Russians until 1935 and is the most comprehensive ethnohistory about a group of Alaskan Athapaskans.[10] These Indians lived along a sector of the lower Yukon river where the fauna, flora, and landscape are much the same as reported for the Kuskokwim Eskimo area. Although the Yukon River is much broader than the Kuskokwim and no Kuskokwim tributary meanders as far through a vast lowland region as the Innoko River drainage exploited by the Yukon area Ingalik, these and other geographical differences are not great. In aboriginal times salmon was a staple in each area, other fishes were important, and big game hunting was prominent. In general, and often in detail, the Anvik-Shageluk Inaglik seasonal round was similar to that described for Kuskokwim Eskimos. In addition, these Indians usually were on friendly terms with Eskimos living farther down the Yukon and had absorbed much of their culture, just as was the case for the Georgetown Ingalik in their contacts with Kuskokwim Eskimos.

Among the Yukon area Ingalik *exploratory access* began with the travels of the Ivanov party (early 1790s), but the travels of Andrei Glazunov (1833–34, 1835) effectively opened the lower Yukon region to Russian colonization. A stage of *transient access* was not represented because of the ease with which the Russians were able to establish themselves in the general region. Mikhailovskiy Redoubt (St. Michael) was founded along Norton Sound (1833), and soon thereafter an odinochka was built at Ikogmiut (Russian Mission) along the lower Yukon (1836). The Anvik-Shageluk Ingalik traveled to these stations and to Kolmakovskiy Redoubt to trade. The first local trading post was built at Anvik during the early American period (1869). A stage of *year-round surface access* was not represented among the Yukon Ingalik; the Iditarod Trail passed to the north of their area and does not seem to have had an impact on their lives. Since VanStone's study ends in 1935, *year-round air access* (early 1930s) is not detailed in his report.

The direct Siberian trade had a profound effect on the Yukon Ingalik long before local contacts were made by the Russians. VanStone suggests that their aboriginal subsistence round had been modified in protohistoric times to include the intense harvest of beaver for the Siberian trade. Furthermore, the data suggest that before direct Russian contact, the Yukon Ingalik settlements had been relocated to optimize their opportunities in the Siberian-Alaskan trade. After Russian traders were established in the region, these Indians became increasingly dependent on imports. Since they received little for their furs and the cost of trade goods was high, the Indians were forced to work harder to obtain imports they desired. Thus it would appear that in late prehistoric and early historic times contacts among the Yukon Ingalik were far greater than among Kuskokwim Eskimos. These Indians were predisposed to intensify their quest for furs, which was not true of Kuskokwim Eskimos for a similar time span.

Soon after the Russians had established themselves in the region, the 1838–39 smallpox epidemic probably led to the deaths of two-thirds of these Indians. Somewhat later an Orthodox church mission was founded in nearby Yukon Eskimo country at Russian Mission (1845); the missionaries stationed there, Netsvetov and Illarion, traveled widely among the Indians to win converts. The Indians initially feared baptism because they incorrectly associated the ritual with smallpox, but their resistance eventually gave way, and most of them appear to have been baptized. However, just as among Kuskokwim Eskimos, there is little evidence that the Anvik-Shageluk Ingalik understood more than the rudiments of Christianity by the time Alaska was sold to the United States.

Following the sale of Alaska, a creole, John E. Orlov, managed the Orthodox church at Russian Mission and served as its priest from 1876 to 1892. Visits by Indians to the mission and yearly trips by the missionary to Anvik-Shageluk Ingalik villages were the Indians' primary contact with the Orthodox faith. By the turn of the century Orthodoxy was declining among most of them. Another factor that made it difficult for the Orthodox church to sustain its influence was competition from other missions. An Episcopalian mission was established at Anvik in 1887, and the Roman Catholics founded a mission at Holy Cross in 1888. Competition between these missions understandably was keen; in general, the Catholics were more successful as a result of their stronger support base and the number of missionaries they fielded at any one time.

As the only major waterway from the Bering Sea leading deep into the interior of northwestern North America, the Yukon River became the major historic access route into this sector. The Russians supplied their lower river station by umiak from St. Michael; thus there were no navigational hazards comparable to supplying the Kuskokwim from the sea. During the early American period the Yukon trade expanded abruptly with the arrival in 1869 of the *Yukon,* the first steam-driven riverboat in the northern Alaskan river trade. The *Yukon* towed barges of goods to lower river posts, which abruptly increased the quantity of imports, enabling local traders to compete more effectively with the direct Siberian trade. The trade expanded on a modest scale until 1887 when steamboats became more numerous and began to travel farther upriver. The traffic increased steadily until the discovery of gold in the Klondike region in 1896 brought an abrupt intensification.

Before the 1880s the Yukon Ingalik were receiving trade goods and imported edibles in great quantities in exchange for furs. The concurrent Kuskokwim trade was miniscule by comparison. However, the number of furbearers along the lower Yukon declined dramatically by the late 1880s, and big game became scarce for a multitude of reasons. The local Indians, seeking alternative income sources, began to work for whites as they passed through the area on their way to the upper Yukon goldfields.

The best access route to the Klondike goldfields was by ship from Seattle to St. Michael and by riverboat up the Yukon. This traffic began shortly before the turn of the century, and by 1906 there were thirty riverboats and forty barges operating along the Yukon. The Fairbanks area gold rush (1903) increased these numbers, but more important to the Yukon Ingalik were the local gold rushes, one into the upper Innoko River area (1906) and another to the Iditarod River region (1908). These rushes and the decline in the fur trade rapidly changed the economic lives of the Yukon Ingalik, who focused on the gold rushes for nearly a generation. Men worked on riverboats as pilots and deckhands, cut cordwood as boat fuel, and freighted for miners as well as working for them in other ways. Whites bought dried salmon as dog food, and a considerable market developed for locally made artifacts, such as sleds, snowshoes, toboggans, fur garments, and curios. By the early 1920s the economic impact of these activities had passed, but while they had been so intense, the Yukon In-galik had become far less dependent on their modified traditional subsistence round and well integrated into a cash economy. While Kuskokwim Eskimos also were affected by gold seekers, their contacts with them were not only of shorter duration but were far less intense.

For the Anvik-Shageluk Ingalik the era of rapid change launched by the gold rushes continued into the 1930s and affected most aspects of village life. Anvik and Holy Cross, each the site of a mission, eventually became home to all the Ingalik living along the Yukon proper, which suggests that these missions had a profound impact on the lives of their converts. The workers at both missions found that activities of shamans and the persistence of the old ceremonial cycle were the greatest barriers to Chris-tianization, and these did not diminish until about 1930. Neither mission encouraged local Indian leadership for its churches, un-like among the Kuskokwim Eskimos where the Moravians and Orthodox fostered the development of leadership within villages. The U.S. Bureau of Education placed its emphasis on day schools to Americanize children, and mission day schools were replaced by those of the bureau in 1895 at Anvik and Holy Cross. Another bureau school opened at Shageluk in 1910. The Catholics and Episcopalians alike placed their major educational emphasis on boarding schools since these schools provided the more con-trolled environment they preferred. The Anvik boarding school operated almost continuously from 1887 to 1935; its students were Ingalik but were few in number, possibly averaging about ten a year. By contrast the Catholic boarding school at Holy Cross, which opened in 1889, flourished through the 1930s. It had 80 students by 1891 and 170 by 1927, yet most of these stu-dents were not Ingalik. Along the Kuskokwim the Moravians had a small-scale boarding school, involving few students, during the early years of their mission and an orphanage that began func-tioning in 1926. During the 1950s it was acknowledged widely by Native Alaskans and whites along the lower Yukon and Kus-kokwim rivers that the Roman Catholic boarding school at Holy Cross provided students with a superior American-style educa-tion; the English-speaking ability of these students was especially notable.[11]

Further affecting this period of change was the series of epidemics occurring between 1898 and 1901. It hit the Anvik-Shageluk Ingalik especially hard, with the influenza epidemic being the most severe one. Holy Cross lost nearly 50 percent of its people between these years, and the influenza epidemic alone killed 20 percent of the people at Anvik. General health care was provided by the Catholic and Episcopalian missionaries, most of it on a nonprofessional basis. A small hospital was built at Holy Cross in 1911, and a medical doctor was stationed in the area by this time. In 1926 a riverboat began serving as a floating clinic; it operated each summer into the 1930s, when increased air service provided a means for transporting serious cases to a hospital at Tanana. For the time period involved, medical care for the Yukon Ingalik seems to have been much the same in quality and intensity as that reported for Kuskokwim Eskimos.

Reindeer herding was introduced among the Yukon Ingalik during this period, but it met with little success. The Catholic mission at Holy Cross received a herd in 1904 or 1905, but the missionaries were unable to recruit Indians as apprentice herders. The Catholics soon became disillusioned with the enterprise but had a difficult time extricating themselves from their responsibility; the animals had disappeared by the late 1930s. Reindeer herding was a temporary success at Shageluk, but there too the herd disappeared by the 1930s. Thus the reindeer industry was of marginal significance among these Indians compared to the relative vigor of the enterprise in the 1910s and 1920s among Kuskokwim Eskimos.

VanStone characterized the cumulative result of Anvik-Shageluk historic contacts with Westerners by 1935 as "deculturative rather than acculturative." [12] To support this conclusion he noted that the traditional religion was gone and had not been replaced by locally supported Christian churches. Health, education, and economic development programs by the government had displaced traditional Indian and subsequent mission involvements but had hardly begun to achieve any of their established goals. The emphasis on trapping as a means to obtain merchandise and imported foods in earlier times had destroyed the subsistence round of old, and as the area became trapped out, no reliable cash-producing alternative emerged. Long-term economic stability was best reflected in subsistence fishing, which had been maintained and now helped to buffer these people from severe hardship. Their active participation in the gold rushes, providing services to gold seekers, had proved to be advantageous in the short-term but not in the longrun. Reflecting on the effect of the gold rushes, VanStone wrote, "Their subordinate role as second-class citizens in their own environment was clearly established at this time."[13] In contrast, among Kuskokwim Eskimos subsistence fishing and trapping remained dominant, despite fluctuations, into the 1930s and later. As a result, they did not experience the deculturative trend identified by VanStone for the Yukon area Ingalik.

Access and Goals   The preceding comparisons of long-term ethnohistorical developments among the Kuskokwim Eskimos, Nushagak Eskimos, and Anvik-Shageluk Ingalik Indians indicate many close parallels, as well they should. These three people not only are geographically near one another, but their habitats are similar, they have shared the same subsistence orientations, and they have exhibited other close cultural ties. Yet substantial differences with far-reaching implications prevailed among them by the late 1930s. Comparative accessibility by Westerners to the people in their respective areas seems to account for the major differences.

To illustrate the critical nature of access, we may for the moment assume that a hypothetical area in the American north was readily accessible to the agents of a trading company that sought to provision a new station at a high and consistent level. Under these favorable circumstances, the institutional basis for developing the trade presumably could be transferred from an old station to a new one without any major changes in the status or role behaviors of its employees; furthermore, clients would be dealt with in standardized and familiar ways. Given this situation, the indigenous people would be the ones required to make the greatest adjustments, changing their behavior to profit from the new situation. Conversely, if access was difficult, creating a low level of maintenance, major adjustments would be expected by company agents; this would diminish the scope of change required on the part of clients. In sum, difficult access is conducive to a slow rate of change among local peoples. Ready access disrupts their culture more abruptly, leaving them bereft of the old before they can settle comfortably into the new.

As has been demonstrated, the remoteness of the Peel River Post among the Eastern Kutchin and Kolmakovskiy Redoubt among the Kuskokwim Eskimos required greater compromises by company employees than by their Native American customers. However, among the Anvik-Shageluk Ingalik, protohistoric and early historic access was far less difficult. Indirect Siberian trade via Koyukuk Indians and coastal Eskimos along Norton Sound had been extensive enough to modify the aboriginal subsistence round long before direct Russian contacts. During the Russian period, the supply line to the major coastal station, St. Michael, posed no major barriers to the entry of Western imports. VanStone stresses the great dependence of these Indians on trade goods and imported foods as the Russian period drew to a close.[14] The Nushagak Eskimo post at Nushagak, which was supplied directly by ship, also was able to import adequate goods for the trade; its decline in importance came primarily because the direct Kuskokwim trade soon offered more furs for exchange. The Anvik-Shageluk trade was more intense than that on the Kuskokwim, again because of the difference in accessibility. The companies involved thus had a differential capacity to supply their stations. Developments during this period were mirrored in the trading networks during the early American period in the respective areas. Although traders were the foremost agents of Western change, missionaries, administrators, and other outsiders were faced with access problems of a similar nature, depending on the sector involved. As a result, until the advent of reliable air travel the Kuskokwim Eskimos, and presumably the Eastern Kutchin, were required to make fewer compromises than were the Nushagak Eskimos and the Anvik-Shageluk Ingalik.

It is now pertinent to consider a further aspect of the impact of access: If differential access has been critical historically for the groups considered, how is it reflected in contemporary conditions? A satisfactory response is not possible because the post-1965 information about Nushagak Eskimos is sketchy, and no studies exist about the Anvik-Shageluk Ingalik after 1935. However, pre-1935 information about all three peoples is suggestive.

By 1935 major differences in the settlement pattern of these

Eskimos and Indians prevailed, indicating a differential impact by Westerners. After the Episcopal and Catholic missions were established along the Yukon, Ingalik villages along the river proper were abandoned as their inhabitants moved to one mission site or the other. This was not true, however, for Ingalik along the Innoko River, where the mission influence was not nearly as strong. Among Nushagak Eskimos, the introduction of canneries brought a relocation of villages along Nushagak Bay; as canneries moved, so did the people. Villages along the Nushagak River itself were more remote and less affected by canneries, though many of their residents were drawn to bayside cannery communities on a seasonal basis. Neither the Yukon Ingalik nor the Nushagak Bay patterning prevailed along the Kuskokwim. Most Kuskokwim villages were relocated as a result of local changes in the habitat or epidemics, and the new villages, which were similar to the old ones, were distinctly Eskimo in character. The only notable exception was Bethel; because of Western developments there, it began to attract numerous Eskimo residents by about 1950. Kuskokwim Eskimo settlements usually have retained their traditional character more than those of the Nushagak Eskimos or the Yukon Ingalik, which began to change dramatically in the early 1900s.

The time at which far-reaching economic changes reached the three groups has led to a differential rate of Americanization among them. The shift from barter to a cash economy, clearly a major marker of Americanization, had begun among the Ingalik by 1900 and among the Nushagak Eskimos by the early 1900s. However, the intense involvement of Kuskokwim Eskimos in a cash economy is largely a post-1940 development. Thus a span of about two generations separated the Kuskokwim group from the others in this respect.

If comparative access is as important as has been maintained, one would expect that for each of the three peoples considered, the residents of the least accessible villages would be the ones least Americanized. We do not know about the Anvik-Shageluk Ingalik in this regard for the recent past. Likewise information about various modern Nushagak Eskimo villages is not sufficient to validate differences among villages depending on their location. For the Kuskokwim there is a detailed study by Susan

Charnley about the economy at Sleetmute in 1982–83.[15] Sleet-mute is the Kuskokwim Eskimo village most remote from the Bethel center and from the more secondary center of Aniak. Charnley found that the Sleetmute residents did not participate in commercial salmon fishing along the river, nor were they employed for wages on a regular basis; trapping was quite important in their economic lives. Twenty-one percent of the households identified with the village did not actually live there but instead maintained single-family hamlets in the area throughout the year, a pattern that was not uncommon along the river earlier in this century. Another 29 percent lived at trapping camps throughout the winter and at Sleetmute during the summer. This indicates that the economic focus at Sleetmute is probably more tradition-ally oriented than that of other contemporary riverine villages, but systematic comparative information for the 1980s is not available. The contrast between Sleetmute and Aniak or Bethel is obvious, however, and would seem to verify the effect of comparative accessibility on particular Kuskokwim populations.

Finally, and most importantly, it is among Kuskokwim Eskimos that a sense of the past extending into the present is most evident. The creation of the Kuskokwim Corporation is one example of a creative Kuskokwim Eskimo response to furthering their identity as Eskimos. There are no counterparts for this among the Nushagak Eskimos or the Yukon area Ingalik. Likewise, it is among Kuskokwim Eskimos that the sovereignty movement has its deepest roots. This is again a novel local approach to retaining their ethnic identity, one that has met persistent opposition from Alaskan politicians and, furthermore, is not supported by the Yukon area Ingalik or the Nushagak Eskimos.

Notes

Abbreviations in Notes

DRHA   Documents Relative to the History of Alaska, 1936–1938.

PSPG   *Proceedings of the Society of the United Brethren for Propagating the Gospel among the Heathen . . .* (year).

RAC:CS   Russian-American Company, Communications Sent . . . (volume, number, date).

Introduction

1. The Eskimo values identified are based largely on observations by Oswalt and others in the 1950s and on statements by Ann Fienup-Riordan (1982: 254–61) about the traditional behaviors of Kuskokwim Eskimos and those living to the west.

2. The origins of ethnohistory are summarized by William C. Sturtevant (1966) and Karl H. Schwerin (1976). As a topical focus, ethnohistory began to crystallize as a result of the Ohio Valley Historical Indian Conference in 1954, which gave rise to the American Indian Ethnohistoric Conference in 1956; during the latter year the journal *Ethnohistory* was founded.

3. Statements about the nature of ethnohistory are included in articles by Wilcomb E. Washburn (1961), William N. Fenton (1962), Robert C. Euler (1972), James Axtell (1979), and Bruce G. Trigger (1986).

4. Richard M. Dorson 1961:16.

5. Fienup-Riordan (1983:193).

6. Ibid., 1983.

7. Crow Village was excavated by Oswalt and James VanStone (1967).

8. Kolmakovskiy Redoubt was excavated by Oswalt (1980a).

9. As Fenton observed (1962:2), "Ethnohistory seems to be an approach and not a discipline—a way of getting at certain problems in culture history."

10. James R. Gibson (1976).

11. Ibid., 1976:216.

12. Shepard Krech III (1976).

13. Robert McGhee (1984).

14. L. H. Neatby (1984).

15. Edward H. Spicer (1962).

Chapter 1

1. Miller Christy 1894: i.
2. James Cook 1967: v. 3, pt. 1, pp. ccxxi–ccxxii.
3. Ibid., 349–51.
4. Ibid., 400–01.
5. Ibid, 402–03.
6. Lydia T. Black 1984:24–27.
7. Helge Larsen and Froelich Rainey 1948:83–84.
8. Dorothy J. Ray 1975:101–02.
9. *United States Coast Pilot 9 Alaska* 1955:519–21.
10. J. C. Beaglehole 1974:613.
11. Steven A. Jacobson 1984:214.
12. Hana U. Lane (1985:628) is the source for the areas and discharge rates for the Kuskokwim and Yukon rivers and the length of the Yukon River. The length of the Kuskokwim and later references to distances between points along this river are based on *Annual Salmon Management Report 1978 Kuskokwim District* 1978:17.
13. *Yukon and Kuskokwim River Basins, Alaska* 1964:35, 97.
14. Kuskokwim area vegetation types are summarized by Leslie A. Viereck and Elbert L. Little, Jr. (1972). The distribution of permafrost is set forth by Philip R. Johnson and Charles W. Hartman (1969:22–23).
15. In this presentation the Kuskokwim River is divided into three segments. The lower river is identified as the sector between Eek Island and the village of Kalskag; the central river is from above Kalskag to Stony River Village, and the upper river extends from there to the headwaters. Furthermore, the *Yukon-Kuskokwim Delta* area is identified as being immediately below the town of Bethel along the Kuskokwim and below Marshall along the Yukon River.
16. Johnson and Hartman 1969:78–79.
17. *Climatography of the United States No. 86–43* 1965:2, 18, 35, 55.
18. Lavrentiy A. Zagoskin (1967:252) reports that the fire at Kolmakovskiy Redoubt occurred in 1843, but Russian records suggest that it probably was in 1842 (RAC:CS, v. 21, no. 549, Sept. 25, 1842).
19. Forest fires seem to have been especially destructive in 1911 when John H. Kilbuck noted that "this year's fires have covered thousands of acres of timber and moss country below and above Georgetown" (Fienup-Riordan 1987a:479).
20. Governor, Alaska 1931:85.
21. Edith Kilbuck letters to J. Kilbuck, Aug. 7, 8, 1911; Ferdinand P. von Wrangell 1980:64.
22. *PSPG* 1891:40, 43.
23. Sleetmute is spelled with "mute," meaning "the people of," rather than with the more widely accepted "miut" because the former suffix appears in the spelling for the post office. In 1830 large caribou herds were reported along the river without reference to specific localities (Wrangell 1980:64). Zagoskin (1967:252, 253, 266) is the source for their distribution along the central river in 1844.

24. *Iditarod Pioneer* Oct. 9, 1910; E. Kilbuck journals, Mar. 23, May 2, 1887.

25. O. J. Murie 1922.

26. Edward H. Hosley 1966:38; Zagoskin 1967:266.

27. From Ketchikan to Barrow Apr. 21, 1941.

28. C. E. Atkinson, J. H. Rose, and T. O. Duncan 1967.

Chapter 2

1. The aboriginal Eskimo population figures cited here and elsewhere are provisional and based on the findings of Oswalt (1979:311–14, Map 1). The 51,000 total probably is best considered as a minimal number.

2. The pioneer Moravian missionary John H. Kilbuck (Fienup-Riordan 1988:5) distinguished between the Downriver and Upriver peoples based on information he obtained from them from 1885 to 1899. Anne Shinkwin and Mary Pete (1984:97) report alternative subgroups of Kuskokwim Eskimos based on fieldwork in 1981 and 1983.

Ethnologists traditionally have designated major Eskimo population segments as *tribes*. A tribe in a strict sense is a group of people with a distinct name, dialect, and well-defined territory. Eskimo tribes are best regarded as somewhat tenuous ethnological constructs rather than as meaningful socio-political units. Dissatisfaction with Eskimo tribal designations led Joan B. Townsend (1973: 409, fn. 2) and Ernest S. Burch, Jr. (1975:10–13; 1980:258–62) to apply the concept of *society* to smaller groups within *tribes*. Each society is regarded by Burch as an autonomous aboriginal socio-territorial unit with a distinct dialect, one or more bases from which members ranged, a distinctive annual round, and a tendency toward endogamy; a society did not necessarily have a name. This framework by Townsend and Burch has been well received and is applied to Kuskokwim Eskimos by Shinkwin and Pete (1984).

3. On a distributional map for aboriginal Alaskan Eskimo groups (Oswalt 1979, Map 1), the Kuskokwim Eskimos collectively are reported as the Kuskowagamiut (Kusquqvamiut), their own generic designation for themselves. However, the 1829 travel journal of the Russian explorer Vasilev indicates that the Kiatagmiut subgroup then found in the Nushagak drainages had the same name as those living from Bethel to Kolmakovskiy along the Kuskokwim (VanStone 1988). Thus the Upriver Eskimos of the Kuskokwim and the Nushagak Eskimos were once one people.

4. In 1830 Vasilev made a hasty exploration of the Kuskokwim Eskimo area and is quoted as reporting a population ranging up to 7,000 (RAC:CS, v. 7, no. 257, Oct. 5, 1830). Ivanov, who traveled along the central portion of the Kuskokwim in the early 1790s, likewise reported up to 7,000 people along the Tutna River, an Indian designation for the Kuskokwim, and stated that there were forty-four villages (Gavriil I. Davydov 1977:201). The population estimate by Vasilev was disputed by Zagoskin (1967:308, fn.), who reached the river in 1843 but was familiar only with the central sector. Furthermore, Zagoskin's observations were made shortly after the 1838–39 smallpox epidemic had resulted in a dramatic population decline. The magnitude of the

population reduction following this epidemic is suggested in figures for the village of Ohagamiut. Ivanov estimated their number as over 200 in the 1790s (Davydov 1977:201), whereas 61 lived there in 1842–44 (Zagoskin 1967:306). Considering this difference, the figure of 7,000 total from the 1790s to 1830 may not be unreasonable.

5. This account about Kuskokwim Eskimos stresses the Upriver People, but most sources do not distinguish between them and the Downriver People. The ethnographic data in this chapter are drawn largely from the 1830 observations by Vasilev as reported by Wrangell (1980:63–68), the 1842–44 travel account by Zagoskin (1967), and especially a manuscript by J. Kilbuck (Fienup-Riordan 1988:2–28) based on observations from 1885 to 1899. In lesser ways field notes collected by Oswalt from 1953 to 1979 have contributed to the data base. An additional source for particulars of village living is the site report about excavations at Crow Village, which was occupied during the Russian and American eras (Oswalt and VanStone 1967). Comments about the context of mask use are from Hans Himmelheber (1987) based on his fieldwork in 1936–37.

6. Morris Swadesh 1951:67.

7. Swadesh 1962:1268.

8. Jacobson 1984:1, 28.

9. Hosley 1968:6–11.

10. Townsend 1979.

11. Wrangell 1980:59–61; Zagoskin 1967:243–44.

12. Townsend 1979:160–62.

13. Wendell H. Oswalt and James W. VanStone 1967:47.

14. Zagoskin 1967:222.

15. Fienup-Riordan (1987b) presents a detailed discussion of dance masks among Kuskokwim Eskimos and others living to the west, based largely on ethnographic data collected in recent years.

Chapter 3

1. Precisely where the war began is unknown, but Edward W. Nelson (1899: 328) states that it was near Ikogmiut (Russian Mission) along the Yukon River. Accounts of the opening episode are included in reports by Mary Black (1975: 1–4), Ferdinand Drebert (n.d.-1), Ann Fienup-Riordan (1984:76–77), John H. Kilbuck (n.d.-1), William Napoka (1977:36–37), Nelson (1899:328), and Joseph H. Romig (in Eva G. Anderson 1940:119). Lydia T. Black (personal communication) notes that the "injured child" theme occurs in Aleut folk tales and among other Eskimos.

2. Romig (in Anderson 1940:119–20) recorded an account of the Bloody Creek Massacre; the legend also was recounted verbally in 1954 by two elderly Kuskokwim Eskimos, Anania Theodore and Sam Simeon (Oswalt field notes). J. Kilbuck (journal, Sept. 13, 1897) is the author reporting the fate of the old man who lagged behind the others. During the 1950s and 1960s Oswalt observed that the Upper Kalskag paddles were marked with red rings, and the villagers told him the reason for the markings. More recently the Bureau of Indian Affairs teacher at Upper Kalskag, Lou Slattery (letter, Sept. 16, 1976), reported

that the custom had been abandoned and that most villagers were unaware of the massacre legend.

3. The attack on Quinhagak and the sequence of hostilities following the War of the Eye is based on the accounts recorded by Romig (in Anderson 1940:119–20).

4. During his Nushagak area explorations in 1829 the Russian Ivan Ya. Vasilev saw the skulls and bones of the Kiatagmiut and was told the date of the massacre (James W. VanStone 1988:91).

5. RAC:CS, v. 3, no. 164, May 4, 1823; v. 9, no. 460, Oct. 31, 1832.

6. Considerable confusion surrounds the protohistoric location of the Aglurmiut and their subsequent movements. Wrangell (1980:64) reports that the Agolegmiut "were driven from their homes on the banks of the Kuskokwim". Presumably he based this statement on information in the 1830 Kuskokwim journal of Vasilev. Reconstructions of early historic Aglurmiut boundaries have been attempted by Don E. Dumond, Leslie Conton, and Harvey M. Shields (1975:50–52) and also by Oswalt (1967:4–5).

The Russian explorer and ethnographer L. A. Zagoskin had read the 1830 Kuskokwim report by Vasilev, but based on his personal findings in 1842–44, Zagoskin (1967:210–11) felt that Vasilev was mistaken about the existence of a settlement called "Agolegma," whose residents were drive south. Zagoskin (Ibid., 210) thought this was "a pure guess, or legend," especially because no one knew the location of the original settlement. Yet so much information exists in the Russian-American Company records about the Aglurmiut as refugees and their conflicts with Kuskokwim and Nushagak Eskimos that it is difficult to accept Zagoskin's conclusion that the story of the dispersal of these people from their homeland in the Kuskokwim region is a fabrication.

7. Ivanov's travels are described by Vasilii N. Berkh (1974:71–72), M. B. Chernenko (Zagoskin 1967:9–10, 29–30, fn. 41) and best by Gavriil I. Davydov (1977:200–02); the original report apparently has been lost. The party appears to have descended the Iloholitna and Holitna rivers to the Kuskokwim and traveled downstream to Tuliuka (Crow Village) and Ukhagmak (Ohagamiut); the actual location of these villages is reversed in Davydov's account.

8. Zagoskin 1967:79.

9. The travels of Korsakovskiy and Rodionov are described by Svetlana G. Fedorova (1973:64–69) and by VanStone (1973:7–8). It is not certain, however, that Rodionov traveled to Ohagamiut along the Kuskokwim; he may have met Kylymbak elsewhere. VanStone (1988) edited a translation of the 1818 Korsakovskiy account.

10. Intermittently the Nushagak station was termed Novo-Aleksandrovskiy to distinguish it from Aleksandrovskiy Redoubt, which was built on Kenai Peninsula in 1786 (Fedorova 1973:63, 128).

11. VanStone 1988:8.

12. RAC:CS, v. 11, no. 72, Apr. 10, 1834.

13. Ibid., v. 3, no. 164, May 4, 1823; Zagoskin 1967:210. From the 1818 Korsakovskiy journal it is apparent that the Aglurmiut were well established along the base of the Alaska Peninsula by that time and were in direct contact

with Russian traders (VanStone 1988). The Aglurmiut of the Nushagak area probably not only anticipated the arrival of Russians but were predisposed to identify with them.

14. RAC:CS, v. 6, no. 114, May 5, 1828.

15. VanStone 1988:94.

16. RAC:CS, v. 2, no. 19, Jan. 17, 1821; v. 2, no. 27, Jan. 18, 1821; v. 2, no. 171, Mar. 15, 1821; v. 2, no. 37, Apr. 27, 1821; VanStone 1972:8–10.

17. VanStone 1988:94–96.

18. RAC:CS, v. 6, nos. 243, 244, Sept. 25, 1829.

19. All dates from the Russian era are recorded in the Old Style (Julian) calendar, which was twelve days behind the New Style (Gregorian) calendar in the nineteenth century.

20. RAC:CS, v. 7, no. 257, Oct. 5, 1830; v. 8, no. 299, May 7, 1831; Petr A. Tikhmenev 1978:181.

21. RAC:CS, v. 7, no. 257, Oct. 5, 1830; Wrangell 1980:63–68; Zagoskin 1967:79–80.

22. RAC:CS, v. 9, no. 321, July 10, 1832.

23. An odinochka consisted of one or more dwellings and outbuildings. Some odinochkas were occupied throughout the year by a few employees, whereas others were seasonal stations or trail houses for travelers.

24. RAC:CS, v. 9, no. 555, Nov. 16, 1832; v. 11, nos. 72, 73, Apr. 10, 1834; Zagoskin 1967:80–81.

25. RAC:CS, v. 9, no. 555, Nov. 16, 1832; v. 11, no. 72, Apr. 10, 1834.

26. Ibid., v. 11, no. 73, Apr. 10, 1834; v. 12, no. 256, Apr. 30, 1835.

27. Ibid., v. 12, nos. 266, 267, May 11, 1835.

28. Ibid., v. 15, no. 455, Nov. 5, 1837; v. 16, nos. 467, 468, Oct. 31, 1838.

29. Ibid., v. 11, no. 273, May 9, 1834.

30. Ibid., v. 12, no. 256, Apr. 30, 1835.

31. Ibid.

32. Ibid., v. 8, no. 192, Apr. 30, 1830.

33. Tikmenev 1978:183.

34. VanStone 1959.

35. RAC:CS, v. 12, no. 328, Oct. 5, 1835.

36. Ibid., v. 17, no. 387, June 4, 1839; v. 17, no. 509, Oct. 24, 1839.

37. Ibid., v. 11, no. 72, Apr. 10, 1834.

38. Katherine L. Arndt n.d.; RAC:CS, v. 16, no. 244, May 1, 1838.

39. RAC:CS, v. 16, no. 479, Nov. 4, 1838.

40. VanStone 1978:68, fn. 37.

41. RAC:CS, v. 17, no. 444, Sept. 6, 1839.

42. Margaret Lantis 1959:4.

43. RAC:CS, v. 18, no. 378, May 31, 1840; Zagoskin 1967:252.

44. Zagoskin 1967:252.

45. Dementiev was born in Russia in 1839, went to Sitka about 1854, and was the last Russian-American Company manager at Kolmakovskiy Redoubt. The Moravian missionary John H. Kilbuck recorded Dementiev's account of the planned attack on Lukin (J. Kilbuck journal, Jan. 20, 1892). The Eskimos ex-

pected Lukin to be alone, and the presence of other company employees no doubt was what dissuaded them from their plan. These men had been sent to warn Lukin and to stay with him after the attack on Russian Mission (RAC:CS, v. 17, no. 512, Oct. 24, 1839).

46. RAC:CS, v. 17, no. 512, Oct. 24, 1839.

47. Vladimir Gsovski 1950:16.

48. RAC:CS, v. 16, no. 479, Nov. 4, 1838.

49. VanStone (1967:56) likewise suggests that the Russian-American Company agents encouraged the indebtedness of local Eskimos.

50. RAC:CS, v. 16, no. 466, Oct. 31, 1838.

Chapter 4

1. RAC:CS, v. 20, no. 43, Feb. 25, 1841.

2. As construction plans developed, Fedor Kolmakov's son Petr was to be the manager, but because he lacked administrative abilities, he soon was replaced by Lukin (Ibid., no. 486, Oct. 15, 1841).

3. Iakov Netsvetov 1984:469–70.

4. RAC:CS, v. 20, no. 43, Feb. 25, 1841

5. Ibid., v. 21, no. 549, Sept. 25, 1842.

6. Zagoskin 1967:252.

7. Zagoskin (1967:251) refers in 1844 to the "gates of the fort"; presumably the stockade had been built the previous year.

8. RAC:CS, v. 21, no. 43, Feb. 11, 1842.

9. Zagoskin 1967:208.

10. In 1966 and 1967 Oswalt (1980a) excavated most of the Russian period structural remains at Kolmakovskiy.

11. Netsvetov 1849; 1984:126.

12. Illarion journal, Sept. 17, 1863.

13. Ibid., Sept. 19, 1861; Jan. 17, 1862.

14. Zagoskin 1967:200, 208, 253.

15. Chernenko, in Zagoskin 1967:11–34.

16. Zagoskin 1967:207.

17. Ibid., 208. In July 1843, before Zagoskin visited Kolmakovskiy, he reported that the fort "carries on a fairly profitable trade in all kinds of European wares" (p. 175), but this was not verified when he visited the fort later in 1843 and again in 1844.

18. Ibid., 256.

19. Ibid., 261.

20. RAC:CS, v. 21, no. 549, Sept. 25, 1842.

21. Ibid., v. 22, no. 577, Oct. 18, 1843.

22. I am indebted to Lydia T. Black (personal communication) for pointing out the class distinction between Russian and creole employees. RAC:CS, v. 21, no. 548, Sept. 25, 1842.

23. Ibid., v. 34, no. 484, June 19, 1853.

24. Zagoskin 1967:208.

25. Ibid., 250.

26. Ibid., 228.
27. The year of Semen Lukin's death appears in Netsvetov (1984:471).
28. E. E. Rich 1960: v. 3, 493–94.
29. Zagoskin 1967:221.
30. RAC:CS, v. 16, no. 467, Oct. 31, 1838.
31. Zagoskin 1967:221.
32. RAC:CS, v. 16, no. 468, Oct. 31, 1838; v. 17, no. 387, June 4, 1839; Zagoskin 1967:221.
33. RAC:CS, v. 20, no. 43, Feb. 25, 1841.
34. Zagoskin 1967:254.
35. Illarion (journal, Oct. 24) refers to the Kihtagamiut Odinochka in 1863. The reason for assuming a founding date of 1853 is that this was the first year a coastal furbearer, the arctic fox, was received at Kolmakovskiy (Petroff 1884:64).
36. Zagoskin 1967:270–71.
37. RAC:CS, v. 30, no. 348, June 4, 1849; v. 31, no. 363, June 6, 1850.
38. Illarion journals, Sept. 25, 1861 to June 1, 1862.
39. Oswalt 1980a:84–85.
40. RAC:CS, v. 23, no. 661, Oct. 11, 1844.
41. Ibid., v. 37, no. 147, Apr. 9, 1856.
42. Ibid., v. 38, no. 115, Apr. 30, 1857; v. 38, no. 266, May 24, 1857.
43. Zagoskin 1967:253–54.
44. RAC:CS, v. 23, no. 648, Oct. 11, 1844; v. 24, no. 271, May 14, 1845.
45. James Alton James 1942:222, 226; Netsvetov 1984:41, 105–06.
46. Illarion journal, Mar. 12, May 21, 1862.
47. Ibid., Dec. 28, 1861; Feb. 20, 1862.
48. Howard I. Kushner 1975:80.
49. Morgan B. Sherwood 1965:89–90.
50. RAC:CS, v. 42, no. 46, Aug. 5, 1860.
51. William H. Dall (1870:276–77) reported that Ivan Lukin went to Fort Yukon in 1863, but Black (in Netsvetov 1984:471) writes that it was in 1862.
52. Zagoskin 1967:82.
53. Nelson 1899:228–32.
54. Zagoskin 1967:247.
55. Ibid., 275.
56. Ibid., 247.
57. Ibid., 102.
58. Ibid., 208, 255.
59. Tikhmenev 1978:350.
60. Illarion journal, Sept. 14, 1861.
61. Tikhmenev 1978:367.
62. Ray 1975:101–02.
63. Illarion journal, Mar. 1, 1862.
64. Nelson 1899:271–85.
65. DRHA, v. 2, 157–59; RAC:CS, v. 11, no. 234, May 10, 1837; Zagoskin 1967:91.
66. James 1942:196–97; Frederick Whymper 1869:154.

67. Robert F. Spencer 1959:156. Zagoskin (1967:101) reported that in the Norton Sound area two greenish-blue beads that were matched and flawless were worth three or four caribou skins.

68. Christopher L. Miller and George R. Hamell 1986.

69. Illarion journal, Nov. 20, 1863.

70. J. Kilbuck journal, Jan. 20, 1892.

71. Zagoskin 1967:255.

72. Oswalt and VanStone 1967.

73. RAC:CS, v. 23, no. 648, Oct. 11, 1844; v. 24, no. 308, May 15, 1845; Zagoskin 1967:81, 275.

74. Sergei Kan n.d.

75. Robert Nichols and Robert Croskey 1972:53.

76. RAC:CS, v. 9, no 460, Oct. 31, 1832.

77. Nichols and Croskey 1972: 53, fn. 38; Zagoskin 1967:206.

78. DRHA, v. 1, 387; Nichols and Croskey 1972:53.

79. RAC:CS, v. 19, no. 147, Sept. 27, 1840.

80. Ibid., v. 21, no. 30, Feb. 11, 1842; Zagoskin 1967:206, 284–85, fn. 5.

81. Netsvetov 1984:4.

82. Ibid., 1–514.

83. Ibid., 484.

84. Illarion journal, Sept. 19, 1861.

85. DRHA, v. 2, 136–37.

86. Illarion journal, Dec. 9, 1866.

Chapter 5

1. Lois D. Kitchener 1954; Frank H. Sloss and Richard A. Pierce 1971.

2. Bernhard Bendel 1987:33, 34, 49.

3. The agreement of employment between Separe and Hutchinson, Kohl & Company is reproduced by Kitchener (1954:37).

4. Bendel 1987.

5. W. Weinland, n.d.

6. American era particulars about Kolmakovskiy are detailed in an archaeological site report about the fort (Oswalt 1980a).

7. W. Weinland journal, June 14, 1884; W. Weinland, n.d.

8. Dunn Poindexter 1889:325.

9. Julius Jette (n.d.) reported that Reinhold Separe died in 1891.

10. Edward Lind was born in Finland or Sweden in 1847 (U.S. Commissioner's records, Aniak, Alaska), and according to Edith Kilbuck (journal, May 22, 1887) he lived in Alaska at the time of the purchase. Edith Kilbuck also provides details about his later life (E. Kilbuck letter to C. Weinland, Nov. 4, 1911).

11. *Iditarod Pioneer* Aug. 24, 1912; Stanford University, Alaska Commercial Company Records, Private Home Office General Ledger, Northern Commercial Company, Aug. 1, 1912. The Alaska Commercial Company records at the California Historical Society, San Francisco, are the source for the sale of Kolmakovskiy in 1917.

12. Sherwood 1965:31, fn. 57; W. Weinland journal, June 28, 1884.

13. W. Weinland journal, June 14, 1884; Oswalt field notes.

14. Netsvetov 1984:478; E. Kilbuck letter to C. and W. Weinland, Mar. 28, 1896; J. Kilbuck journal, Aug. 12, 1890; Oswalt field notes.

15. Bethel Mission Log, Aug. 2, 1898.

16. Oswalt field notes.

17. E. Kilbuck journal, Sept. 8, 1888.

18. W. Weinland ms., Jan. 20, 1887.

19. Poindexter 1889:399–400.

20. Josiah E. Spurr 1900:261–62.

21. W. M. Cady et al. 1955:109–16; Hans Nelson et al. 1977:820.

22. DRHA, v. 2, 146.

23. J. Arthur Lazell (1960) published a biography of Jackson, and more recently Ted C. Hinckley (1972) has written about Jackson's work in Alaska.

24. S. H. Gapp 1928:84–85; W. Weinland ms., Apr. 19, 1926.

25. The 1884 travel journal of Hartmann was published twice (1884–85; 1886). Extracts of the journal by Weinland were published in 1885–86.

26. Kamilakojhin was born about 1836 and married an Aglurmiut, Anisia Chinauk, in 1861 (DRHA, v. 1, 220–21; Netsvetov 1984:418).

27. James W. Henkelman and Kurt H. Vitt 1985:358–65.

28. Henkelman and Vitt 1985:84–95; Oswalt 1963a:23–50, Anna Buxbaum Schwalbe 1951:10–15.

29. *Periodical Accounts of the United Brethren* 1885:429.

30. Ibid., 1886:465.

31. W. Weinland journal, June 18, 1884.

32. E. Kilbuck journal, May 5, 1889.

33. E. Kilbuck letter to Mary E. Yost, Feb. 2, 1886.

34. E. Kilbuck journal, Feb. 4, 1887.

35. *PSPG* 1889:21, 30, 31.

36. Ibid., 30.

37. *Periodical Accounts of the United Brethren* 1886:465.

38. William Henry Weinland's obituary appears in *PSPG* (1930:74–77).

39. *PSPG* 1887:15.

40. Ibid., 1888:35–36.

41. Ibid., 20–23.

42. E. Kilbuck journal, Mar. 4, 1889; *PSPG* 1888:21.

43. *PSPG* 1889:23–24.

44. Ibid., 1890:21.

45. Ibid., 1891:22.

46. Ibid., 1894:27.

47. Ibid., 1933:43.

48. Anderson 1940:24, 27, 281; Schwalbe 1951:47, 68.

49. *PSPG* 1890:20–21.

50. Fienup-Riordan 1988:73–76.

51. *Moravian Conference, Kuskoqwim River* 1895.

52. *Bethel Mission Log* July 25, 1898, Dec. 18, 1899; Fienup-Riordan 1987a:305.

53. Bishop Gregory (Afonsky) 1977:76.

54. DRHA, v. 1, 155.
55. DRHA, v. 1, 249–50; Barbara S. Smith 1974:57; Barbara S. Smith 1980:131.
56. Oswalt 1980b:35–36.
57. Ibid., 69–70.

Chapter 6

1. A. G. Maddren (1910:33) records that the *Albatross* arrived in 1889, but in a journal entry for June 23, 1890, E. Kilbuck noted the arrival of a passenger from the vessel.
2. E. Kilbuck journals, Sept. 19, 24, 1900.
3. *Bethel Mission Log* Aug. 14, 25, 1900.
4. Ferdinand Drebert n d.-2; *PSPG* 1906.48.
5. *PSPG* 1905:106.
6. Ibid., 1908:75.
7. John R. Bockstocc 1977:104, 107; John W. Felder, ms.; C. W. Kutz 1912:1–5.
8. *Iditarod Pioneer* May 13, 1916.
9. Boats and barges used in lightering and transport operations are described by Henkelman and Vitt (1985), Schwalbe (1951), and in the annual reports of the Moravian Church (*PSPG*).
10. Lee R. Dice ms., n.d.:85, 92; *PSPG* 1911:85.
11. *Bethel Mission Journal* May 18, 1907.
12. *Iditarod Pioneer* Aug. 28, Sept. 11, 1910.
13. Iditarod Pioneer June 3, 1916; E. Kilbuck journal, June 18, 1916.
14. *Alaska Daily Press* Jan. 11, 1936; C. Michael Brown 1985:252.
15. Charlie Guinn 1976:4.
16. Fienup-Riordan 1987a:481.
17. *The Iditarod Trail and Other Alaskan Gold Rush Trails* 1977:26, 33.
18. Kenneth Gideon 1967.44.
19. *PSPG* 1927:41, 1933:40.
20. Drebert n.d.-2:3; *PSPG* 1941:32.
21. Particulars about the 1900 epidemic are recorded by Schwalbe (1951:84–85) and in accounts by Romig (in Anderson 1940:190–205; *PSPG* 1901:25–36).
22. J. Kilbuck 1913:22.
23. *PSPG* 1894:57.
24. Ibid., 1902:25; 1905:57; 1916:41; 1917:43–44.
25. E. Kilbuck journals, Sept. 19, 24, 1900; Maddren 1915:299–300.
26. *PSPG* 1900:52–53.
27. Philip S. Smith 1933: table facing p. 96.
28. Maddren 1910:21–23.
29. David H. Sleem 1910:298–99.
30. George C. Martin 1922:149.
31. John S. Brown 1926:127–28.
32. Maddren 1915:300; H. W. Reeth 1924:7.
33. Oswalt 1980b:67.

34. Fienup-Riordan 1987a:478; Oswalt 1980b:41.

35. *Iditarod Pioneer* Jan. 10, 1914; Maddren 1915:301–02; Smith 1942:54.

36. Melvin B. Ricks 1965:2, 4, 7, 23, 59.

37. Accounts by white prospectors along the Kuskokwim and adjacent sectors of the Yukon have been published by Charles Lee Cadwallader (n.d.), Gideon (1967), Floyd R. Marsh (1976), and Harold and Zora Peckenpaugh (1973).

38. *Iditarod Nugget* Feb. 22, 1911.

39. *Iditarod Pioneer* Mar. 4, 11, Apr. 1, 1916.

40. *PSPG* 1911:64.

41. Ray 1975:226–40.

42. The Moravian request for reindeer was reproduced by Jackson (1897: 131–32), and the agreement between the Moravians and the federal government appears in U.S. Congress, Hearings of the Reindeer Committee (1931, Feb. 28, p. 52).

43. Fienup-Riordan 1987a:516–36.

44. The development of Kuskokwim reindeer herding is described by Gapp (1928:54–58), Henkelman and Vitt (1985:306–11), Schwalbe (1951:125–38), H. Dewey Anderson and Walter C. Eells (1935:196–97), the journal *Eskimo* (1942, v. 9, no. 1; 1947, v. 14, no. 1), and the Moravian Church publication *PSPG* (1926:69–72).

45. A. C. Kinsley 1931:143.

46. Adolph Stecker 1929.

47. Ivan J. Donaldson and Frederick K. Cramer 1971:7–8.

48. Charles H. Gilbert and Henry O'Malley 1921:143; John Nathan Cobb 1931:484–85.

49. Long-term white and Eskimo residents along the river in the 1950s are the undocumented source for the first Kuskokwim fish wheel (Oswalt field notes). The earliest written reference to Kuskokwim wheels may be the one by J. Kilbuck (Fienup-Riordan 1987a:476) dating from 1911. Records also indicate that wheels were used along the lower Yukon River by 1913 (J. W. Chapman 1913:50).

50. Dice (ms., n.d.:108) records that fish traps were used widely in 1912 but that fish wheels also prevailed.

51. *Iditarod Pioneer* July 18, 1914; E. Kilbuck journals, June 22, 25, 1914.

52. O'Malley 1932:22.

53. W. Weinland journal, June 21, 1884.

54. Ivan Petroff 1884:13.

55. Robert P. Porter 1893:104, 253.

56. Anderson 1940:47.

57. *PSPG* 1907:63, 73.

58. Fienup-Riordan 1987a:173, 178, 185, 334–35.

59. *PSPG* 1904:60, 61; 1905:51; 1908:74.

60. Gapp 1928:23–24.

61. These companies were especially prominent in the early twentieth-

century trade, but there were others. The information about trading companies presented is from the journal of John W. Felder (ms.).

62. These and other founding dates for Kuskokwim trading posts are detailed by Oswalt (1980b).

63. Maurcie M. Gould et al. 1965:15–16; Guinn 1976:5.

64. James Wickersham 1938:235.

65. C. D. Scott 1909:425.

66. Dice ms., n.d.:68–69.

67. John Kilbuck, in writing about the Georgetown to Sleetmute area in 1911, noted that "Game and fur bearing animals are rapidly disappearing before the onslaught of white hunters and trappers, and the destructive fires" (Fienup-Riordan 1987a:480). However, his statement seems to be an exaggeration designed to foster the development of Native "colonies" in the area. The statement about the minor importance of white trappers by Harry J. Christoffers and Dice (1914:111) seems to be more accurate.

68. RAC:CS, v. 16, no. 377, May 30, 1838; no. 468, Oct. 31, 1838; Zagoskin 1967:268, 269. Lydia T. Black (personal communication) kindly pointed out the source of guns during the Russian period.

69. W. Weinland journal, July 5, 1884.

70. E. A. Hitchcock 1900.

71. RAC:CS, v. 16, no. 468, Oct. 31, 1938; v. 17, no. 387, June 4, 1839; Zagoskin 1967:221.

72. Nelson and F. W. True 1887:247, 279.

73. J. Kilbuck journal, Nov. 22, 1897.

74. *PSPG* 1915:41.

75. Ibid., 1920:42.

76. Ibid., 1921:47, 54–55; 1927:44.

77. Ibid., 1927:44.

78. Oswalt field notes.

Chapter 7

1. Oswalt 1980b:19.

2. Ibid., 54, 71–72.

3. Jim Kari ms.

4. BIA records, 1953, Bethel, Alaska.

5. Lynn Douglas Mason 1972:21–23.

6. Fienup-Riordan 1987:67–68.

7. *PSPG* 1891:20–21; 1896:20.

8. Oswalt and VanStone 1967:13–15.

9. *PSPG* 1911:63.

10. Ibid., 1906:57.

11. Ibid., 1926:59–60.

12. Economic survey of Kwethluk, Alaska, 1939.

13. Oswalt 1963b:123.

14. Fienup-Riordan 1987a:604–05.

15. Jim Payne, Regina Soiffer, and P. J. Wyatt 1981.

16. Oswalt field observations.
17. Payne, Soiffer, and Wyatt 1981:25.
18. Ibid., 16.
19. Ibid., 18.
20. Alfred Mongin 1979:63, 66, 67–68.
21. Ibid., 67.
22. Oswalt 1980b:25, 37, 54.
23. Ibid., 35–36.
24. *PSPG* 1887:17; 1905:111; 1906:49.
25. *Moravian* Nov. 1958, p. 5.
26. *PSPG* 1892:20; 1896:23.
27. Ibid., 1912:45.
28. Ibid., 1913:35; 1914:40; 1917:41.
29. The best discussion of Moravian translations into Yupik is by Vitt (In Henkelman and Vitt 1985:38–46), and the best overview of translations by Christian missionaries for Alaskan Eskimos is by Michael E. Krauss 1980.
30. Fienup-Riordan 1987a:491, 502, 560, 597.
31. Francis M. Menager 1943; J. B. Tennelly 1939.
32. Oswalt 1980b:25.
33. Henkelman and Vitt 1985:374–83.
34. E. Kilbuck journal, Sept. 11, 1886.
35. Fienup-Riordan 1987a:472–617.
36. *PSPG* 1919:64.
37. Ibid., 1925:50–54.
38. *Moravian Messenger* Sept. 1974, p. 211.
39. David H. Getches 1977:3–10.
40. Oswalt 1980b:20, 25, 30, 37, 38; *Tundra Drums* June 10, 1982.
41. The information about village schools is based primarily on Oswalt's observations at the BIA school at Napaskiak in 1955–56 (Oswalt 1963b:37–38) and his observations of schools along the Kuskokwim in the 1950s.
42. Frank Darnell 1979:432, 435–36; Gerald A. McBeath et al. 1983.
43. *BIA School Turnover* 1984.
44. Fienup-Riordan 1982:291–93.
45. Darnell 1979:437.
46. Ibid., 438–40.
47. Osahito Miyaoka 1980:185; *Tundra Times* Nov. 4, 1970.
48. Miyaoka 1980:187–88.
49. John A. Kruse 1984:4, 7–8.
50. *Tundra Drums* May 29, 1980; Elaine Warren 1974:1, 6.
51. Betsy Brenneman 1976:1, 7; *Chuathbaluk* 1979; *Crooked Creek* 1979; Kruse 1984:4, 7–8; *Red Devil* 1979; *Sleetmute* 1979.
52. *Tundra Drums* Aug. 21, 1980.
53. Kruse 1984:7–8.
54. Wallace Turner 1985; Thomas D. Snyder 1988:133.
55. Anderson and Eells 1935:407–10.
56. Schwalbe 1951:46, 67–68, 88, 257.

57. Edith Kilbuck's work on behalf of Kuskokwim Eskimos is well documented throughout the account about John and Edith Kilbuck by Fienup-Riordan (1988).

58. Anderson and Eells 1935:407–10; Otto George 1979:30, 95.

59. Governor, Alaska 1919:14.

60. *PSPG* 1919:46.

61. VanStone 1967:103–04.

62. *PSPG* 1919:46–47; Schwalbe 1951:153–54.

63. Fienup-Riordan 1987a:591, 600, 604.

64. Governor, Alaska 1934:33–34.

65. Elvon G. Skeen 1959:15; Louise Lear 1955:1100–02; *Tundra Drums* Aug. 21, 1980.

66. *Tundra Times* Jan. 12, 1968.

67. *Tundra Drums* Dec. 4, 1976.

68. Joseph A. Aronson 1940:31–32; Petroff 1884:43.

69. F. S. Fellows 1934:294.

70. M. Walter Johnson 1973:247.

71. Thomas Parran 1954:III, Fig. 4.

72. Johnson 1973:249–51.

73. Mason 1972.

74. Alcohol consumption in the Bethel area before World War II is best documented in Moravian missionary reports (e.g., *PSPG* 1894:57; 1902:25; 1905:57–58; 1915:45; 1917:43–44; 1927:44–45; 1930:48; 1936:36; 1939:28, 32–33).

75. *Economic survey of Kwethluk, Alaska* 1939.

76. Oswalt 1963b:116–18.

77. *Moravian* Nov. 1960:5; Aug. 1967:5, 7; *Moravian Messenger* Aug. 1977:460.

78. *Tundra Drums* Sept. 21, 1974.

79. Ibid., Oct. 18, 1975; July 3, 1983.

80. Oswalt field notes.

81. Slinkwin and Pete 1980.

82. *Tundra Drums* Aug. 18, 1983.

83. *Statewide Village Status Report* 1983.

84. Cities/villages which have voted to ban the sale & importation of alcoholic beverages 1985.

85. Mary Lenz 1986g.

Chapter 8

1. John Collier, Jr. 1973:69; Fienup-Riordan 1982:417.

2. Susan Charnley 1984:254–68.

3. VanStone 1967:67.

4. Steven Pennoyer, Kenneth R. Middleton, and Melvan E. Morris, Jr. 1965:1–5, 38–43.

5. Fienup-Riordan 1987a:556–58.

6. VanStone 1967:63–82.

7. *PSPG* 1944:37.

8. Pennoyer, Middleton, and Morris 1965:42.

9. Richard A. Berg 1965:64–65.

10. Alaska Department of Fish and Game, Division of Commercial Fisheries 1966:11.

11. Alaska Department of Fish and Game, Division of Commercial Fisheries 1978; Fienup-Riordan 1982:408–09; *Tundra Times* July 18, 1979; *Tundra Drums* July 28, 1983.

12. *City of Bethel comprehensive development plan* 1984: v. 30, 10–12.

13. *PSPG* 1933:facing p. 39.

14. Alaska Department of Fish and Game, Division of Commercial Fisheries 1978:57–58.

15. *Tundra Drums* Sept. 11, 1986.

16. Robert B. Gibson, Aug. 6, 1957.

17. Oswalt field notes.

18. Fienup-Riordan 1987a:512–13.

19. George 1979:98.

20. Virginia Newton 1985:2.

21. Governor, Alaska 1903:63.

22. *Iditarod Pioneer* Aug. 12, 1911.

23. Christoffers and Dice 1914:111.

24. Ward T. Bower 1921:9–11.

25. *PSPG* 1926:60; 1927:44.

26. Sherwood (1981) thoroughly discusses the issues regarding subsistence hunting by Native and other Alaskans.

27. *Iditarod Pioneer* Sept. 28, 1912; *PSPG* 1913:33–34.

28. *Iditarod Pioneer* July 17, 1915.

29. Fienup-Riordan 1987a:546.

30. Ibid., 553, 563, 565.

31. Thomas A. Morehouse, Gerald A. McBeath, and Linda Leask 1984:177.

32. *Corporate Charter of the Organized Village of Kwethluk* 1941; *Corporate Charter of the Akiachak Native Community Alaska* 1950; *Corporate Charter of the Akiak Native Community Alaska* 1950.

33. Oswalt 1963b:70.

34. John Japheth 1951.

35. Arthur E. Hippler and Stephen Conn (1973:31) found this to be true of Eskimo councils in northern Alaska, and it seems to apply equally as well to those in the Kuskokwim area.

36. Ibid., 44–46.

37. Marvin R. (Muktuk) Marston 1972: Governor, Alaska 1943:3–4.

38. Governor, Alaska 1949:51–52.

39. Although Oswalt's (1963b:77) observations were at Napaskiak, there is every reason to believe that the same patterning prevailed in Eskimo villages farther up the Kuskokwim.

40. *Kuskokwim Kronicle* Apr. 19, 1973; *Tundra Times* Apr. 12, 1968.

41. McBeath and Morehouse 1980:30–31; *Kuskokwim Kronicle* Jan. 25, 1973.

42. Morehouse, McBeath, and Leask 1984:173–77.

43. *Alaska Blue Book* 1985:165–76.

44. Russian America 1868:8.

45. Robert D. Arnold et al. 1978:69.

46. Ibid., 68–71, 80–81.

47. *Tundra Drums* Dec. 29, 1983.

48. McBeath and Morehouse 1980:19–37.

49. Ibid., 39–56.

50. Stewart French 1972.

51. Arnold et al. 1978:145–62; French 1972.

52. Arnold et al. 1978:182.

53. *Tundra Drums* Sept. 2, 1982.

54. Terence Armstrong, George Rogers, and Graham Rowley 1978:140, Table 13.

55. Lenz 1986e:1, 22.

56. The communities included in this management corporation were Aniak, Chuathbaluk, Crooked Creek, Georgetown, Lime Village, Lower Kalskag, Napamiut, Red Devil, Sleetmute, Stony River, and Upper Kalskag.

57. Information about the origins of the Kuskokwim Management Corporation, the Kuskokwim Corporation, and the Kuskokwim Native Association is drawn from their reports and a 1979 interview with Jan Fredericks.

58. U.S. Bureau of the Census 1982:3, 73–75.

59. *PSPG* 1894:57; 1902:25; 1905:57; 1910:46. The "basest animal lust" quotation appears in *PSPG* 1911:64, and the "devil's frolic" quote appears in *PSPG* 1916:41.

60. Ibid., 1916:41.

61. Fienup-Riordan 1987a:605.

62. U.S. Bureau of the Census 1914:573; Porter 1893:6; U.S. Bureau of the Census 1952: v. 1, pp. 51–56.

63. Linda L. Stout 1982:8.

64. Oswalt 1963b:8–9; Skeen 1959.

65. Wien Consolidated 1971; Wien 1980.

66. *Tundra Times* Aug. 9, 23, 1965.

67. McBeath and Morehouse 1980:31–32.

68. McBeath and Morehouse 1980:30–31; *Tundra Drums* Oct. 19, 1974.

69. *Bethel Housing Project . . .* 1970; Lael Morgan 1974:199–200; Raymond Otis Youdan 1970:74–76.

70. Morgan 1975:36–39, 50–51.

71. *City of Bethel* 1984:27–28, 30.

72. Richard Goldstein 1979:1, 18; Peter Friend 1982:13; Morgan 1975:38.

73. Stout 1982:10, 12.

74. Fienup-Riordan 1982:213, 229.

75. *City of Bethel* 1984:15.

76. Fienup-Riordan 1982:166–67.

77. Ibid., 214.
78. Mary Lenz and James H. Barker (1985) have written the most comprehensive history of Bethel.

Chapter 9

1. Jacobson 1984:678–85.
2. Ibid., 686–87.
3. Harold Sparck and David Friday 1983.
4. Ibid.
5. Krauss ms. 15–24.
6. Taylor Brelsford 1986.
7. Oswalt 1972:83.
8. Fienup-Riordan (1982:210–12) stresses the insular nature of contemporary villages as she observed it in the Yukon-Kuskokwim Delta, but her conclusions seem to apply equally as well to riverine Kuskokwim villages above Bethel.
9. *Kusko Times* Sept. 22, 1928; Jan. 5, 1929; Aug. 29, 1931.
10. The *N C Co. Flag* (June 1957) includes a comparatively recent discussion of Klutuk, as does an article by Fred Hatfield (1984); the latter presentation is unreliable.
11. Anthony F. C. Wallace 1956:265.
12. *Tundra Drums* Mar. 27, 1986.
13. *Kuskokwim Drift* 1986.
14. Lenz 1986c:4, 5.
15. ANCSA 1985 Study 1984:16–21.
16. Bernard Segal et al. 1983.
17. Bobbie Garthwaite 1986:1, 24.
18. Akiachak 1984: *Tundra Drums* Apr. 12, July 12, 1984.
19. Michael Fagan 1986a:8–9.
20. *Tundra Drums* Apr. 12, July 12, 1984.
21. Ibid., July 31, 1986.
22. Lenz 1986a:1, 32; *Tundra Drums* Sept. 24, 1987.
23. *Tundra Drums* Oct. 2, 1986.
24. Lenz 1986a:1, 32.
25. Lenz 1986d:1, 22.
26. *Tundra Drums* Oct. 16, 1986.
27. Ted Stevens 1986:3, 30.
28. Thomas R. Berger 1986.
29. Lenz 1986b:1, 27.
30. Fagan 1987.
31. Alaska Native Claims Settlement Act Amendments of 1987, 1988.
32. *Tundra Drums* Sept. 17, Oct. 1, 1987; Lenz 1988.
33. *Tundra Drums* Nov. 25, 1987.

Chapter 10

1. Krech (1984) discusses the era approach in ethnohistorical presentations.
2. Gary C. Anders 1980; Richard White 1983.

3. Gibson 1976.

4. For a comparatively few years after air transport was initiated it was sporadic but soon was maintained on a year-round basis; the distinction does not seem critical in this presentation.

5. From 1841 to 1844 Kolmakovskiy was supplied by dog team during the winter from Nushagak, but the expense was so great that it was discontinued.

6. Krech 1976.

7. VanStone 1967.

8. VanStone, personal communication, Oct. 23, 1987.

9. John S. Petterson et al., 1984; Robert J. Wolfe et al., 1984.

10. VanStone 1979.

11. Oswalt field notes.

12. VanStone 1979;254

13. Ibid., 249.

14. Ibid., 98–100.

15. Susan Charnley (1984) worked at Sleetmute and Chuathbaluk, and for each factor cited in the text, the Sleetmute residents represented a more conservative position than did the people at Chuathbaluk. For example, fewer Chuathbaluk residents were involved in trapping than were residents at Sleetmute.

References

Akiachak
  1984   *Alaska Native News* Jan.:26–28. Anchorage.
Alaska Blue Book
  1985   Ed. Scott Foster, 7th ed. Juneau: Dept. of Education, Div. of State
          Libraries.
Alaska Daily Press (Juneau newspaper)
  1936   Jan. 11.
Alaska Department of Fish and Game, Division of Commercial Fisheries
  1966   *Annual Report, Arctic-Yukon-Kuskokwim Area.* Anchorage: Alaska
          Dept. of Fish and Game.
  1978   *Annual Salmon Management Report, 1978, Kuskokwim District.*
          Anchorage: Alaska Dept. of Fish and Game.
Alaska Native Claims Settlement Act Amendments of 1987
  1988   Public Law 100–241—Feb. 3, 1988.
ANCSA 1985 Study
  1984   *Alaska Native News* Dec.:16–21. Anchorage.
Anders, Gary C.
  1980   Theories of Underdevelopment and the American Indian. *Journal
          of Economic Issues* 14(3):681–701.
Anderson, Eva G.
  1940   *Dog-team Doctor.* Caldwell, Ida.:Caxton.
Arndt, Katherine L.
  n.d.   The Russian-American Company and the Smallpox Epidemic of
          1835 to 1840. (ms.)
Anderson, H. Dewey, and Walter C. Eells
  1935   *Alaska Natives.* Stanford, Ca.: Stanford Univ. Press.
Armstrong, Terence, George Rogers, and Graham Rowley
  1978   *The Circumpolar North.* London: Methuen.
Arnold, Robert D., et al.
  1976   *Alaska Native Land Claims.* Anchorage: Alaska Native
          Foundation.
Aronson, Joseph D.
  1940   The History of Disease among the Natives of Alaska. *Transactions*

   & Studies of the College of Physicians of Philadelphia. Fourth
   Series 8(1): 27–34. Baltimore, Md.: Coll. Med. Philad. Inst.
Atkinson, C. E., J. H. Rose, and T. O. Duncan
  1967 Salmon of the North Pacific Ocean—Part IV, Spawning
    Populations of North Pacific Salmon. *Internatl. North Pacific
    Fisheries Commission Bull.* 23:43–223.
Axtell, James
  1979 Ethnohistory. *Ethnohistory* 26(1): 1–13.
Beaglehole, J. C.
  1974 *The Life of Captain James Cook.* Stanford, Ca.: Stanford Univ.
    Press.
Bendel, Bernhard
  1987 *1870 Kuskokwim Expedition.* Kurt H. Vitt, ed. Bethel: Moravian
    Seminary & Archives.
Berg, Richard A.
  1965 The Economic Base and Development of Alaska's Kuskokwim
    Basin With Particular Emphasis Upon the Period 1950–1964.
    Fairbanks: Univ. of Alaska. (M.S. thesis)
Berger, Thomas R.
  1986 *Village Journey.* New York: Hill & Wang.
Berkh, Vasilii N.
  1974 *A Chronological History of the Discovery of the Aleutian Islands.*
    Tr. Dmitri Krenov, ed. Richard A. Pierce. Kingston, Ontario:
    Limestone.
Bethel Housing Project Economic Impact Study
  1970 Institute of Social, Economic, and Government Research.
    Fairbanks: Univ. of Alaska.
Bethel Mission Journal
  1907 Moravian Archives. Bethlehem, Pa.
Bethel Mission Log
  1898–1900 Moravian Archives. Bethlehem, Pa.
BIA School Turnover
  1984 Bureau of Indian Affairs. Juneau. (chart)
Black, Lydia T.
  1984 The Yup'ik of Western Alaska and Russian Impact. *Études/Inuit/
    Studies* 8 (H.S.): 21–43.
Black, Mary
  1975 The War and the Sickness. *Kaliikaq Yugnek* 2(1): 1–4. Bethel.
Bockstoce, John R.
  1977 *Steam Whaling in the Western Arctic.* New Bedford, Mass.: Old
    Dartmouth Historical Society.
Bower, Ward T.
  1921 Alaska Fishery and Fur-seal Industries in 1922. *Report of the U.S.
    Commissioner of Fisheries for 1923,* app. 4. Bureau of Fisheries
    Document no. 951. Washington, D.C.: Govt. Print. Off.

Brelsford, Taylor
  1986   Personal communication.
Brenneman, Betsy
  1976   Molly Hootch Case Settled. *Tundra Times* Sept. 22.
Brown, C. Michael
  1985   Alaska's Kuskokwim River Region. Bureau of Land Management.
          Anchorage. (mimeograph)
Brown, John S.
  1926   The Nixon Fork Country and Silver-Lead Prospects Near Ruby.
          U.S. Geological Survey Bull. 783-D:97–150. Washington,
          D.C.: Govt. Print. Off.
Burch, Ernest S., Jr.
  1975   *Eskimo Kinsmen.* St. Paul: West.
  1980   Traditional Eskimo Societies in Northwest Alaska. *Senri
          Ethnological Studies* 4: 253–304.
Cadwallader, Charles Lee
  n.d.   Reminiscences of the Iditarod Trail. (mimeograph)
Cady, W. M., et al.
  1955   The Central Kuskokwim Region, Alaska. *U.S. Geological Survey
          Professional Paper* 268. Washington, D.C.: Govt. Print. Off.
Chapman, J. W.
  1913   A Message from Anvik. *Alaskan Churchman* 7(2): 49–50.
Charnley, Susan
  1984   Human Ecology of Two Central Kuskokwim Communities.
          Technical Paper Number 81. Anchorage: Alaska Dept. of Fish
          and Game.
Christoffers, Harry J., and Lee R. Dice
  1914   Minor Fur Industries. *Report of the Commissioner of Fisheries for
          the Fiscal Year 1912 and Special Papers,* pp. 99–123. Bureau
          of Fisheries. Washington, D.C.: Govt. Print. Off.
Christy, Miller
  1894   *The Voyages of Captain Luke Foxe and Captain Thomas James.* 2
          vols. London: Hakluyt Society.
Chuathbaluk
  1979   Alaska Dept. of Community and Regional Affairs. (brochure)
Cities/villages which have voted to ban the sale and importation of alcoholic
  beverages
  1985   List. Anchorage: Alcoholic Beverage Control Board, State of
          Alaska.
City of Bethel
  1984   Comprehensive Development Plan, v. 30: The Bethel Economy.
          (mimeograph)
Climatography of the United States No. 86–43
  1965   Washington, D.C.: U.S. Dept. of Commerce, Weather Bureau.
Cobb, John N.
  1931   Pacific Salmon Fisheries. *Report of the U.S. Commissioner of*

Fisheries 1930, pp. 409–704. U.S. Department of Commerce,
Bureau of Fisheries. Washington, D.C.: Govt. Print. Off.

Collier, John, Jr.
1973   *Alaskan Eskimo Education.* New York: Holt, Rinehart and
Winston.

Cook, James
1967   *The Voyage of the Resolution and Discovery, 1776–1780.* Vol. 3,
pt. 1 of *The Journals of Capt. James Cook on his Voyages of
Discovery,* ed. J. C. Beaglehole. 4 vols. in 5. 1955–74.
Cambridge, Eng.: Published for the Haklyut Society at the
University Press.

Corporate Charter of the Akiachak Native Community, Alaska.
1950   U.S. Dept. of the Interior, Bureau of Indian Affairs. Washington,
D.C.: Govt. Print. Off.

Corporate Charter of the Akiak Native Community, Alaska
1950   U.S. Dept. of the Interior, Bureau of Indian Affairs. Washington,
D.C.: Govt. Print. Off.

Corporate Charter of the Organized Village of Kwethluk
1941   U.S. Dept. of the Interior, Office of Indian Affairs. Washington,
D.C.: Govt. Print. Off.

Crooked Creek
1979   Alaska Dept. of Community and Regional Affairs. (brochure)

Dall, William H.
1870   *Alaska and Its Resources.* Boston, Mass.: Lee and Shepard.

Darnell, Frank
1979   Education among the Native Peoples of Alaska. *Polar Record*
19(122): 431–46.

Davydov, Gavriil I.
1977   *Two Voyages to Russian America, 1802–1807.* Ed. Richard A.
Pierce, tr. Colin Bearne. Kingston, Ontario: Limestone.

Dice, Lee R.
n.d.   Interior Alaska in 1911 and 1912. University of Alaska Archives.
Fairbanks. (ms.)

Documents Relative to the History of Alaska
1936–38   Alaska History Research Project. Vols. 1 and 2. Fairbanks:
Univ. of Alaska. (mimeograph)

Donaldson, Ivan J., and Frederick K. Cramer
1971   *Fishwheels of the Columbia.* Portland, Ore.: Binford & Mort.

Dorson, Richard M.
1961   Ethnohistory and Ethnic Folklore. *Ethnohistory* 8(1): 12–30.

Drebert, Ferdinand
n.d.-1   Drebert's War Story. (recorded by Barbara Lipton, The Newark
Museum; ms.)
n.d.-2   A Brief History of Bethel Alaska. (mimeographed ca. 1942)

Dumond, Don E., Leslie Conton, and Harvey M. Schields
  1975   Eskimos and Aleuts on the Alaska Peninsula. *Arctic Anthropology*
          12(1): 49–67.
Economic Survey of Kwethluk, Alaska
  1939   Dept. of the Interior, Office of Indian Affairs. Federal Archives and
          Records Center, Seattle. (mimeograph)
Elliott, Henry W.
  1886   *Our Arctic Province.* New York: Scribner's.
Eskimo (journal, published intermittently between 1916 and 1947 at Nome,
  Alaska, Eugene, Oregon, and Seattle, Wash.)
Euler, Robert C.
  1972   Ethnohistory in the United States. *Ethnohistory* 19(3): 201–07.
Fagan, Michael
  1986a   VPSO (Village Public Safety Officers). *Tundra Drums* Jan. 9.
  1986b   AVCP Convention. *Tundra Drums* Oct. 16.
  1987   AVCP & Tanana Chiefs Drop AFN. *Tundra Drums* Oct. 29.
Fedorova, Svetlana G.
  1973   *The Russian Population in Alaska and California.* Ed. and tr.
          Richard A. Pierce and Alton S. Donnelly. Kingston, Ontario:
          Limestone.
Felder, John W.
  ca. 1949 Travel Journals. In possession of Margaret Felder Holland. (ms.)
Fellows, F. S.
  1934   Mortality in the Native Races of the Territory of Alaska, with
          Special Reference to Tuberculosis. *Public Health Reports* 49(9):
          289–98. U.S. Treasury Dept. Washington, D.C.: Govt. Print.
          Off.
Fenton, William N.
  1962   Ethnohistory and Its Problems. *Ethnohistory* 9(1): 1–23.
Fienup-Riordan, Ann
  1982   Navarin Basin Sociocultural Systems Baseline Analysis. *Technical
          Report #70, Alaska OCS Socioeconomic Studies Program,
          Bureau of Land Management.* Alaska Outer Continental Shelf
          Office. Springfield, Va.: Natl. Technical Information Service.
  1983   *The Nelson Island Eskimo.* Anchorage: Alaska Pacific University
          Press.
  1984   Regional Groups on the Yukon-Kuskokwim Delta. *Études/Inuit/
          Studies* 8 (H.S.): 63–93.
  1987a   The Real People and the Children of Thunder. (ms.)
  1987b   The Mask. *Arctic Anthropology* 24(2):40–55.
  1988   *The Yup'ik Eskimos.* Kingston, Ontario: Limestone Press.
French, Stewart
  1972   *Alaska Native Claims Settlement Act.* Washington, D.C.: Arctic
          Institute of North America.

Friend, Peter
1982   Incidence of Rape Doubles in State. *Tundra Drums* May 6.
From Ketchikan to Barrow
1941   *Alaska Sportsman* Apr. 21.
Gapp, S. H.
1928   *Where Polar Ice Begins.* Bethlehem, Pa.: Comenius Press.
Garthwaite, Bobbie
1986   Grand Jury Issues Special Report on Child Sexual Abuse. *Tundra
        Drums* Jan. 23.
George, Otto
1979   *Eskimo Medicine Man.* Oregon Historical Society.
Getches, David H.
1977   *Law and Alaska Native Education.* Fairbanks: Center for Northern
        Educational Research, University of Alaska.
Gibson, James R.
1976   *Imperial Russia in Frontier America.* New York: Oxford University
        Press.
Gibson, Robert B.
1957   Letter to Area Director, Bureau of Indian Affairs, Juneau, Alaska.
        Aug. 6. Record Group No. 75. Federal Archives and Records
        Center, Seattle.
Gideon, Kenneth
1967   *Wandering Boy.* Washington, D.C.: Merkle.
Gilbert, Charles H., and Henry O'Malley
1921   Investigation of the Salmon Fisheries of the Yukon River. *Report
        of the U.S. Commissioner of Fisheries for 1921,* app. 4. Bureau
        of Fisheries. Washington, D.C.: Govt. Print. Off.
Goldstein, Richard
1979   Bethel Tops Nation in VD Rate. *Tundra Drums* Aug. 23.
Gould, Maurice M., Kenneth Bressett, Kaye and Nancy Dethridge
1965   *Alaska's Coinage Through the Years,* 2nd ed. Racine, Wis.:
        Whitman.
Governor, Alaska
1885–1931   *Annual Report.* Dept. of the Interior. Washington, D.C.:
        Govt. Print. Off.
Gregory (Afonsky), Bishop
1977   *A History of the Orthodox Church in Alaska (1794–1917).*
        Kodiak: St. Herman's Theological Seminary.
Gsovski, Vladimir
1950   Russian Administration of Alaska and the Status of the Alaskan
        Natives. *81st Congress, 2nd Session, Senate Document no. 152.*
        Washington, D.C.: Govt. Print. Off.
Guinn, Charlie
1976   Mamterilleq (Old Bethel). *Kaliikaq Yugnek* 2(2): 1–7. Bethel.

Hatfield, Fred
  1984   Of Traps and Treasures: Klutuk. *Alaska Magazine* Sept.,
          pp. 10–13, 61, 63.
Henkelman, James W., and Kurt H. Vitt
  1985   *Harmonious to Dwell.* Bethel: Moravian Seminary & Archives.
Himmelheber, Hans
  1987   *Eskimo Artists.* Zurich: Museum Rietberg.
Hinckley, Ted C.
  1972   *The Americanization of Alaska, 1867–1897.* Palo Alto, Ca.:
          Pacific Books.
Hippler, Arthur E., and Stephen Conn
  1973   Northern Eskimo Law Ways and Their Relationship to
          Contemporary Problems of "Bush Justice." *Institute of Social,
          Economic and Government Research Occasional Papers* no. 10.
          Fairbanks: Univ. of Alaska.
Hitchcock, E. A.
  1900   Letter to Alaska Commercial Company from the Dept. of the
          Interior. Alaska Commercial Company Records, University of
          Alaska Library, Fairbanks.
Hosley, Edward H.
  1966   Factionalism and Acculturation in an Alaskan Athapaskan
          Community. Los Angeles: Univ. of California. (Ph.D.
          dissertation)
  1968   The Kolchan. *Arctic* 21(1): 6–11.
Iditarod Nugget (newspaper)
  Sept. 1910 to June 1918.
Iditarod Pioneer (newspaper)
  July 1910 to Sept. 1919.
The Iditarod Trail and Other Alaskan Gold Rush Trails
  1977   Seward to Nome Route (Iditarod Trail), pp. 21–82. Bureau of
          Outdoor Recreation, U.S. Dept. of the Interior.
Illarion, Hieromonk [Peremezhko]
  1861–68 Journals. Alaska Church Collection, U.S. National Archives.
          (ms.)
Jackson, Sheldon
  1897   Report on Introduction of Domestic Reindeer into Alaska . . .
          1896. *54th Congress, 2nd Session, Senate Document no. 49.*
          Washington, D.C.: Govt. Print. Off.
Jacobson, Steven A., comp.
  1984   *Yup'ik Eskimo Dictionary.* Fairbanks: Alaska Native Language
          Center, Univ. of Alaska.
James, James Alton
  1942   The First Scientific Exploration of Russian America and the
          Purchase of Alaska. *Northwestern University Studies in the
          Social Sciences,* no. 4. Evanston: Northwestern Univ.

Japheth, John
    1951   Letters to George A. Morlander, April 6, 9, 13, 19; June 10.
            Record Group No. 75. Federal Archives and Records Center,
            Seattle.
Jette, Julius
    n.d.   Notes about Children. Oregon Province Archives of the Society of
            Jesus, Crosby Library. Spokane, Wash.: Gonzaga Univ. (ms.)
Johnson, M. Walter
    1973   Results of 20 Years of Tuberculosis Control in Alaska. *Health
            Services Reports* 88(3): 247–54.
Johnson, Philip R., and Charles W. Hartman
    1969   *Environmental Atlas of Alaska*. Institute of Arctic Environmental
            Engineering, Institute of Water Resources. Fairbanks: Univ. of
            Alaska.
Kan, Sergei
    n.d.   Russian Orthodox Church in Alaska. (ms.)
Kari, Jim
    1974   Linguistic data. Unpublished.
Kilbuck, Edith
    1886–1916   Journals. Kilbuck Papers. Bethlehem, Pa.: Moravian
            Archives. (ms.)
    1886–1911   Letters. Kilbuck Papers. Bethlehem, Pa.: Moravian Archives.
            (ms.)
    1896, 1911   Letters to Caroline Weinland. San Marino, Ca.: Huntington
            Library. (ms.)
Kilbuck, John Henry
    1890–97   Journals. Kilbuck Papers. Bethlehem, Pa.: Moravian Archives.
            (ms.)
    1913   Annual Report of the United States Public School at Akiak, a
            Remote Village on the Kuskokwim River, Hitherto without a
            School. *U.S. Bureau of Education Bull.*, 1913, no. 36:19–22.
            Washington, D.C.: Govt. Print. Off.
    n.d.-1 A Piece of Native History. Kilbuck Papers. Bethlehem, Pa.:
            Moravian Archives. (ms.)
    n.d.-2 Something About the Innuit of the Kuskokwim River, Alaska.
            Kilbuck Papers. Bethlehem, Pa.: Moravian Archives. (ms.)
Kinsley, A. C.
    1931   General Report, Reindeer Investigations, Kuskoquim Area. In
            Documents Relative to the History of Alaska. 1936–38. Vol.
            15:134–49. Fairbanks: Univ. of Alaska. (mimeograph)
Kitchener, Lois D.
    1954   *Flag Over the North*. Seattle: Superior.
Krauss, Michael E.
    1980   *Alaska Native Languages*. Alaska Native Language Center.
            Fairbanks: Univ. of Alaska.
    n.d.   Central Yupik. (ms.)

Krech, Shepard, III
  1976   The Eastern Kutchin and the Fur Trade, 1800–1860. *Ethnohistory*
          23(3): 213–35.
  1984   Introduction. *The Subarctic Fur Trade*. Shepard Krech III, ed.,
          pp. ix–xix. Vancouver: University of British Columbia Press.
Kruse, John A.
  1984   Changes in the Well-being of Alaska Natives Since ANCSA.
          Alaska Review of Social and Economic Conditions 21(3): 1–12.
Kushner, Howard I.
  1975   *Conflict on the Northwest Coast.* Contributions in American
          History Number 41. Westport, Conn.: Greenwood.
Kuskokwim Drift (shareholder report)
  1986   Vol. 6, no. 1. Anchorage: Kuskokwim Corp.
Kuskokwim Kronicle (Bethel, Alaska, newspaper, published 1969–73).
Kusko Times (McGrath and Takotna, Alaska, newspaper, published 1921–35).
Kutz, C. W.
  1912   Entrance to Kuskokwim River, Alaska. *62nd Congress, 3rd
          Session, House Documents,* vol. 26, no. 1051:3–5.
          Washington, D.C.: Govt. Print. Off.
Lane, Hana U., ed.
  1985   *The World Almanac and Book of Facts 1985.* New York:
          Newspaper Enterprise Assoc.
Lantis, Margaret
  1959   Folk Medicine and Hygiene. *Anthropological Papers of the
          University of Alaska* 8(1): 1–75.
Larsen, Helge, and Froelich Rainey
  1948   Ipiutak and the Arctic Whale Hunting Culture. *Anth. Papers of
          Amer. Mus. of Nat. Hist.,* vol. 42. New York: American
          Museum of Natural History.
Lazell, J. Arthur
  1960   *Alaskan Apostle.* New York: Harper & Brothers.
Lear, Louise
  1955   Tundra Hospital. *American Journal of Nursing* 55(9): 1100–1102.
Lenz, Mary
  1986a   Kasayulie and Yupiit Nation to Lobby Congress. *Tundra Drums*
          Feb. 6.
  1986b   ANCSA 1991 Legislation Introduced. *Tundra Drums* Feb. 13.
  1986c   Alaska Native Teens are Nation's Highest Risk Suicide Group.
          Tundra Drums Mar. 6.
  1986d   Yupiit Nation Leaders in, Richards out with AVCP. *Tundra Drums*
          Mar. 27.
  1986e   Calista Reports $7.5 Million Loss. *Tundra Drums* Apr. 3.
  1986f   Why Villages Want Self-Government. *Tundra Drums* Apr. 17.
  1986g   Bone Dry Local Option Approved for Villages. *Tundra Drums*
          May 15.
  1988   Calista Sale of Sheraton. *Tundra Drums* June 30.

Lenz, Mary, and James H. Barker
    1985   *Bethel.* Bethel: Yugtarvik Regional Museum.
McBeath, Gerald A., and Thomas A. Morehouse
    1980   *The Dynamics of Alaska Native Self-Government.* Lanham, Md.:
            Univ. Press of America.
McBeath, Gerald A., Judith S. Kleinfeld, G. William McDiarmid, E. Dean
Coon, and Carl E. Shepro
    1983   *Patterns of Control in Rural Alaska Education.* Center for Cross-
            Cultural Studies, Dept. of Political Science, and Inst. of Social
            and Economic Research, Univ. of Alaska, Fairbanks.
            Washington, D.C.: U.S. Dept. of Education, Natl. Inst. of
            Education.
McGhee, Robert
    1984   Contact Between Native North Americans and the Medieval Norse.
            American Antiquity 49(1): 4–26.
Maddren, A. G.
    1910   The Innoko Gold-Placer District, Alaska. *U.S. Geological Survey
            Bull.* 410. Washington, D.C.: Govt. Print. Off.
    1915   Gold Placers of the Lower Kuskokwim, with a Note on Copper in
            the Russian Mountains. *U.S. Geological Survey Bull.* 622,
            pp. 292–360. Washington, D.C.: Govt. Print. Off.
Marsh, Floyd R.
    1976   *20 Years a Soldier of Fortune.* Portland, Ore.: Binford & Mort.
Marston, Marvin R. (Muktuk)
    1972   *Men of the Tundra.* New York: October House.
Martin, George C.
    1922   Gold Lodes in the Upper Kuskokwim Region. In *Mineral
            Resources of Alaska, 1920* by A. H. Brooks et al. *U.S.
            Geological Survey Bull.* 722:149–61. Washington, D.C.: Govt.
            Print. Off.
Mason, Lynn Douglas
    1972   Disabled Fishermen. Los Angeles: Univ. of California. (Ph.D.
            dissertation)
Menager, Francis M.
    1943   Plan for Bethel Church. Oregon Province Archives of the Society
            of Jesus, Crosby Library. Spokane, Wash.: Gonzaga Univ.
Miller, Christopher L., and George R. Hamell
    1986   A New Perspective on Indian-White Contact. *Journal of American
            History* 73(2): 311–28.
Miyaoka, Osahito
    1980   Alaska Native Languages in Transition. In *Alaska Native Culture
            and History,* Yoshinobu Kotani and William B. Workman, eds.,
            pp. 169–203. Senri Ethnological Studies no. 4. Osaka, Japan:
            Natl. Museum of Ethnology.

Mongin, Alfred
　1979　The Russian Orthodox Churches of Alaska. *Orthodox Alaska*
　　　　8(3 & 4): 15–72.
Moravian (Moravian Church periodical)
Moravian Conference, Kuskoquim River
　1895　Minutes. Bethlehem, Pa.: Moravian Archives.
Moravian Messenger (Moravian Church periodical)
Morehouse, Thomas A., Gerald A. McBeath, and Linda Leask
　1984　*Alaska's Urban and Rural Governments*. Lanham, Md.: University
　　　　Press of America.
Morgan, Lael
　1974　*And the Land Provides*. Garden City, N.Y.: Doubleday.
　1975　Bethel. *Alaska Magazine* Sept.
Murie, O. J.
　1922　Journals: Physiography, Birds, and Mammals. Feb. 10–
　　　　March 18. (ms.)
Napoka, William
　1977　The War. *Kalikaq Yugnek* 3(1): 36–37. Bethel.
N C Co. Flag (Northern Commercial Company quarterly)
Neatby, L. H.
　1984　Exploration and History of the Canadian Arctic. In *Handbook of
　　　　North American Indians, Arctic*, David Damas, ed., v. 5,
　　　　377–90. Washington, D.C.: Smithsonian Institution.
Nelson, Edward W.
　1899　The Eskimo about Bering Strait. *Bureau of American Ethnology,
　　　　18th Annual Report, pt. 1*. Washington, D.C.: Govt. Print. Off.
Nelson, Edward W., and F. W. True
　1887　Mammals of Northern Alaska. In *Report upon Natural History
　　　　Collections Made in Alaska* by Edward W. Nelson, pt.
　　　　2:227–93. Arctic Series of Publications issued in Connection
　　　　with the Signal Service, U.S. Army, No. 3. Washington, D.C.:
　　　　Govt. Print. Off.
Nelson, Hans, et al.
　1977　Mercury Dispersal from Lode Sources in the Kuskokwim River
　　　　Drainage, Alaska. *Science* 198:820–24.
Netsvetov, Iakov
　1849　Report. Alaska Church Collection, National Archives. Washington,
　　　　D.C.
　1984　*The Journals of Iakov Netsvetov*. Tr. Lydia T. Black, ed. Richard
　　　　A. Pierce. Kingston, Ontario: Limestone.
Newton, Virginia
　1985　Alaska Court Records, 1884–1960. *Alaska History News* 16(5): 2.
Nichols, Robert, and Robert Croskey, tr. and ed.
　1972　The Condition of the Orthodox Church in Russian America. From
　　　　Innokentii Veniaminov's *History of the Russian Church in
　　　　Alaska. Pacific Northwest Quarterly* 63(2): 41–54.

O'Malley, Henry
  1932   *Report of the United States Commissioner of Fisheries for the
          Fiscal Year 1931.* Bureau of Fisheries. Washington, D.C.: Govt.
          Print. Off.
Oswalt, Wendell H.
  1963a   *Mission of Change in Alaska.* San Marino, Ca.: Huntington
          Library.
  1963b   *Napaskiak.* Tucson: Univ. of Arizona Press.
  1967   *Alaskan Eskimos.* San Franciso: Chandler.
  1972   The Eskimos (Yuk) of Western Alaska. In *Modern Alaskan Native
          Material Culture,* Wendell Oswalt, ed. pp. 73–95. Fairbanks:
          Univ. of Alaska Museum.
  1979   *Eskimos and Explorers.* Novato, Ca.: Chandler & Sharp.
  1980a   Kolmakovskiy Redoubt. *Monumenta Archaeologica,* vol. 8.
          Institute of Archaeology. Los Angeles: Univ. of California, Los
          Angeles.
  1980b   Historic Settlements along the Kuskokwim River, Alaska. *State
          Library Historical Monograph,* no. 7. Juneau: Alaska Division
          of State Libraries and Museums.
  n.d.   Field notes and observations.
Oswalt, Wendell H., and James W. VanStone
  1967   The ethnoarcheology of Crow Village, Alaska. *Bureau of
          American Ethnology Bull.* no. 199. Washington, D.C.: Govt.
          Print. Off.
Parran, Thomas
  1954   *Alaska's Health.* Pittsburgh, Pa.: Graduate School of Public
          Health, Univ. of Pittsburgh.
Payne, Jim, Regina Soiffer, and P. J. Wyatt
  1981   Final Research Report on Village Systems of Social Control in the
          Mid-Kuskokwim Region. Kuskokwim Native Assn. (photocopy)
Peckenpaugh, Harold and Zora
  1973   *Nuggets and Beans.* New York: Carlton.
Pennoyer, Steven, Kenneth R. Middleton, and Melvan E. Morris, Jr.
  1965   Arctic-Yukon-Kuskokwim Area Salmon Fishing History.
          Information Leaflet 70. Juneau: Dept. of Fish and Game, State
          of Alaska.
*Periodical Accounts Relating to the Missions of the Church of the United
Brethren Established among the Heathen.*
  1884–86   London: Printed for the Brethren's Society for the Furtherance of
          the Gospel among the Heathen.
Petroff, Ivan
  1884   *Report on the Population, Industries, and Resources of Alaska.*
          Dept. of the Interior, Census Office. Washington, D.C.: Govt.
          Print. Off.
Petterson, John S., et al.
  1984   *Sociocultural/Socioeconomic Organization of Bristol Bay.* Minerals

        Management Service Alaska Outer Continental Shelf Region
        Leasing and Environment Office. Springfield, Va.: National
        Information Service.

Poindexter, Dunn
    1889   Fur-seal Fisheries of Alaska. *50th Congress, 1888–89, 2nd
            Session, Reports of the Committees of the House of
            Representatives vol. 2, report 3883.* Washington, D.C.: Govt.
            Print. Off.

Porter, Robert P.
    1893   *Report on Population and Resources of Alaska at the Eleventh
            Census: 1890.* Dept. of the Interior, Census Office. Washington,
            D.C.: Govt. Print. Off.

*Proceedings of the Society of the United Brethren for Propagating the Gospel
among the Heathen* (annual reports)
    1885–1947   Bethlehem, Pa.: Moravian Publication Office.

Ray, Dorothy Jean
    1975   *The Eskimos of Bering Strait, 1650–1898.* Seattle: Univ. of
            Washington Press.

Red Devil
    1979   Alaska Department of Community and Regional Affairs.
            (brochure)

Reeth, H. W.
    1924   The Kuskokwim River. *Pathfinder of Alaska* 5(10): 7–8.

Rich, E. E.
    1960   *Hudson's Bay Company, 1670–1870.* 3 vols. Toronto: McClelland
            and Stewart.

Ricks, Melvin B.
    1965   *Directory of Alaska Postoffices and Postmasters.* Ketchikan,
            Alaska: Tongass Publ.

Russian America
    1868   *40th Congress, 1867–68, 2nd Session, House of Representatives
            Executive Document vol. 13, no. 177.* Washington, D.C.: Govt.
            Print. Off.

Russian-American Company
    1818–65   Correspondence of the Governors General. U.S. National
              Archives, Washington, D.C., Microfilm Group 11.

Schwalbe, Anna B.
    1951   *Dayspring on the Kuskokwim.* Bethlehem, Pa.: Moravian Press.

Schwerin, Karl H.
    1976   The Future of Ethnohistory. *Ethnohistory* 23(4): 323–41.

Scott, C. D.
    1909   Opportunities of the Kuskokwim. *Alaska-Yukon Magazine* 8(6):
            423–26.

Segal, Bernard, Jill McKelvy, Dani Bowman, and Theodore Mala
    1983   *Patterns of Drug Use.* Anchorage: Center for Alcohol and
            Addiction Studies.

Sherwood, Morgan B.
   1965   *Exploration of Alaska 1865–1900.* New Haven, Conn.: Yale Univ.
            Press.
   1981   *Big Game in Alaska.* New Haven, Conn.: Yale Univ. Press.
Shinkwin, Anne, and Mary Pete
   1980   Alaskan Villagers' Views on Problem Drinking. *Human
            Organization* 41(4): 315–22.
   1984   Yup'ik Eskimo Societies. *Études/Inuit/Studies* vol. 4,
            supplementary issue, pp. 95–112.
Skeen, Elvon G.
   1959   *Bethel, Alaska.* Anchorage: Color Art.
Slattery, Lou
   1976   Personal communication.
Sleem, David H.
   1910   Great Kuskokwim a New Land of Promise. *Alaska-Yukon
            Magazine* 10(5): 295–301.
Sleetmute
   1979   Alaska Department of Community and Regional Affairs. (brochure)
Sloss, Frank H., and Richard A. Pierce
   1971   The Hutchinson, Kohl Story. *Pacific Northwest Quarterly* 62(1): 1–6.
Smith, Barbara S.
   1974   *Preliminary Survey of Documents in the Archives of the Russian
            Orthodox Church in Alaska.* Boulder, Colo.: Western Interstate
            Commission for Higher Education.
   1980   *Russian Orthodoxy in Alaska.* Alaska Historical Commission.
            Anchorage: Van Cleve.
Smith, Philip S.
   1933   Past Placer-Gold Production from Alaska. *U.S. Geological Survey
            Bull.* 875-B. Washington, D.C.: Govt. Print. Off.
   1942   Mineral Industry of Alaska in 1940. *U.S. Geological Survey Bull.*
            933-A. Washington, D.C.: Govt. Print. Off.
Snyder, Thomas D.
   1988   Digest of Education Statistics 1988. Washington, D.C.: Govt.
            Print. Off.
Sparck, Harold, and David Friday
   1983   *Arctic Haze and Bush Alaskan Villages.* Bethel, Alaska: Nunam
            Kitlutsisti.
Spencer, Robert F.
   1959   The North Alaskan Eskimo. *Bureau of American Ethnology.* Bull
            171. Washington, D.C.: Govt. Print. Off.
Spicer, Edward H.
   1962   *Cycles of Conquest.* Tucson: University of Arizona Press.
Spurr, Josiah E.
   1900   A Reconnaissance in Southwestern Alaska in 1898. *Twentieth
            Annual Report of the United States Geological Survey* 1898–99,
            pt. 7: 31–264. Washington, D.C.: Govt. Print. Off.

Statewide Village Status Report
1983   Alaska Legal Services Corp. Alcohol Project. Anchorage: Alaska
        Legal Services Corp.
Stecker, Adolph
1929   Introduction of Reindeer into the Kuskokwim River Country.
        In Documents Relative to the History of Alaska, 1936–38,
        vol. 15:150–54. Fairbanks: Univ. of Alaska. (mimeograph)
Stevens, Ted
1986   The Importance of the 1991 Amendments to Alaska. *Tundra
        Drums* Aug. 28.
Stout, Linda L.
1982   *1982 Bethel City Census, Population Summary and Analysis.* City
        of Bethel Planning Office.
Sturtevant, William C.
1966   Anthropology, History, and Ethnohistory. *Ethnohistory* 13(1–2):
        1–51.
Swadesh, Morris
1951   Kleinschmidt Centennial III: Unaaliq and Proto Eskimo.
        International Journal of American Linguistics 17(1): 66–70.
1962   Linguistic Relations Across Bering Strait. *American
        Anthropologist* 64(6): 1262–91.
Tennelly, J. B.
1939   Letter to Francis M. Menager regarding Aniak Church. Oregon
        Province Archives of the Society of Jesus, Crosby Library.
        Spokane, Wash.: Gonzaga Univ.
Tikhmenev, Petr A.
1978   *A History of the Russian-American Company.* Tr. and ed. Richard
        A. Pierce and Alton S. Donnelly. Seattle: Univ. of Washington
        Press.
Townsend, Joan B.
1973   Ethnoarchaeology in Nineteenth Century Southern and Western
        Alaska. *Ethnohistory* 20(4): 393–412.
1979   Indian or Eskimo? *Arctic Anthropology* 26(2): 160–82.
Trigger, Bruce C.
1986   Ethnohistory. *Ethnohistory* 33(3): 253–67.
Tundra Drums (Bethel, Alaska, newspaper, 1969—)
Tundra Times (Fairbanks and later Anchorage newspaper, 1962—)
Turner, Wallace
1985   Alaska Native Leaders Say Education System is Failing. *New York
        Times* Oct. 27.
United States Bureau of the Census
1914   *Thirteenth Census of the United States.* Statistics for Alaska. U.S.
        Dept. of Commerce, Bureau of the Census. Washington, D.C.:
        Govt. Print. Off.
1952   *Seventeenth Census of the United States.* U.S. Dept. of Commerce,
        Bureau of the Census. Washington, D.C.: Govt. Print. Off.

1982   *1980 Census of Population. General Population Characteristics,*
        Alaska. Vol. 1, chapt. B, part 3. U.S. Dept. of Commerce,
        Bureau of the Census. Washington, D.C.: Govt. Print. Off.
United States Coast Pilot 9. Alaska
1955   Sixth (1954) edition. Washington, D.C.: Govt. Print. Off.
United States Commissioner's Records. Aniak.
United States Congress
1931   *Hearings of the Reindeer Committee in Washington, D.C.,*
        February-March, 1931. Dept. of the Interior. (mimeograph)
VanStone, James W.
1959   Russian Exploration in Interior Alaska. *Pacific Northwest*
        Quarterly 50(2): 37–47.
1967   *Eskimos of the Nushagak River.* Seattle: Univ. of Washington
        Press.
1972   Nushagak. *Fieldiana Anthropology,* vol. 62.
1973   V. S. Khromchenko's Coastal Explorations in Southwestern
        Alaska, 1822. *Fieldiana Anthropology,* vol. 64.
1978   E. W. Nelson's Notes on the Indians of the Yukon and Innoko
        Rivers, Alaska. *Fieldiana Anthropology,* vol. 70.
1979   Ingalik Contact Ecology. *Fieldiana Anthropology,* vol. 71.
1988   Russian Exploration in Southwest Alaska. Tr. David H. Kraus.
        Fairbanks: University of Alaska Press.
1987   Personal communication Oct. 23.
Viereck, Leslie A., and Elbert L. Little, Jr.
1972   *Alaska Trees and Shurbs.* Agriculture Handbook No. 410.
        Washington, D.C.: United States Dept. of Agriculture, Forest
        Service.
Wallace, Anthony F. C.
1956   Revitalization Movements. *American Anthropologist* 58(2):
        264–81.
Warren, Elaine
1974   Boarding Programs are Proven Failures. *Tundra Times* Feb. 6.
Washburn, Wilcomb E.
1961   Ethnohistory. *Ethnohistory* 8(1): 31–48.
Weinland, William H.
1884   Journal. San Marino, Ca.: Huntington Library. (ms.)
1887   Manuscript, draft. San Marino, Ca.: Huntington Library.
1926   Apr. 19. San Marino, Ca.: Huntington Library. (ms.)
n.d.   Life Amongst the Natives of the Kuskokwim River, Alaska. San
        Marino, Ca.: Huntington Library. (ms.)
White, Richard
1983   *The Roots of Dependency.* Lincoln, Neb.: University of Nebraska
        Press.
Whymper, Frederick
1869   *Travel and Adventure in the Territory of Alaska.* New York: Harper
        & Brothers.

Wickersham, James
  1938   *Old Yukon.* Washington, D.C.: Washington Law Book.
Wien.
  1980   System Time Table.
Wien Consolidated.
  1971   Complete System Timetable.
Wolfe, Robert J., et al.
  1984   *Subsistence-Based Economies in Coastal Communities of
          Southwest Alaska.* Anchorage: Division of Subsistence, Alaska
          Department of Fish and Game and Minerals Management
          Service, Alaska Region, U.S. Department of the Interior.
Wrangell, Ferdinand P. von
  1980   *Russian America Statistical and Ethnographic Information.*
          Translated from the German edition of 1839 by Mary Sadouski
          and edited by Richard A. Pierce. Kingston, Ontario: Limestone.
Youdan, Raymond Otis
  1970   A Descriptive Study of the Process of Social Change Among
          Alaska Natives at Bethel, Alaska. Pullman: Washington State
          Univ. (M.A. thesis)
Yukon and Kuskokwim River Basins, Alaska, Interim Report No. 7
  1964   88th Congress, 2nd Session, House Document No. 218.
          Washington, D.C.: Govt. Print. Off.
Zagoskin, Lavrentiy A.
  1967   Lieutenant Zagoskin's Travels in Russian America, 1842–1844.
          Ed. Henry N. Michael. *Arctic Inst. of North America,
          Anthropology of the North, Translations from Russian Sources,
          no. 7.* Toronto, Ontario: Univ. of Toronto Press.

Index